IDAHO
THE WHITEWATER STATE

A GUIDEBOOK

grant amaral

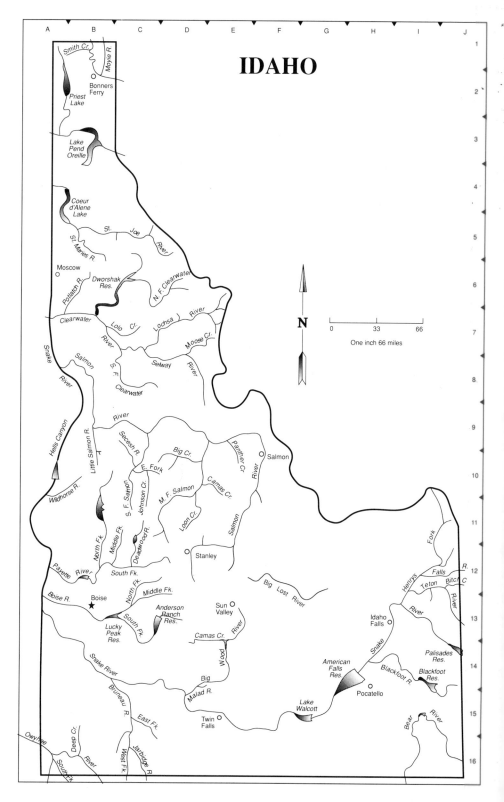

IDAHO

One inch 66 miles

II

III

Idaho — The Whitewater State: a guidebook

©1990 by Grant Amaral

Printed in the United States of America by:
BookCrafters, Chelsea, Michigan

For information address:
Watershed Books, PO Box 111, Garden Valley, Idaho, 83622

First Printing, 1990
Second Printing, 1992
Third Printing, 1995
Fourth Printing, 1998

ISBN 0-9622344-0-0

Editors: Doug Ammons, Laura Andrews

River descriptions: Doug Ammons, Dave Becker, Jeb Blakely, Martin Bochenek, Tony Brennan, Bozo Cardozo, Jim Ciardelli, Slater Crosby, Jim Good, Alan Hamilton, Stan Kolby, Phil Lansing, Clinton La-Tourette, Rob Lesser, Peter Palmer, Roger Rosentredder, Steve Sherick, Craig Stoenner, Roy Piskadlo, Tom Wittaker, John Wasson, Dick Wold

Maps and graphs: Grant Amaral, Todd Rumps, Katrina Stein

All photographs: Grant Amaral unless otherwise noted

Contributing Photographers: Rob Lesser, Glen Oakley, Paul Faulkner, Jack Weinberg, Jim Ciardelli, Eric Straubhar

Cover photo: Mark Lisk

Layout: Grant Amaral, Mary Jones

Thanks:
       Idaho River Sports, Stan Kolby and Joe Cassin
       Canoe Sport Idaho, Phil Lansing
       Cascade Raft Co., Steve and Mary Jones
       Idaho Department Water Resources, Bill Ondrechen
       BSU Library: Karin Eyler, Mary Carter
       ISU OAP
       UI OAP
       Greg Amaral
       Ron Waters
       Mark Torf
       Idaho Transportation Department

Introduction

It would be easy for kayakers living in or near Idaho to be spoiled and start taking its amazing resources for granted. There are hundreds of miles of wilderness class III and IV rivers; myriad free-spirited steep creeks cascading down wild canyons; rivers with 15,000 cfs of clean water sparkling along at 15 mph — forming river wide surfwaves and bouncing holes; hundreds of deep, swirling eddies on dozens of rivers for squirtists to ply their trade; romping class V virtually nonstop from spring until fall; and remote, still canyons whose serene waters will calm you. Even when you spend all your time out here, it seems like there's always some new place to explore. Chances are, if you get a little off the beaten track in time or place, you'll see hardly anyone else. Is this a kayaker's paradise? Well Grant, I, and other Idaho paddlers think so.

Having mentioned your guide for the upcoming pages, I'll introduce him from my point of view. Over the years, Grant and I have shared lots of paddling hours in all kinds of situations — backsurfing on big Lochsa waves, pirouetting our endos into the twilight on the S. F. Payette, thumping and scozzling down big class V on the N. F. Payette, and steep creekin' in places dear to our hearts. He knows his stuff about these rivers, and he's carefully crammed as much as he can in this book for your pleasure and information. If you're not well-informed by the end of the book, well, you should be. The writing is clear and it's amusing — even after most of his wisecracks and hyperkinetic quirks of humor have been edited out or toned down, so as not to offend good taste and morals of youth.

Those of us who live in Idaho know that on any given spring or summer day we have our pick of dozens of great rivers. Everyone who's spent time paddling here will rave about the whitewater. So, since people already know about some of the best rivers, and since this entire book is filled with careful, enthusiastic descriptions of these and other excellent runs, I want to use this opportunity to speak of the downside — so readers will realize there are also many outstanding places they don't know about, some of which we are in danger of losing.

The information gathered in this book, and the willing help of various paddlers represents a recent change in the Idaho paddling community's attitude. For years, we had all this great whitewater to ourselves and didn't particularly want to share it with a lot of outside people. Grant had been gathering information for a long time, but he didn't finally decide that it would be a good idea to write a book encouraging popular use until a few summers ago. To me, advertising my favorite spots without being able to personally screen the prospective paddlers seemed ridiculous. But, like most of our other paddling buddies, we've found within the last few years that some of these places have been threatened and some nearly ruined, and we had no effective way to protect them. We've found that our smug secretiveness has begun to backfire on us. Without people from outside knowing what is here, many of the outstanding runs on lesser known rivers have had very few allies.

Modern progress has been chipping away at Idaho's country, streams, and rivers for a century. There are dozens of dams and many hundreds of square miles of ugly, unredeemed clearcuts; the Snake river has been almost completely civilized and the N.F. Clearwater forests thoroughly brutalized.

Some of the most outstanding rivers have been protected by law as Wild and Scenic, but several have been lost, and many have been saved thusfar only because power and timber companies have been too busy elsewhere. Our civilization is now baring its teeth and threatening some of these remaining unprotected river drainages. There are plans to plug up rivers and run them down pipes, so we can mindlessly feed the energy to the insatiable blight of the West coast and Southwest. The once seemingly endless forests have had huge swaths hacked down to sell overseas and to make all the toothpicks we'll ever need into the 25th century, and always, more is planned. Idaho, Montana and the Northwest have been made into a Third World country— decimating many of their beauties to sell raw timber to Japan, provide a few hours of air conditioning for overheated office workers in Phoenix, and run hairdryers in Eugene, Oregon. Sometimes it makes you mad enough to dream of blowing up a Boise-Cascade mill or wish for a 8.0 earthquake that targets all those dams on the Snake— but these juvenile fantasies aren't solutions. At any rate, the mills and dams would be rebuilt, the power still run out of state, the trees still mowed down, and you'd have 50 years to spend in the slammer.

So we've changed our minds, and agreed that if enough paddlers, river people, and other folk come to know and love the great popular runs — as well as the more secluded and beautifully unspoiled areas — we can gain enough clout to save them before they are fed into the maw of a voracious civilization. Better to have a river crowded with happy paddlers and rafters (a still unlikely prospect for many places in Idaho) than to have it destroyed by a dam, or its canyon stripped bare of trees.

The particular issues and places that have made me change my own mind are the N.F. Payette project, and what is now happening to Smith Creek and the upper Lochsa. The following is a short synopsis of each.

The N.F. Payette Project. This is a dam proposal which has been revived by Gem Irrigation of Boise. It would flood a beautiful valley and a bunch of ranches. In addition, it would virtually dewater the Cabarton run and the great Smith's Ferry to Banks thumper. In their place we would have a big muddy bathtub and mostly dry rocks downstream. Nearly all that bathtub water would be sent down a pipe to make scads of little electron thingies to be bottled up, and zinged down to the southwest in a huge, unsightly powerline. This is not a reasonable trade, but it is an all too real prospect. The valley, ranches, and whitewater, don't count for much, and 16 miles of world famous class IV+ and V rapids may be turned into 16 miles of moss-covered boulders.

Smith Creek's dam and proposed logging. Smith Creek is a small "unnavigatable" river hidden up a very quiet, pretty canyon in the northern-most part of the Panhandle. The run has sustained gradients up to 500 fpm, with polished granite waterslides, wildly steep boulder drops, waterfalls, and a huge, fast spring runoff that has to be caught just right - but when you do catch it, you will find Steep Creek Heaven. Starting this fall, however, there's a new low-head dam syphoning out water at the top of the run (to power the electric toothbrushes of a city that should know better — Eugene, Oregon), a widened road and pipe corridor slashed out of the forest to provide spring-time mud slides in the loose granitic soil, and 17 proposed timber sales in the canyon — eight of them down to the streambed right alongside the most spectacular part of the run. All this might not turn out to be a total disaster in the end — I hope not. But it is the beginning of a very, very sad transition from a beautiful, forested canyon and stunning steep creek to a "managed" resource which is on the verge of losing most of its unique charm and beauty. This is an unknown canyon with a world class whitewater run, and we're watching it get ruined right before our eyes. The more people who know what is happening, the better.

Upper Lochsa logging. The Lochsa area borders the Selway-Bitterroot Wilderness in northeast Idaho. It has quiet, ceder-scented forests and crystalline-clear streams slipping around granite boulders; springtime's warmth brings a rush of sun-sparkled water and shades of green beyond imagining. The main Lochsa River has 50+ miles of class II, III, and IV rapids in a beautiful, pristine canyon, and there are great wilderness steep creek runs on all of its major tributaries. While the lower 60 miles of the river corridor is designated Wild and Scenic - and is as pretty a river as you'll ever find - there are large sections of private timber company land in the White Sands, Crooked Fork, and Brushy Fork drainages which have been and are being heavily logged. In what looks like a worst case scenario for the forest's scenic beauty, Plum Creek Co. has apparently decided to "convert" it's holdings, which means to a viewer, scything down the forest in big sections. Although they are well within their rights to do this, the visual impact of commercial timber management in this spectacular area will make you sick. As you drive over Lolo Pass at the head of the drainage, where unbroken forest stood there are miles of gaping bare spots covered with stumps, slash heaps and splintered debris. In addition, timber access to the roadless land bordering the 15 miles of the lower White Sands run is being considered. After all the cuts are made, what will be left of the drainages? Will the crystalline water of the lower Lochsa still run clear? Will the quiet ceder and pine forests along the steep creeks be ruined? If you are a pessimist like me — having seen what's already been done to the North Fork Clearwater forests — you wonder if the slogans of the militant loggers say it all: "Buttwipe and toothpicks — not wilderness." "Loggers — the true environmentalists."

So there you have it, the N.F. Payette, Smith Creek and the upper Lochsa, three reasons why I decided to change my mind and help Grant all I could to invite the use of the outstanding paddling runs I know and love. I thank him for his huge effort in putting this book together so that out-of-state people can discover the fantastic paddling that we have, as well as what our problems are. Idaho is still a whitewater and wilderness paradise, but we are losing ground to "progress". The threat of abuse is not from overcrowding, but from the lack of a voice to protect these places. The awareness this guidebook awakens may help turn the tide. I hope so.

Idaho- the Whitewater State; for those of us who take part in its flow, it is a state of mind as well as a place. Come and paddle, enjoy these wonderful streams and rivers, and the land that cradles them. You will be much the richer for it. Please take part and help keep them beautiful for all of us, and our children.

Doug Ammons
Missoula, Montana

Rivers such as the Payette, the Salmon, and Snake are constantly being threatened by new and unnecessary dams, ditches, diversions and development. Idaho Rivers United represents the public interest and your concerns, whenever Idaho rivers are threatened. Together we can make a difference. If you love a river join Idaho Rivers United.

Idaho Rivers United
P.O. Box 633, Boise, Id. 83701

Author's Foreword

River Travel has been a way of life in Idaho since it was first explored by Europeans at the start of the 19th century and probably by the Indians before then. Explorers used canoes to cross the Snake River Plain. Lewis and Clark made the Salmon River famous by not running it. A hundred years later miners used the Salmon to float supplies and loggers turned the rivers into flumes. Today kayakers, canoeists and rafters use the same rivers for recreation, exploration, adventure and relaxation. Until now, in typical Idaho style, river runners simply had to wing it, relying on word of mouth descriptions from other boaters and a handful of guidebooks focused on individual rivers.

For 10 years I've been winging it on the rivers of Idaho, but I've also been writing it down. The result is this guidebook. It is your key to unlocking the whitewater secrets of Idaho. It is only one key and hundreds of whitewater runs remain to be explored and unlocked. There's a lot of me in this book. I'm a thorough person and you'll find this book complete and well researched. I like to talk and joke, so you'll find some tall tales and an underlying vein of humor. Finally, many of these runs, I selfishly (and foolishly) consider mine— please treat them with care.

The information contained in this book is the end product of a profound love of rivers, mountains, books and maps, but most of all whitewater. This book is an outgrowth of my desire to understand and apply order to the apparent chaos of whitewater. You will find no stroke by stroke rapid descriptions in this book. With the exception of noting most of the major rapids, hazards and portages, once on the river you're on your own. Even if I were along on your run, I probably wouldn't tell you how to run a rapid. Use this book as a means of finding rivers, knowing what to expect and being there at the right time. By writing this guidebook, hopefully I've saved you some tedious hours in the library, a few wrong turns on the road and increased your time on the water.

I put together the first draft of this book back in 1985. The reaction of the whitewater crowd ran from enthusiastic to appalled. Most of the appalled reactions came from my close friends. After all we were living in our own private Idaho of whitewater bliss: big water, lots of rivers and all of it to ourselves. Why share it? So I shelved my notebooks and went kayaking. Then low-head hydro came into venture-capital vogue. And while I don't mind sharing a wave with other boaters, I sure as hell don't like to share my rivers with penstocks and turbines. Two of the best defenses against dam builders are a large group of river users and a written record of use. A guide book serves both purposes: introducing people to new rivers and documenting use. In fact on popular runs it may actually reduce crowding by presenting boaters with new alternatives. It's a trade-off, but I don't think sharing the river with dams is really sharing.

This is a small book, but it's the result of a big effort. What you can't see are the piles of notebooks, the miles of computer printouts, the stacks of maps and all the help from my friends. I've set the record for map use at BSU, worn out four kayaks, outgrown two computer systems, broken two camera bodies and three lenses, spent a small fortune, and swam several nasty rapids. I hope you find these efforts useful. I've had a lot of fun.

How to use this book

For people unfamiliar with Idaho, finding a river can be a headache, and even for those of us who live here, other parts of the state can be as foreign as another language. This book is organized around the Snake River and moves upstream. With the exception of the Panhandle rivers and the Bear River (in the state's southeast corner), every river in Idaho eventually ends up in the Snake. Imagine you're following the Snake river upstream starting where it crosses the western Idaho border and every time you pass a tributary you follow it to its end and in turn to the end of it's tributaries. After you've explored all the runs, you go back to the Snake and continue upstream.

The book moves upstream, because on maps it's easy to find big rivers and follow them upstream to a small creek, but it's hard to find a small creek unless you already know where it is. Therefore, if you know the major rivers in Idaho you can use this book.

I've divided the state into 13 basins, moving up along the Snake first to the Clearwater, then all the way up the Salmon: lower Salmon, South Fork Salmon, Middle Fork Salmon, upper Salmon. Back to the lower Snake, Payette, Boise, Owyhee, Bruneau, the Magic Valley, upper Snake (including the Bear), and then to the north and the Panhandle. The Main Salmon and the Snake have been divided into upper and lower basins, because, for example, the extreme of the upper Snake is over 500 miles from the extreme of the lower Snake — it would be ridiculous to keep them together. Runs close together in the book are usually nearby in reality. Turning the page is the same as driving up the road.

If you're familiar with Stanley and Holbek's guidebook to California it's obvious I've borrowed heavily from their layout. This isn't a rip-off, but a tribute to what I find to be an easy to read page. The layout of this book is intended to make it simple to find a river, both in the book and the field. To find a river look at the map and index in the very front of the book. Find the page number and turn to the description. The descriptions will always start on the left page and the corresponding map on the opposite page, except in the case of one map serving more than one description. To find a missing map turn back through the pages to the precedent. In most cases all the information on a river is lumped together: description, map and graph. Unfortunately, in some places I was forced to put the graph several pages away. The directions on where to find it are at the end of the description.

Key to River Descriptions

Class: The ratings in this book are a reflection of the popularly agreed upon classification. Idaho is in the West, so the common Western convention regarding class VI is followed throughout the book: a class VI rapid is an unrun rapid. By no means should the ICF scale ever be used as a substitute for your own judgment.

Class I: Moving water with a few riffles and small waves, Few or no obstructions.

Class II: Easy rapids with waves up to three feet, and wide, clear channels that are obvious without scouting. Some maneuvering is required.

Class III: Rapids with high, irregular waves often capable of swamping an open canoe. Narrow passages that often require complex maneuvering. May require scouting from shore.

Class IV: Long, difficult rapids with constricted passages that often require precise maneuvering in very turbulent waters. Scouting from shore is often necessary, and conditions make rescue difficult. Generally not possible for open canoes. Boaters in covered canoes and kayaks should be able to Eskimo roll.

Class V: Extremely difficult, long,and very violent rapids with highly congested routes which nearly always must be scouted from shore. Rescue conditions are difficult and there is significant hazard to life in event of a mishap. Ability to Eskimo Roll is essential for kayaks and canoes.

Class VI: Difficulties of Class V carried to the extreme of navigability. Nearly impossible and very dangerous. For teams of experts only, after close study and with all precautions taken. (As mentioned above, the common Western convention regarding class VI is followed throughout the book: a class VI rapid is an unrun rapid.)

Any time a classification is written down, an argument starts. As with any standard, the ICF scale is merely a symbolic model, it is not the river.

Another Idaho outdoorsman says it best:

> Then there is the other secret. There isn't any symbolism. The sea is the sea. The old man is an old man. The *river* is a *river* and the fish is a fish. The *rapids* are all *rapids* no better and no worse. All the symbolism that people say is shit. What goes beyond is what you see beyond when you know. — Ernest Hemingway (sort of)

Level: The discharge of the river as expressed in cubic feet per second (cfs). If the difficulty of the run changes at different levels this is expressed as well. The discharge on some Idaho rivers is expressed in feet. On these rivers the height scale is correlated to difficulty in the same method used for cfs ratings. Usually the rating table is provided as well.

Length: Length is expressed in miles, beginning at the put-in and ending at the river's mouth or the take-out, whichever comes first. If there are two numbers with the second in parenthesis, this indicates the run ends in another river or a lake and paddling out is required. The first number is the entire length, the sum of both rivers. The second number is the length of the river being described. If you want to know how long the paddle out is subtract the latter from the former.
In computing gradient if both sections were computed together the gradient figure was often radically deceptive. Therefore, the profile and gradient ends at the mouth of the first river and the paddle out is ignored.

Gradient: Gradient is expressed in feet per mile (fpm). All elevations are water level. The elevation at the take-out is subtracted from the elevation at the put-in and divided by the length of the run. If the river flows into another river and the run includes paddling out on the latter, the gradient is computed using the confluence as the take-out.

Time: Time is expressed in hours or days. This is the minimum amount of time necessary to kayak the run at medium flows.

Put-in: Starting point and elevation.

Take-out: Finishing point and elevation.

Shuttle: Expressed in miles from the put-in to the take-out. Occasionally time is expressed as well. Dirt or pavement is explained in the descriptions and on the maps.

Craft: Refers to whether the river is runnable in kayaks, rafts, or canoes. Canoe refers to open canoes.
The words "raft " or "canoe" do not imply all rafts or canoes are capable of making the run. They indicate the run has been successfully run in those craft.

Portages: The number is not a recommendation. It is a record of the **minimum** number of portages known to have been made on a run. It is by no means a guide to the number of portages an individual may expect or a substitute for individual judgement. If the portage number is followed by the word **logs** and a number in parenthesis, this is an indication of logs or logjams that must be portaged as part of the total number of portages. The distinction between a log portage and a rapid portage is important due to the changing nature of logs and logjams.

Season: Most Idaho rivers are free flowing. This means the river season coincides with spring run-off. On the average, peak run-off starts in April and ends in June. Seasons, naturally, vary from river to river and those with dams usually have a longer season.

Gauge: Simply whether there is a gauge on the river. Most rivers have more than one gauge, so the one relating to the specific run is named. Since science has taken a back seat to business, most of the gauges presently in use, are on rivers that supply irrigation water. Many of the gauges on the small and more remote creeks are no longer maintained, but their historic records are still available. These are listed as "historic." Rivers with a usable stick gauge are noted as well. The rating table is provided in the appendix. The rating tables change from year to year, but the difference is marginal. All the hydrographs are summaries of the entire period of record for the gauge. The data was supplied by the Idaho Department of Water Resources.

Permit: "Yes" if you need one. Read the description for the details.

Maps: The USGS topographical maps are listed followed by the national forest maps (in italics).
There are three different types of maps used in this guide:
The State Map: The big picture — shows major highways, cities, rivers and mile markers
Basin Maps: show rivers, primary access routes and major geographic features in the area.
River Maps: show the specific river, the put-in, take out and access roads. Every effort has been made to insure the accuracy of these maps. They are computer traces of Idaho Department of Transportation county maps.
While the most of the major rapids and portages are marked, the river maps do not show every rapid nor portage. In addition to helping locate the river, the rapids and the hazards the maps are provided to assist floaters in tracking their progress on the run.
Forest Service and BLM land use maps are scaled to make useful shuttle guides. In addition, they are current. I recommend carrying the forest service map for the area you are boating in. Most of them run $2.00. You can get the travel map for free. They are identical to the forest map, but lack campground information. I don't recommend topographic maps because they are expensive and are scaled in a size that only shows segments of any shuttle or river. They are excellent maps for elevations and detail, but since the profiles are included in this book, you don't really need them. Neverless, I've listed the topographic maps for reference.

Character: Character is a brief outline of the river, distinguishing riverbed, rapid type, hazards, trails, roads, scenery, and man's impact. It is an abstract of the **description** below.

Description: The big picture — The description gives a detailed account of what to expect on the river: rapids, hazards, camping, points of interest and any other information which will help make your trip more enjoyable. While I may be unwilling to tell you how to run a rapid, I'm more than willing to tell you how to drive —every description includes detailed shuttle directions.

Graphs: The graphs show both the flow and profile of the river. They're double Y axis plots. If you've dealt with them before, they should be easy to understand. The river's **profile** is represented by one line and the **flow** by the other. A double Y axis has a constant horizontal axis and two independent vertical axes. The horizontal axis represents miles, starting at 0, the put-in, and ending at the take-out. In addition, the months of the year correlate to the numbers 1-12.

The left vertical axis represents elevation expressed in feet. The profile line represents the river's gradient at mile intervals. This line starts in the graph's upper left corner (the put-in) and descends to the right (the take-out). The graph lines represent 100 foot intervals. They are the constant factor in all the graphs. If the lines are close together, the river usually has a high gradient. The run's average gradient is stated as well.

The right vertical axis represents the river's monthly discharge in cubic feet per second (cfs). In almost every graph, the discharge line, looks like a standard bell curve. It starts in the lower left corner, climbs towards the center, and then descends towards the lower right corner. The gauges statistical records, such as, "peak" — the river's record discharge and date, "drainage area" — the size of the river basin expressed in square miles, and the mean elevation, when available, are all stated within the graph. All flows are based on the historic average unless noted otherwise.

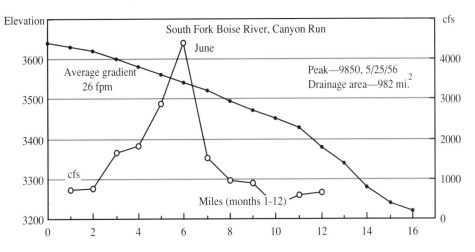

South Fork Boise River, Canyon Run

Clearwater Basin

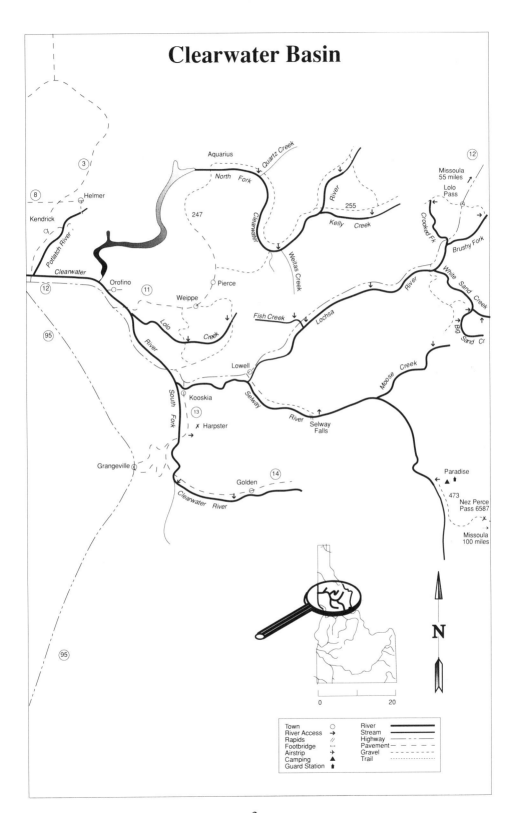

BIG BEAR CREEK

CLASS	LEVEL	LENGTH	GRADIENT	TIME
IV-V	500 cfs	16 miles	98 fpm	8 hours

PUT-IN: Highway 8 Bridge, west of Deary 2 miles (2,600 ft.)
TAKE-OUT: Kendrick High School (1,320 ft.)
SHUTTLE: 18 miles
CRAFT: Kayak
PORTAGES: 1 fence
SEASON: Peak (April)
GAUGE: No
PERMIT: No
MAPS: Juliatte, Little Bear Rdg., Texas Rdg., Deary
CHARACTER: Extreme steep-creek, granite and basalt canyons, blind corners, falls, secluded.

DESCRIPTION: This run has only been done once due to the usual lack of water in this creek. There is no gauge, because, usually, the flow is too insignificant to warrant one. If the river gets bank-full, or the runoff in the surrounding area is going wild, then Big Bear is probably running. Jim Good and Gary Bordeaux made an exploratory run the spring of 1985.

The river starts off with class II-III whitewater for the first third of the run. There is a fence that must be portaged in the first mile. Dry Creek enters from the right seven miles down. Within the next mile a class IV drop has been created by a slide from the right filling the stream with rubble. A little further downstream the river goes around a blind corner to the left. Just around the bend there is a horizon line with several breaking waves just above it. There is a small must-make eddy just above the horizon line. This is Bordeaux Falls — run once — accidently, upside down and without scouting by Gary Bordeaux. Luckily, it has a plunge pool. Portage this drop or scout it on the right. Below the falls there are several more big drops with a long class IV approximately a mile below the falls. After the big gravel island, a long staircase of ledges runs along the base of a prominent cliff. The rest of the trip is a clean run-out.

The shuttle is easy. To find the put-in from Kendrick go north on highway 3 approximately 14 miles to Deary, then turn left and go two miles to the first bridge. Start here or follow the little road paralleling the first two miles of the run on the left side. To find a suitable take-out, follow the road by the high school upstream and choose your spot.

Little Bear Creek has been run as well. From the bridge in Troy, it starts with a mile of willows, followed by class II swift water for the rest of the run.

J.G.

See graph page 13.

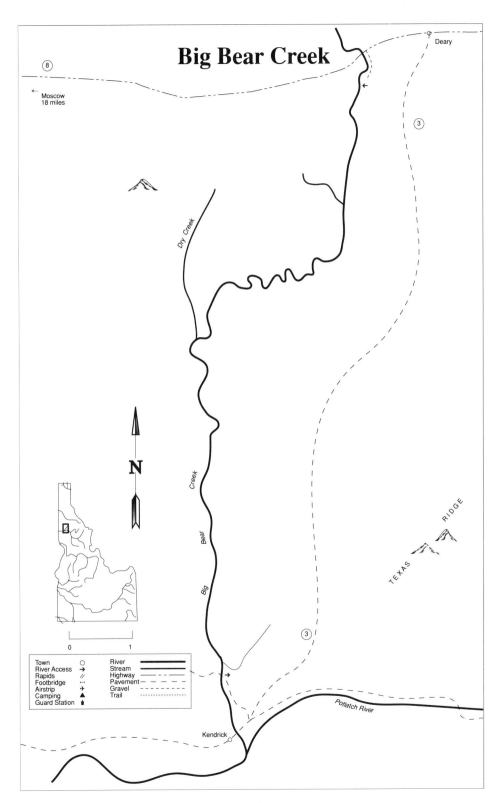

Big Bear Creek

Deary

③

← Moscow
18 miles

Dry Creek

N

Big Bear Creek

RIDGE

TEXAS

③

Town	○	River	
River Access	→	Stream	
Rapids	∥	Highway	
Footbridge	⊣⊢	Pavement	
Airstrip	⤳	Gravel	
Camping	▲	Trail	
Guard Station	⬧		

0   1

Kendrick

Potlatch River

POTLATCH RIVER, LOWER RUN

CLASS	LEVEL	LENGTH	GRADIENT	TIME
II-III	300-1,000 cfs	8 miles	45 fpm	3 hours
III	>1,000 cfs			

PUT-IN:	Frog Pond
TAKE-OUT:	Kendrick High School
SHUTTLE:	5
CRAFT:	Kayaks, canoes, small rafts
PORTAGES:	Fence
SEASON:	February, March, April
GAUGE:	Kendrick
PERMIT:	No
MAPS:	Juliatte, Lenore, Little Bear Rdg.
CHARACTER:	Rock garden changing to easy swift water, road, developed.

DESCRIPTION: There are many possible put-ins and take-outs in the lower Potlatch canyon. The most interesting section begins at the highest point you can drive to, upstream from Kendrick before the road leaves the river (locals call this the "Frog Pond") There is a class III drop at this put-in, which was the site of the slalom race at the '86 North Idaho Whitewater Festival. There are a couple of surf waves in the next two miles that get better as the water rises.

If you go beyond the first bridge there is no public access and almost no whitewater until you get to Kendrick High School (access only no whitewater). Local boaters take out at this bridge and run the top two miles over and over. Below this bridge the river meanders through cow pastures and grain fields down to Kendrick. Look out for fences and other agricultural by-products in this stretch of the river. Behind the grain silos in Kendrick, a shallow ledge forms a play wave at higher flows.

The riverbanks along the lower canyon are all private property, please respect property owners at all times. The man living next to the Frog Pond (on the switchback above the put-in) is happy to grant permission to use his access, but insists that people ask first.

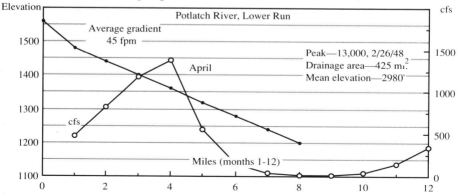

Potlatch River

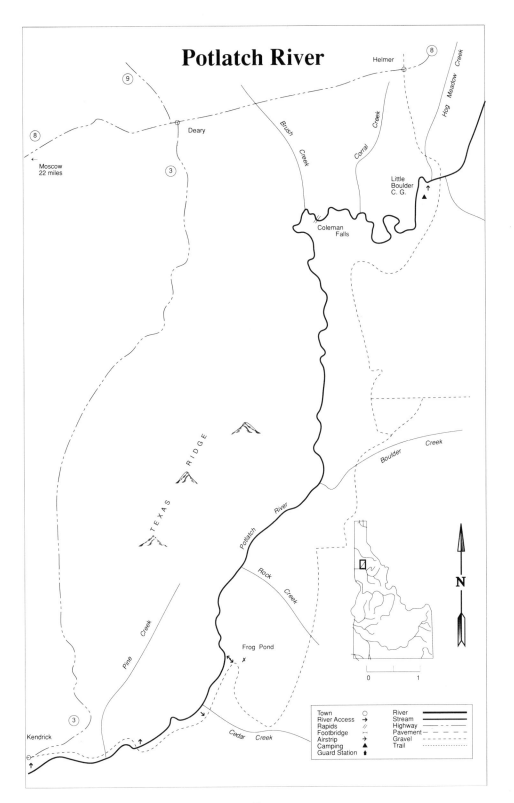

Helmer

⑧

Hog Meadow Creek

⑨

⑧

Deary

Moscow
22 miles

③

Brush Creek

Corral Creek

Little
Boulder
C. G.

Coleman
Falls

Boulder Creek

Potlatch River

T E X A S   R I D G E

Rock Creek

Pine Creek

Frog Pond

Kendrick

③

Cedar Creek

Town	○	River	
River Access	→	Stream	
Rapids	//	Highway	— · —
Footbridge	)(	Pavement	— —
Airstrip	✦	Gravel	- - -
Camping	▲	Trail	····
Guard Station	♠		

N

0   1

POTLATCH RIVER, CANYON

CLASS	LEVEL	LENGTH	GRADIENT	TIME
IV (V)	500-1,600 cfs	15 miles	72 fpm	1 day
V	>1600 cfs			

PUT-IN:	Little Boulder Campground (2,580 ft.)
TAKE-OUT:	Cedar Creek (1,440 ft.)
SHUTTLE:	28 miles
CRAFT:	Kayak
PORTAGES:	0
SEASON:	Spring
GAUGE:	Kendrick (historic)
PERMIT:	No
MAPS:	Juliatte, Lenore, Little Bear Rdg., Texas Rdg.
CHARACTER:	Small river, technical, rock gardens, gorge, logs, wilderness.

DESCRIPTION: The Potlatch canyon has a wilderness character that can't be found on the popular wilderness rivers in Idaho. Just downstream from the put-in, the river drops into a deep basalt gorge. The canyon sides are covered by a lush forest of pine and fir. An old roadbed follows the river for the first couple miles and some logging roads are visible in the lower half of the canyon, but they do not provide access to the river. It is possible, but difficult, to reach a road on the ridge by climbing out of either side of the canyon.

The Potlatch Canyon begins with a couple of miles of class I and II whitewater which lead into a constricted granite gorge. The biggest drop in the gorge is a long class V known as Coleman Falls. This rapid consists of a series of sticky ledges, so look carefully at it and in particular, note the undercut on the left at the rapid's end. Lots of people choose to portage on the right, bring a rope and be careful. A raft could probably be lined down the right, if not the portage would probably take a couple hours.

The steep walled granite gorge continues for about five miles. You will know you are close to the end of the gorge when the walls come together to create a kind of exit gate. At this point a mile of difficult whitewater remains. The geology changes to a deep, and progressively more open basalt canyon. After the last major rapid, you still have a long paddle out in class II-III swift water. At high water there are some excellent surf waves in this stretch. However, unless you like paddling in the dark, you had better keep your boat pointed downstream.

The shuttle is easy. To find the put-in from Kendrick go north on highway 3 approximately 14 miles to Deary, then turn right and continue east four miles to Helmer. On the south side of the road a national forest campground sign marks the turn to the put-in. Follow this road south 2.5 miles to Little Boulder Campground. The take-out is seven miles up from Kendrick at the little turnout 100 meters down from Cedar Creek. Cedar Creek is less than a mile down from where the road leaves the river.

The upper canyon had a notorious reputation among Moscow area boaters in the early '80s following several unsuccessful expeditions that destroyed several fiberglass boats. Water levels may fluctuate dramatically in a few days. If the water is touching the bridge abutments at the put-in, the whitewater will be challenging. Above this, the Potlatch is a much more difficult run. Below this, it is a very long day, so start early.

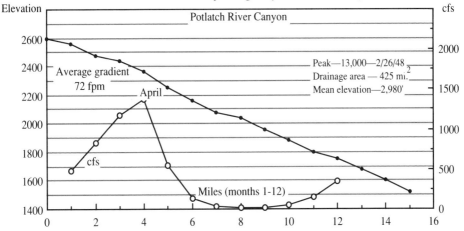

Potlatch River Canyon

Average gradient 72 fpm

April

cfs

Miles (months 1-12)

Peak—13,000—2/26/48
Drainage area — 425 mi.^{2}
Mean elevation—2,980'

Bob Powell in the Potlatch Canyon.

NORTH FORK CLEARWATER, QUARTZ CREEK RUN

CLASS	LEVEL	LENGTH	GRADIENT	TIME
III	1,000-15,000 cfs	9 miles	19 fpm	4-6 hours

PUT-IN: Quartz Creek (1,860 ft.)
TAKE-OUT: Aquarius Campground (1,680 ft.)
SHUTTLE: 9 miles
CRAFT: Kayak, canoe, raft
PORTAGES: 0
SEASON: May, June, July
GAUGE: Canyon Ranger Station
PERMIT: No
MAPS: Sheep Mtn., Clark Mtn., The Nub, *Clearwater NF*
CHARACTER: Big river, big waves and rapids, ledges and boulder gardens, scenic, road.

DESCRIPTION: Like most roadside rivers, the put-in and the take-out on the North Fork of the Clearwater are up to the individual. The North Fork could be run from the Cedars to Aquarius for a total trip of over 60 miles. As a precaution make sure you top off your gas tank before dropping into the North Fork canyon, because this is one of the most remote areas in Idaho. If you're going to do more than one or two of the runs in this area, bring a jerrican of gas.

Over the years boaters have informally divided the river into three runs, plus Kelly Creek. The lower run, from Quartz Creek to Aquarius is class III at almost all levels. As the volume increases, the waves grow in size, but the rapids lose some of their character. Kayakers can camp and put in at the mouth of Quartz Creek. Rafters can camp here too, but the creek is too small for most rafts. The alternate put-in is just downstream from Quartz Creek.

The river is fairly flat to Skull Creek, but picks up downstream with three good class III rapids. Lost Pete Rapid has some big waves and good surfing, Cougar Rapids are about a mile downstream, and the last rapid, Aquarius, is a good class III rock garden with some surfing, just above the take-out.

The take-out on the right. The camping is good at Aquarius with the usual forest service fee. If you want a precise water level reading, there is a stick gauge on the left bank, upstream of the bridge. See the appendix for the rating table.

See graph page 13.

North Fork Clearwater River

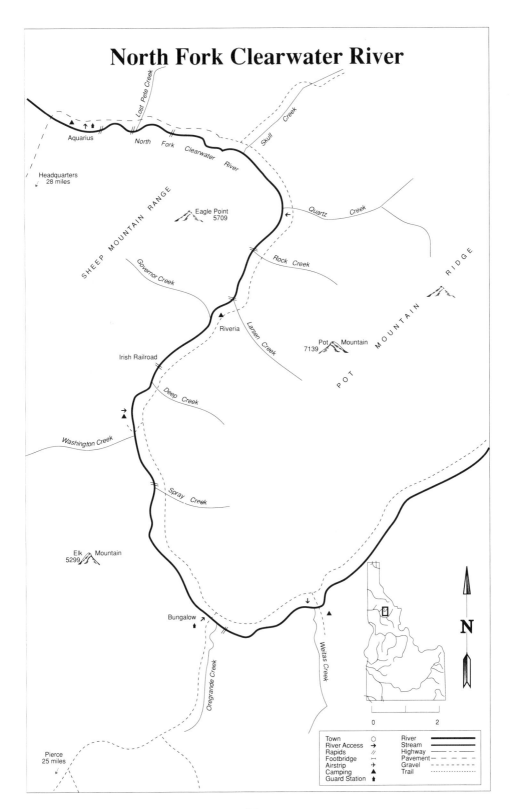

NORTH FORK CLEARWATER RIVER, BUNGALOW RUN

CLASS	LEVEL	LENGTH	GRADIENT	TIME
III (V)	3,000-15,000 cfs	20 miles	23 fpm	6-8 hours

PUT-IN:	Weitas Creek Campground (2,320 ft.)
TAKE-OUT:	Quartz Creek (1,860 ft.)
SHUTTLE:	20 miles
CRAFT:	Kayak, canoe, raft
PORTAGES:	0
SEASON:	May, June, July
GAUGE:	Canyon Ranger Station
PERMIT:	No
MAPS:	Sheep Mtn., Clark Mtn., The Nub, *Clearwater NF*
CHARACTER:	Big river, big waves and rapids, boulder gardens, scenic, road.

DESCRIPTION: The upper run on the North Fork of the Clearwater has several big rapids, including Irish Railroad, a huge boulder-choked class IV-V drop. During high water most of the current feeds into a hole in the center. If you look at it, I think you will agree it would be unwise to go into this hole, so look for the sneak route down the right, which is there at most levels. Washington Creek Campground is a good access point to either avoid or attempt Irish Railroad. Get out here if you want to avoid it, start here if you want to run it. Above Irish Railroad there are two other major drops, the first is Spray Creek and the other is just up from the bridge at Oregrande Creek (note one of the few Spanish names in Idaho). The wave train in the run-out contains one of the best surf waves in Idaho. When the waters high there's an eddy on the right which will auto-load you directly onto a 10 footer.

Most people put-in below Irish Railroad. Downstream there are lots of play holes and rapids. One of the standouts is Governor Creek, a long class III rock garden. The campgrounds are secluded. For the gauge location check the Quartz Creek Run description.

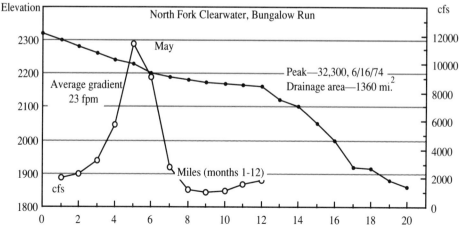

12

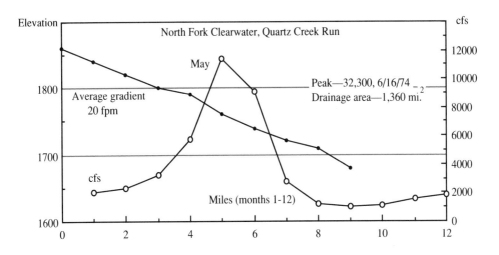

North Fork Clearwater, Quartz Creek Run

Average gradient
20 fpm

Peak—32,300, 6/16/74
Drainage area—1,360 mi.^{2}

May

cfs

Miles (months 1-12)

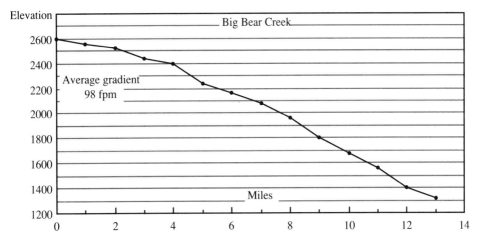

Big Bear Creek

Average gradient
98 fpm

Miles

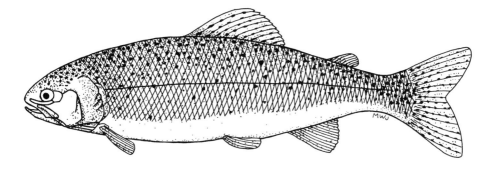

RAINBOW TROUT
Salmo gairdneri

NORTH FORK CLEARWATER RIVER, BLACK CANYON

CLASS	LEVEL	LENGTH	GRADIENT	TIME
III-IV	1,000 cfs	11 miles	54 fpm	3 hours

PUT-IN: Hidden Creek Campground (3,330 ft.)
TAKE-OUT: Kelly Forks Campground (2,740 ft.)
SHUTTLE: 11 miles
CRAFT: Kayak, canoe, raft
PORTAGES: 0
SEASON: May, June
GAUGE: No
PERMIT: No
MAPS: Junction Mtn., Moose Mtn., Scurvy Mtn., *Clearwater NF*
CHARACTER: Small river, swift, rock gardens, logs, secluded, road.

DESCRIPTION: At the Kelly Forks Ranger Station, the North Fork of the Clearwater takes on a different character. The gradient picks up and the flow is cut in two. Kelly Creek, to the south, is a major tributary of the North Fork and at this point, nearly equal in volume.

Upstream, the North Fork enters a deep canyon with some magnificent scenery. The whitewater is busy class II and III rock gardens for most of the run. Below Hidden Creek the run starts with fast and splashy swift water. About a mile down is the first rapid of significance, a class III S-turn. The canyon sides are covered by a maze of avalanche paths which dump hundreds of logs into the river every winter. Some of the river channels are completely choked by logjams. At Elizabeth Creek the whitewater picks up and doesn't let off until a mile from the take-out. In addition to the many class III rapids, there is a long class III-IV rock garden in this stretch.

The shuttle is next to the river and most of the rapids can be road scouted. Look for new logjams on the way up.

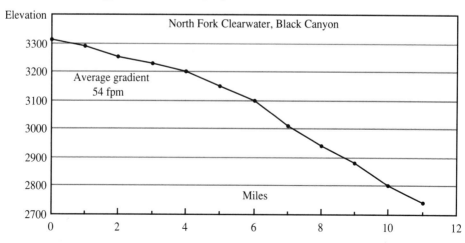

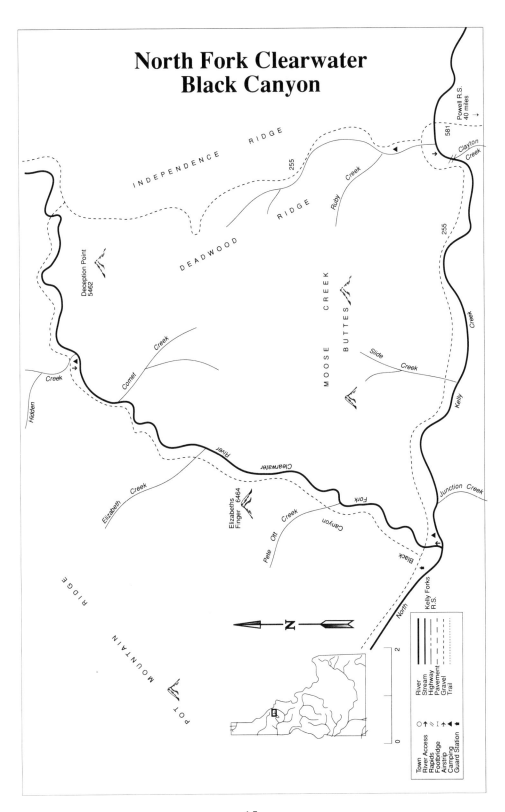

North Fork Clearwater
Black Canyon

KELLY CREEK

CLASS	LEVEL	LENGTH	GRADIENT	TIME
III-IV	1,000 cfs	10 miles	45 fpm	2-3 hours

PUT-IN: Clayton Creek (3,140 ft.)
TAKE-OUT: Kelly Forks Campground (2,740 ft.)
SHUTTLE: 11 miles
CRAFT: Kayak
PORTAGES: 0
SEASON: May, June,
GAUGE: No
PERMIT: No
MAPS: Junction Mtn., Moose Mtn., Scurvy Mtn., *Clearwater NF*
CHARACTER: Small river, swift, rock gardens, logs, secluded, road.

DESCRIPTION: This little creek offers a kayakers a interesting change from the wide open character of the other runs in the area. Kelly Creek is a tight little run, in a deep canyon. The scenery is scarred from the big fire of 1910. Do your stretches at the put-in, because the most difficult rapid on Kelly Creek is just around the first bend at Clayton Creek. At high flows a river wide hole forms at the entrance of the rapid. The run-out is a long chute with a tight line. About a half-mile downstream a big class III-IV starts where the creek makes a turn to the left. The next rapid is a long and rocky class IV. Downstream, there are three straight forward rapids, and then the river changes to a wide splashy ride to the take-out.

All the rapids can be scouted from the road. The put-in is in the flat water just upstream of Clayton Creek. The camping is good at the take-out and the put-in.

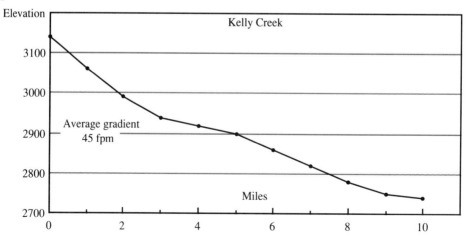

When the water's high the North Fork offers some superlative surfing.

LOLO CREEK, LOWER RUN

CLASS	LEVEL	LENGTH	GRADIENT	TIME
III-V	300-600 cfs	15 miles	75 fpm	4 hours

PUT-IN:	Cottonwood Flats (2,200 ft.)
TAKE-OUT:	Clearwater Confluence (1,080 ft.)
SHUTTLE:	25 miles
CRAFT:	Kayak
PORTAGES:	0
SEASON:	May, June
GAUGE:	Lolo Creek
PERMIT:	No
MAPS:	Sixmile Cr., Woodland, Weippe South, *Clearwater NF*
CHARACTER:	Small river, rock gardens, ledges, technical, logs, secluded.

DESCRIPTION: Lolo Creek is one of the best whitewater runs in Idaho. I can't quite believe it remained unrun until 1989. There are two reasons for its undeserved lack of use: first, it's hard to find; even with maps and even if you know where it is (it's buried under the Clearwater County line on maps and in the field it's hidden in a deep canyon surrounded by wheat fields); second, a couple of kayakers claimed to have run it and described it as, full of brush, logs and lacking any significant whitewater. Nothing could be further from the truth, but, their "first descent" left such a stigma with north Idaho boaters that for years no one bothered to look at the maps let alone peek into the canyon.

I saw the maps before I started asking about the run. The logs, brush, and bull story cooled my enthusiasm for four years, but the topos and the profile gnawed away in the back of my mind. All it took was one look at the creek to fire up my enthusiasm. The top of Lolo Creek is wide and swift. The brush is off the banks and all the logs are either standing or riding on the back of a truck. The canyon consists of jointed-basalt bluffs and is covered with a dense cedar forest. It even smells good — like those little cedar boxes you buy at national forest tourist traps. I drove to the take-out, it looked even better there, so I camped.

At six the next morning I carried my kayak and equipment back to the "main" road and stuck out my thumb. People are a little different in north Idaho. It took an hour to get my first ride, but everyone waved and smiled at me. The ride I finally got stopped in Weippe and I was left, with a cup of coffee and a wave, sitting on top of my kayak in the middle of an Idaho prairie. After about an hour of people waving at me I began to feel a little foolish. I was planning on paddling 26 miles of unknown river, with an average gradient of 67 fpm and two 160 foot miles, alone. I looked at my watch and figured I had 15 minutes to catch a ride, after then the chance of being caught on the river after dark would be too great. At that moment a pick-up pulled to a stop in front of me. I stuck my head in the window. The driver, an old logger, gave me a

Lolo Creek

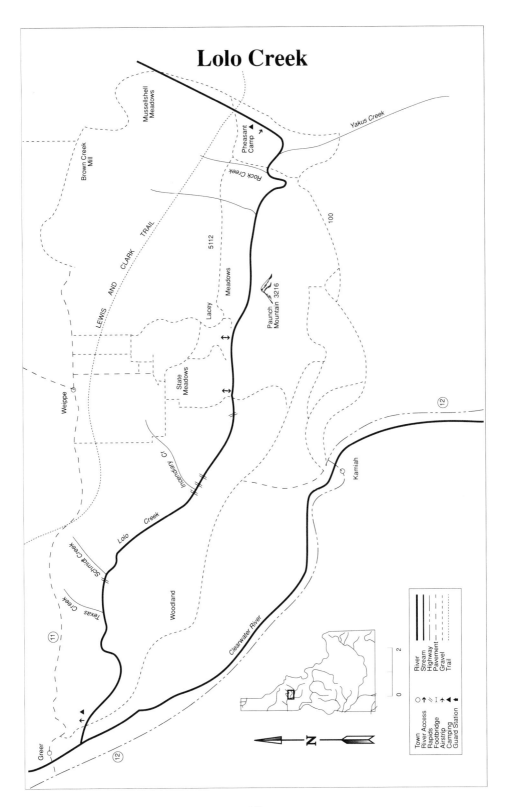

big grin and said, "Just what in the hell do you think your doing?" I knew it was my lucky day. I explained my plan and said "I'll give you ten bucks to drive me to Lolo Creek."

"Put your money away and throw that boat in back."

Starting at State Meadows, Lolo Creek flows through a beautiful wide meadow, where the canyon closes in, and the rock turns to granite, brace yourself for some whitewater. The rapids start with a bang. I named the first one Shamrock, in honor of the other first descent. It's a mile-long series of class IV-V ledges and only a sampler of what's downstream. The next landmark is a county bridge on a good road. If it's been raining and you can't drive down the State Meadows road start at this bridge.

The next six miles are a nonstop whitewater blur. The canyon closes in on the river and the further you go, the tougher things get. Most of the rapids consist of complex ledges and steep chutes. They are formed by boulders choking off the river bed. As the river continues down into the canyon the rapids become progressively more difficult. This section of the canyon ends with a series of three boulder-filled class Vs. The first is called Maniac. It's a mess of a rock garden. Check the sneak route down the right. The next big rapid I named Mad Bear. It's a dangerous class V with a tight chute pressed between a log and an overhanging boulder. Because I was alone, I'd of probably portaged this one. Instead I was forced to run it blind after being chased out of the eddy just above it by an angry momma bear with cubs. I could have eddied out on the other side of the creek, but the bear was hopping around in such a frenzy I thought she was going to jump in the river and swim after me. Lame Duck, is just downstream. A simple move, but if you blow it, you're going into a guillotine undercut.

After these rapids, the canyon opens up a little and the whitewater backs off as well, but don't start celebrating too early — Big Schmidt, a class V jumble of rocks, is downstream. The last four miles are a series of easy class III rock gardens.

To get to the take-out go seven miles south of Orofino on highway 12 and cross the Clearwater at Greer. Continue south through Greer about a mile on highway 11 to a large turnout and a gravel road leading down to the river and the take-out. To reach the put-in continue 16 miles on highway 11 to Weippe. Go straight through Weippe about 100 yards to the Three-mile Road. Take this to the south a little over two miles until you come to a Y in the road. Keep to the right and follow this road a mile to the next intersection, then go to the east for a half-mile and take the second road to the south, for a mile, through State Meadows and continue down into the canyon. You won't be able to drive all the way to the river. When you can go no further, get out and walk. If you want to drive to the river and miss two miles of great whitewater, go back to the gravel and go to the west for a little over a half-mile. Then go south and follow the main road down into the canyon to the bridge.

Elevation — Lolo Creek, Lower Run — cfs

May

Peak—3,920, 5/26/80
Drainage area—243 mi.^{2}

Average gradient
75 fpm

cfs

Miles (months 1-12)

Lolo Creek just below the bridge. Photo: Jim Ciardelli

LOLO CREEK, UPPER

CLASS	LEVEL	LENGTH	GRADIENT	TIME
II+	600 cfs	12 miles	50 fpm	4 hours

PUT-IN:	Lolo Campground (2,810 ft.)
TAKE-OUT:	Cottonwood Flats (2,200 ft.)
SHUTTLE:	28 miles
CRAFT:	Kayak
PORTAGES:	1 log
SEASON:	May, June
GAUGE:	Lolo Creek
PERMIT:	No
MAPS:	Weippe South, Browns Cr. Rdg., *Clearwater NF*
CHARACTER:	Small river, swift water, gorge, logs, secluded.

DESCRIPTION: The first nine miles of Lolo Creek are a beautiful swift water tour through a deep cedar-filled canyon. The creek winds between steep cliffs mixed with wide open meadows. There are cabins in some of the meadows and fences running along the river-bank. The rapids, are class I-II swift water. Be careful of blind corners due to the amount of deadfall in the area. There are two corners where the current swings under overhanging basalt cliffs. A log spans the entire width of the river about four miles down and must be portaged on the left. However, all of these obstacles are easily spotted and avoided. At Cottonwood Flats, the canyon opens up and the river winds slowly through a maze of logjams and islands. There are thousands of logs, but the current is slow and shallow. The biggest hazard here is taking the wrong channel and being forced to hike back to the main channel. Geese and blue herons live in the meadow and on the islands.

When the canyon begins to close back in, it's time to look for the take-out. The road from State Meadows winds down the north side of the canyon at the downstream end of the valley. It can be seen on the open hillsides. Make sure you can get down this road before committing to the run. Even when the conditions are good, you have to hike up the hill a couple hundred feet. If it's been raining the road becomes impassable and you'll be forced to paddle or portage the two miles of class IV before the next possible take-out at the bridge.

The put-in is east of Weippe. Driving on highway 11 from the west into Weippe, continue due east where the main street turns to the north. Follow this road 18 miles through Browns Creek Mill, Mussellshell and to the south along Lolo Creek to Lolo Campground. See the lower run description to find the take-out.

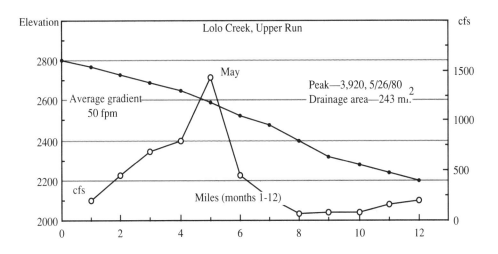

Lolo Creek, Upper Run

Elevation

cfs

2800

1500

May

Peak—3,920, 5/26/80
Drainage area—243 mi.²

2600

Average gradient
50 fpm

1000

2400

500

2200

cfs

Miles (months 1-12)

2000

0

0   2   4   6   8   10   12

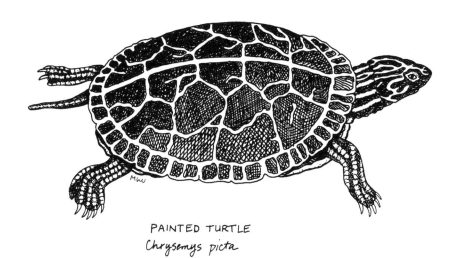

PAINTED TURTLE
Chrysemys picta

SOUTH FORK CLEARWATER RIVER, LOWER

CLASS	LEVEL	LENGTH	GRADIENT	TIME
III	600-1,200 cfs	13 miles	44 fpm	4 hours
III-IV	1,200-3,000 cfs			

PUT-IN:	Bully Creek (2,200 ft.)
TAKE-OUT:	Highway 13 junction (1,600 ft.)
SHUTTLE:	13 miles
CRAFT:	Kayak, canoe, raft
PORTAGES:	0
SEASON:	May, June
GAUGE:	Near Stites
PERMIT:	No
MAPS:	Harpster, Grangeville E., Goodwin Meadows, Hungry Rdg. , *Clearwater NF*
CHARACTER:	Small river, rock gardens, logs, road, secluded.

DESCRIPTION: The locals call this the Mickey Mouse Run. While not as difficult as the canyon upstream, this is still a challenging run. A canoeist drowned in this stretch in 1988. In addition, dozens of rafts have been wrapped on the rocks and experienced kayakers have lost boats on this run. It contains four large rapids, including, Blackerby, right below the bridge, which is close to a mile in length.

Because it is roadside, the entire run can be road scouted and the put-in and the take-out are arbitrary. A Bully Creek start offers rafters access to the river. The best river access for rafters is two miles above Harpster. Just upstream from the junction where highway 13 climbs up to Grangeville, look for a gravel bar with an unimproved road down to the river. There are lots of take-outs above here for a concentrated whitewater run.

There is an old bridge abutment in the river at Harpster with a river runner's scale painted on it. Between 2 and 3 are good levels. Two feet equals approximately 2000 cfs at Stites. Four feet equals approximately 4000 cfs. Above 3.5 feet the river becomes extremely pushy, particularly on the Golden Canyon Run. Below 3 on the Harpster gauge, the rocks start showing their teeth. The gauge at Stites is across the bridge and back upstream. See the appendix for the rating table.

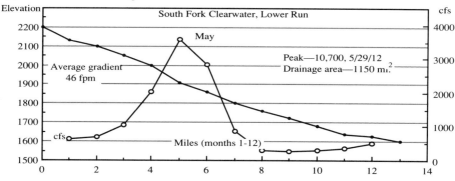

South Fork Clearwater, Lower Run

Peak—10,700, 5/29/12
Drainage area—1150 mi.^{2}

Average gradient 46 fpm

Miles (months 1-12)

South Fork Clearwater River

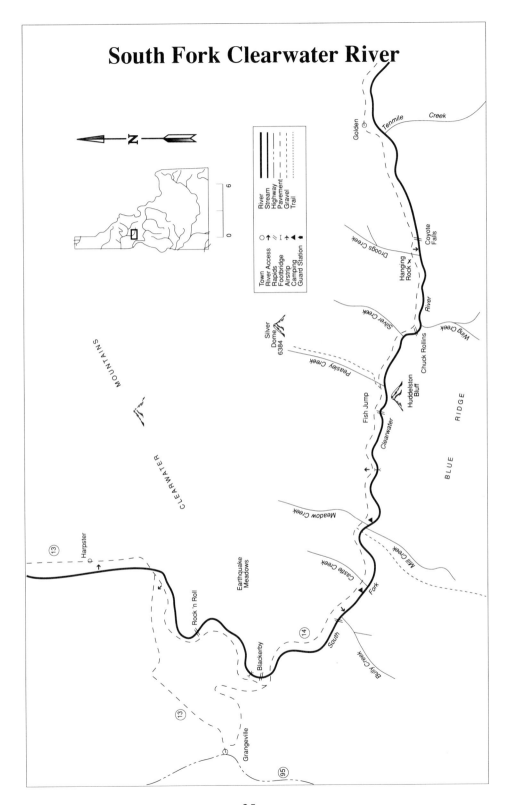

SOUTH FORK CLEARWATER RIVER, GOLDEN CANYON

CLASS	LEVEL	LENGTH	GRADIENT	TIME
IV-V	600-1,500 cfs	10 miles	98 fpm	3-5 hours
V	>1,500 cfs			

PUT-IN:	Hanging Rock, mile 28 (3,200 ft.)
TAKE-OUT:	Pack Bridge, mile 19 (2,380 ft.)
SHUTTLE:	9 miles
CRAFT:	Kayak, raft
PORTAGES:	0
SEASON:	May
GAUGE:	Near Stites
PERMIT:	No
MAPS:	Hungry Rdg., Huddleston Blf., Golden, *Clearwater NF*
CHARACTER:	Steep mountain river, technical, continuous, constricted rock gardens, logs, road, secluded.

DESCRIPTION: This is a run with two faces. High water packs some power and a disappearing horizon line that you can never catch. If the water is brown be prepared for a strong class V run. When the water is low and clear (it never gets crystal clear because of all the dredge tailings upstream), the South Fork is a fun, but technical river with hundreds of great eddies and lots of steep drops.

There are three outstanding rapids on this run. Most people put in below the first one, Coyote Falls. This drop has been run by several people (Rob Lesser, Mark Fraas, and Rick Williams). They were very selective of the flow. Even then, at best, it is a stunt. In 1982 an Easterner, Chuck Rollins, drowned here. If you're quick with numbers you've undoubtably noticed the graph and the above statistics don't agree. Let me explain — I had to include Coyote Falls in the profile and in turn the length, however since I'm unwilling to run Coyote Falls, I don't feel comfortable telling people to start above Hanging Rock (the rock hanging over the road, not a criminal's nemesis).

About half way down the run is the next significant drop, erroneously called Chuck Rollins because of the common misconception that he drowned here (myself included). It is identified by the huge overhanging boulder on the right, the big waves in the river and the hole at the end. Close to the run's end is the other named drop, a river wide hole known as Fish Jump. The feasibility of running this drop increased dramatically in 1988 when the forest service dynamited it to aid upstream fish migration. In the good old days this was one nasty rapid, now it's only semi-nasty (it's still a keeper). I would never dream of dynamiting a rapid, but I can't stop the grin that spreads over my face when I think of this rapid's fate, since the worst swim of my life was out of this hole. On a bit-too-nonchalant run, I went straight into it, and after a good mix of windowshades and endos I realized that it wasn't going to release me without some work on my part. The first step involved getting out of my boat — which isn't too easy while doing uncontrolled endos. Once out of my boat, I'd

26

surface at the crest of the backwash, get sucked upstream into the pour-over, exchange love taps with my boat (which was showing the folks on shore an unmanned endo demonstration) and then be hammered to the bottom — which, I can testify, is covered with fine, soft sand. It took about five cycles to totally cleanse my ego. For those of us with psychological scars, there is a nice turn-out just above this drop in which to leave a shuttle car.

The camping in this canyon is beautiful. Castle Creek, downstream from the take-out is a good spot with river access. See the Lower Run description for gauge details.

Fish Jump, South Fork of the Clearwater. Grant Amaral matching wits with the Salmon. Photo: Paul Faulkner

SELWAY RIVER, LOWER RUN

CLASS	LEVEL	LENGTH	GRADIENT	TIME
III	1,000-20,000 cfs	7 miles	14 fpm	2-5 hours

PUT-IN:	Below Selway Falls (1,680 ft.)
TAKE-OUT:	Boyd Creek Campground (1,580 ft.)
SHUTTLE:	8 miles
CRAFT:	Kayak, canoe, raft
PORTAGES:	0
SEASON:	May, June, July
GAUGE:	Lowell
PERMIT:	No
MAPS:	Selway Falls, Stillman Point, *Selway Bitterroot Wilderness*
CHARACTER:	Big gentle river, low gradient, road, secluded.

DESCRIPTION: There is an easy day run on the lower Selway, below Selway Falls. If you're in the area, have lots of time and want an easy float, consider this run. It's a good beginner run with a few easy rapids. The routes are plentiful and wide. Below each rapid the river pools, allowing plenty of recovery room. There are two class III rapids: Fall Creek about two miles down from the put-in and Rock Island, about a mile from the take-out. This is a gentle run, but during high water (15,000 cfs) it does pack some punch. Everything can be scouted from the road. Boyd Creek provides good camping, however, there is a fee.

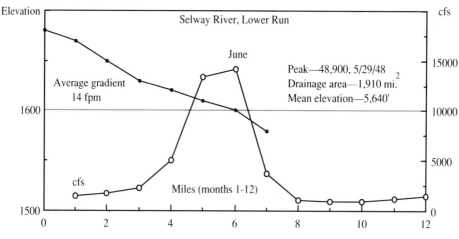

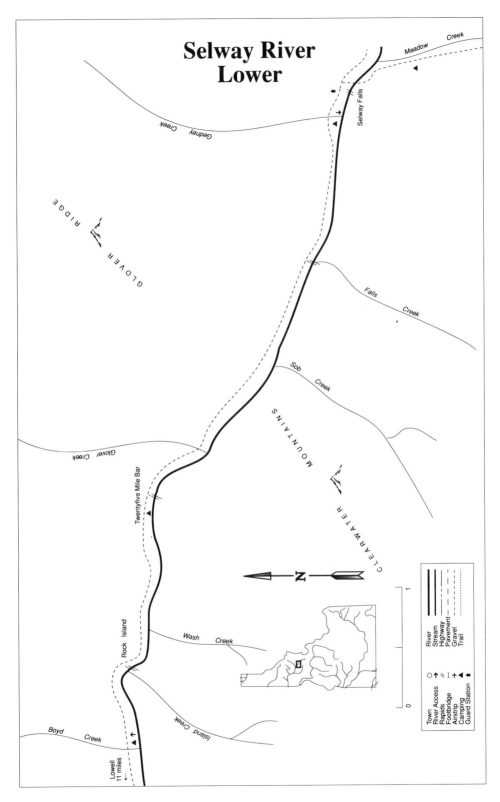

Selway River
Lower

Meadow Creek

Gedney Creek

Selway Falls

GLOVER RIDGE

Falls Creek

Sob Creek

Glover Creek

Twentyfive Mile Bar

CLEARWATER MOUNTAINS

Rock Island

Wash Creek

Island Creek

Boyd Creek

Lowell
11 miles

N

River
Stream
Highway
Pavement
Gravel
Trail

Town
River Access
Rapids
Footbridge
Airstrip
Camping
Guard Station

29

THE SELWAY

CLASS	LEVEL	LENGTH	GRADIENT	TIME
III-IV	1'-3'	46 miles	29 fpm	2-6 days
IV	3'-6'			
IV-V	>6'			

PUT-IN: Paradise Guard Station (3,050 ft.)
TAKE-OUT: Meadow Creek (1,720 ft.)
SHUTTLE: 255 miles
CRAFT: Kayak, canoe, raft
PORTAGES: 0
SEASON: May, June
GAUGE: Paradise
PERMIT: Yes
MAPS: Selway Falls, Fog Mtn., Moose Ridge, Dog Cr., Mink Pk., Gardiner Pk., Burnt Strip Mtn., *Selway Bitterroot Wilderness*
CHARACTER: Wild and Scenic River, boulder-choked rapids, cedar forest, fire scarred canyon, trail, wilderness.

DESCRIPTION: The Selway is another of Idaho's Big Three along with the Salmon and the Snake. Of these three, the Selway is the extreme of limited access and wilderness. The odds on drawing a Selway permit are slim. If someone offers you a spot on a Selway permit — take it. Permits are limited to one launch a day and each year only 62 private permits are issued. Commercial outfitters fill out the control season with an additional 16 starts. May permit holders will usually find the road to the put-in blocked by snow, unfortunately by late July the Selway is usually reduced to a small creek with barely enough water to float a kayak or canoe. Although if it has been a good water year, outstanding open canoe trips are possible just after the permit season (gauge .5'-1').

If you don't draw a permit, the other option is to show up before permit season officially opens, May 15, and poach a launch. It is legal and still a relatively unknown way of getting on the river. The only problem with this approach is Nez Perce Pass is often closed well into permit season and if it is open, the water is usually high and the river pushy and dangerously loaded with logs (sharing a hole with a 60 foot pine tree may not be everyone's idea of fun). At these times you are still required to conform to all river regulations. Finally, you can phone in for cancellations on a first-come, first-served basis. The number for information on cancellations is (406) 821-3269.

If Paradise is still snowbound on your launch date, it is possible to fly into Shearer Airstrip, 15 miles downstream. See the appendix for information on back country flying in Idaho. Once you're on the river, you may be discouraged to discover air traffic is completely unrestricted in the wilderness.

Once you've conquered the mountain of Selway paperwork and you're on the river, you can finally relax. The Selway is different from the rest of the

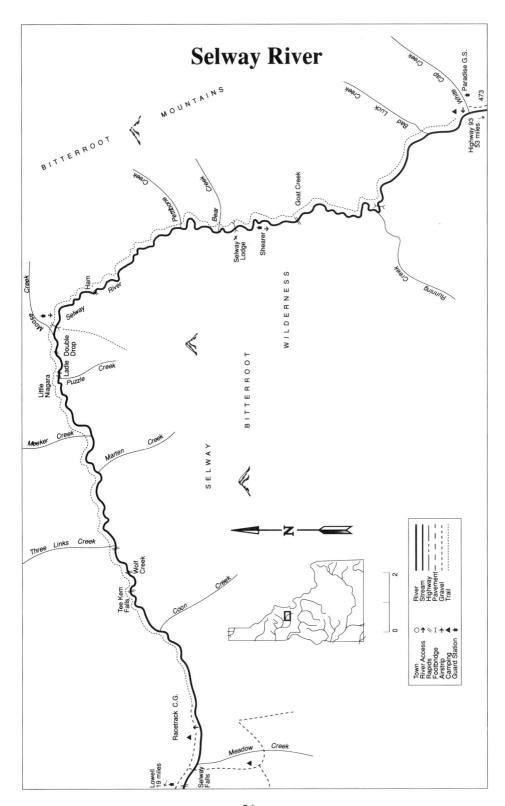

Selway River

Big Three, it runs through a totally different type of landscape. The Snake runs through an arid canyon, the Salmon through pines and sage and the Selway through ceder and fir. Unfortunately, because it also runs through the Selway-Bitterroot Wilderness, much of the Selway's cedar and fir is burned due to the Wilderness "let burn" policy.

The rapids are different as well. They are big and can be tricky. At most flows they are not as big as legend would have them, but when the water's high, the waves and holes conform to the epic scale. At least 10 named rapids lie between the put-in and Moose Creek. Ham is the first of the big rapids, about 15 miles down from Paradise. Below Moose Creek, the flow nearly doubles and the gradient picks up. Some of the biggest drops are just downstream. Double Drop, Ladel and Little Niagara equally divide the next three miles. Ladle is the trickiest of these and should be scouted. Be careful in this stretch, especially when the waters high.

For a permit and a map with all the details contact the West Fork Ranger Station, Darby, Montana, 59829. To find the put-in drive 73 miles south of Missoula on highway 93. Go west at Conner, 53 miles, on road 473 up over Nez Pierce Pass and down along the Selway. The take-out is 129 miles west of Missoula on highway 12. At Lowell follow the Selway another 19 miles upstream.

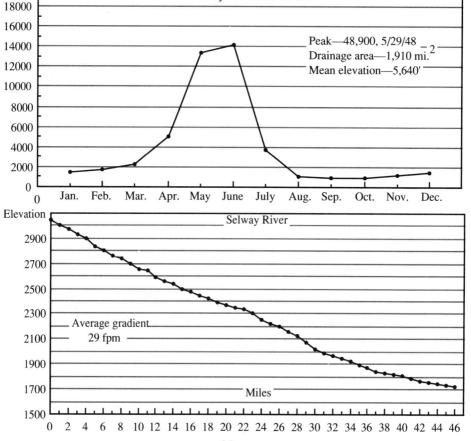

Selway River near Lowell

Peak—48,900, 5/29/48
Drainage area—1,910 mi.^{2}
Mean elevation—5,640'

Selway River

Average gradient
29 fpm

Miles

The tail end of Ladle at medium flows. Photo: Rob Lesser

MOOSE CREEK

CLASS	LEVEL	LENGTH	GRADIENT	TIME
III-IV	700-1500 cfs	43 (22) miles	53 fpm	3 days

PUT IN: Dolph Creek (3,325 ft.)
TAKE OUT: Meadow Creek {(confl. 2,160 ft.) 1,720 ft.}
SHUTTLE: 115 miles (6 mile hike)
CRAFT: Kayak
PORTAGES: Logs
SEASON: June, July
GAUGE: No
PERMIT: Yes*
MAPS: Cedar Ridge, Wahoo Pk., Freeman Pk., Shissler Pk., Moose Ridge, Grave Pk., *Selway Bitterroot Wilderness*
CHARACTER: Large mountain stream, meanders with logjams, changing to boulder gardens, wilderness, trail.

DESCRIPTION: Moose Creek is one of those logistically difficult runs that leaves you with a real sense of accomplishment; if you pull it off. A combination of factors makes this run difficult. The whitewater, though good, is the least of these problems. Perhaps the biggest obstacle is the Selway River. Moose Creek is a tributary of the Selway and to boat the Selway you need a permit. To get a permit, allocated through a complex lottery, you'll need a lot of luck. Next, to get to the put-in, the road must be clear of snow and if the road is clear, there is a good chance Moose Creek will be an irrigated boulder field. Once you reach the end of the road, the put-in is a six mile downhill hike, until you are on the river. It's no wonder only a few groups have done this run. Rob Lesser, Bo Shelby and Ron Fry, designed the plan and made the first descent in June of 1979.

The river starts off meandering through a log-choked alpine meadow and many of the logs must be portaged. The river runs through a series of emerald green pools surrounded by a dense cedar forest. Downstream the whitewater picks up and the scenery is scarred with the signs of a large forest fire. Because of the fire the camping from Elbow Bend almost all the way to the Selway isn't spectacular. Once on the Selway, 21 miles remain to the take-out at Meadow Creek. Remember to bring your Selway permit with you on the river.

To get there turn off highway 12 onto Elk Summit Road one mile east of Powell Ranger Station. Drive over the White Sand and Crooked Fork bridges to forest service road 360. Continue approximately 20 miles over Savage Pass and Elk Summit to Hoodoo Lake. At Hoodoo Lake follow the road 486 to the fork with trail 939. This is where the hiking starts. Go to the left, down into Moose Creek. To drive to the take-out, return to highway 12. From here the directions are the same as the Selway take-out.

*You'll need a permit to float out on the Selway. R.W.L.

See graph page 41.

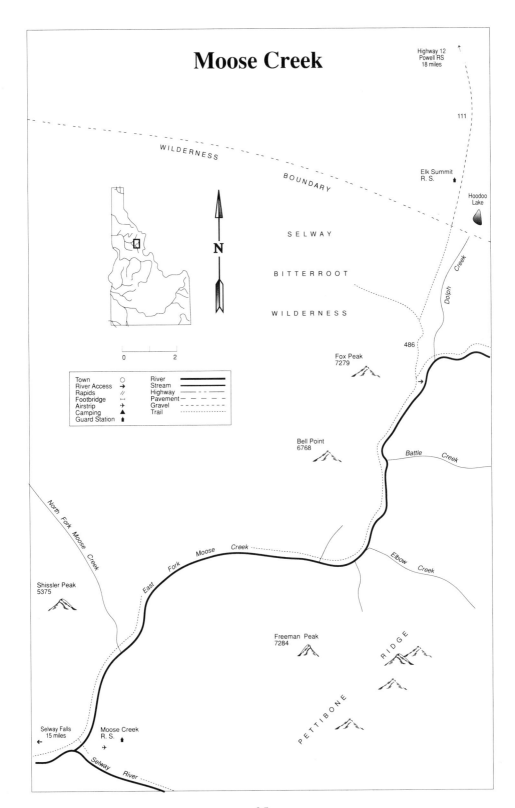

Moose Creek

LOCHSA RIVER, LOWER RUN

CLASS	LEVEL	LENGTH	GRADIENT	TIME
III-IV	0'-10' feet	9 miles	29 fpm	3 hours

PUT-IN: Mile 120, Fish Creek (1,980 ft.)
TAKE-OUT: Mile 112, Split Creek Pack Bridge (1,720 ft.)
SHUTTLE: 8 miles
CRAFT: Kayak, canoe, raft
PORTAGES: 0
SEASON: April, May, June, July
GAUGE: Lowell
PERMIT: No
MAPS: McLendon Btt., Huckleberry Btt., *Clearwater NF*
CHARACTER: Big river, rock and boulder gardens, holes, big waves, road.

DESCRIPTION: The Lochsa (a Flathead Indian word meaning "rough water") rates as one of the best Idaho whitewater runs. It is clear, clean and accessible. The locals call this the Goat Range Run. The rapids are full of big waves, big holes and house-size boulders. The streambed is wide and there is at least one clean line through every rapid.

The Lochsa offers kayakers some great surfing and more than 20 class III and IV rapids. Rafters will enjoy the big waves and recovery pools. The stand out rapids start about four miles down with House Wave. Grim Reaper is just downstream. Another four miles downstream, Lochsa Falls is one of the bigger rapids on the run. Below the surf wave, Termination and Split Creek are good rapids. I've been told Termination flips more rafts than any other rapid on the Lochsa. Unfortunately, I've never paddled the last couple miles of this run, because always I seem to get trapped in the hole at the surf wave for several hours.

This is one of the best surf waves in Idaho. It's at approximately mile 114, about 100 meters upstream of Old Man Creek. It is a one shot wave, as most of the Lochsa waves are. At some flows, 2.5'-3' and 5.25'-6', it is possible to work up the eddy on river right. At other levels, it's worth getting out of your boat and carrying around the rocks for another chance. As the river drops the wave becomes a hole and it is just as good sideways as head on. Between 2.5 and 3' the hole offers a variety of surfing possibilities including spins and polish endos, however as dropping flows approach two feet, it becomes very difficult to get out of. At flows of about 1.5 and less, it is next to impossible to get out of the hole with any dignity. Above 5' it's about as good a surf wave as you can imagine.

Camping on the Lochsa is great. Most of the cedar groves are developed, but there are still some untouched meadows, well off the highway. The meadows are covered with lush green grass and protected by willows, pine and some cedar. The canyon walls are covered by a thick green forest.
See graph page 41.

Lochsa River
Lower Run

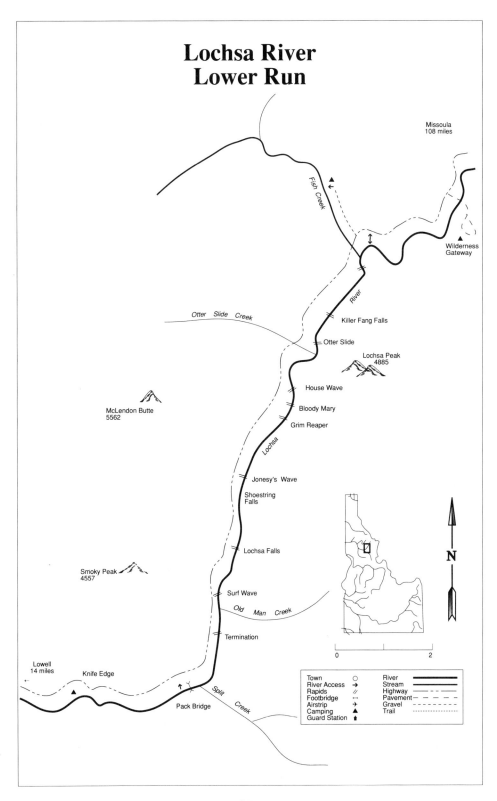

Missoula
108 miles

Fish Creek

Wilderness
Gateway

River

Killer Fang Falls

Otter Slide Creek

Otter Slide

Lochsa Peak
4885

House Wave

Bloody Mary

McLendon Butte
5562

Grim Reaper

Lochsa

Jonesy's Wave

Shoestring
Falls

Lochsa Falls

Smoky Peak
4557

Surf Wave

Old Man Creek

Termination

Lowell
14 miles

Knife Edge

Split Creek

Pack Bridge

N

Town	○	River	
River Access	→	Stream	
Rapids	//	Highway	
Footbridge	⊢⊣	Pavement	
Airstrip	✈	Gravel	
Camping	▲	Trail	
Guard Station	⚲		

0   2

LOCHSA RIVER, UPPER RUN

CLASS	LEVEL	LENGTH	GRADIENT	TIME
III-IV	2'-4'	17 miles	39 fpm	4-6 hours
IV+	>4'			

PUT-IN:	Whitepine, mile 138.5 (2,640 ft.)
TAKE-OUT:	Fish Creek, Mile 120 (1,980 ft.)
SHUTTLE:	18 miles
CRAFT:	Kayak, canoe, raft
PORTAGES:	0
SEASON:	April, May, June, July
GAUGE:	Lowell
PERMIT:	No
MAPS:	Huckleberry Btt., Greenside Btt., Holly Cr. , *Clearwater NF*
CHARACTER:	Big river, gravel bed changing to rock and boulder gardens, holes, big waves, road.

DESCRIPTION: The upper Lochsa has a different character than the lower. It is swifter and more technical whitewater, however this does not mean more difficult. Instead of the pools the lower has, these rapids are linked by swift water. There are a lot of big waves and big holes, but there is plenty of room and time to get around most of them. The road is less of an intrusion as well. Be forewarned, some of the bigger rapids are away from the road, so road scouting will not give you a true indication of the run.

My favorite rapid on this stretch is Castle Creek a long class IV with some sizable holes, lots of rocks and a big breaking wave capable of flipping rafts and crushing kayaks. Other than this and Ten Pin, downstream, all the rapids up here seem to fade into an indistinct blur of boulders, waves and holes. Not because they lack character, but because they flow into one another.

As the flows on the Lochsa approach six feet, the slack time between the rapids diminishes. The recovery pools vanish at close to 6.5 and kayakers who swim or rafters who flip could be in for a long swim in cold water. Commercial rafters put in at mile 130, below Three Hole, when the flow is greater than 6.5.

Put in at mile 138.5 by the large turn out. There's a gauge here and another on Eagle Mountain Pack Bridge which correlate with the primary gauge on the Lowell Bridge.

Upstream from the put-in there are some excellent hot springs, At mile 142, on the north, Weir Hot Springs are a short hike up Weir Creek. At mile 151, Jerry Johnson Hot Springs are on the south, over the bridge and up Warm Springs Creek less than a mile. Please take care of these spots, they are becoming popular and are in danger of being thrashed.

Take out anywhere, the last miles to Fish Creek are undefined swift water. Fish Creek offers the best access for rafters. There is good camping up Fish Creek, at Wilderness Gateway and on many of the undeveloped gravel bars between the river and the road.

See graph page 41.

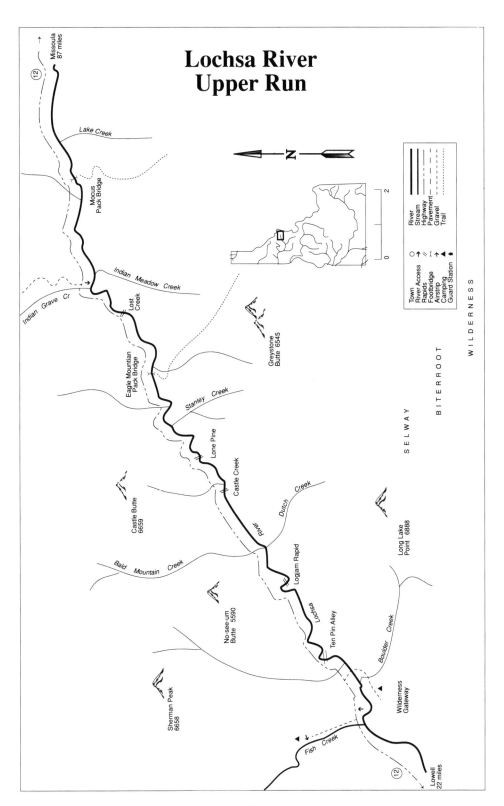

Lochsa River
Upper Run

N

Legend:
River
Stream
Highway
Pavement
Gravel
Trail

Town
River Access
Rapids
Footbridge
Airstrip
Camping
Guard Station

2

0

Missoula
87 miles

12

Lake Creek

Mocus
Pack Bridge

Indian Meadow Creek

Indian Grave Cr

Lost
Creek

Greystone
Butte 6545

Eagle Mountian
Pack Bridge

Stanley Creek

Lone Pine

Castle Creek

Castle Butte
6659

Dutch Creek

River

Bald Mountain Creek

Logjam Rapid

Long Lake
Point 6888

No-see-um
Butte 5590

Lochsa

Ten Pin Alley

Boulder Creek

Sherman Peak
6658

Wilderness
Gateway

Fish Creek

12

Lowell
22 miles

SELWAY

BITERROOT

WILDERNESS

FISH CREEK

CLASS	LEVEL	LENGTH	GRADIENT	TIME
III-IV	600-800 cfs	1 mile	180 fpm	1/2 hour
IV	800-1,500 cfs			

PUT-IN: End of road (2,160 ft.)
TAKE-OUT: Lochsa Confluence (1,980 ft.)
SHUTTLE: 1 mile
CRAFT: Kayak
PORTAGES: 0
SEASON: April, May, June
GAUGE: Fish Creek
PERMIT: No
MAPS: Huckleberry Btt., *Clearwater NF*

CHARACTER: Short steep-creek, rock gardens, road, secluded.

DESCRIPTION: Fish Creek is a great kick start for a Lochsa run. This is a very good introduction to technical class IV kayaking for solid intermediate kayakers. Any time the Lochsa is 2.5 feet or higher Fish Creek is runnable. There are several good drops towards the bottom, scout them with due caution, there are some potential broach and piton spots due to the narrow river-bed and shallow conditions.

Presently, the camping up Fish Creek is a pristine oasis; off the highway along the Lochsa. The Forest Service recently improved the road and trail. The gauge on Fish Creek is not included in state water resources data. The graph shows historic flows from the previous gauge.

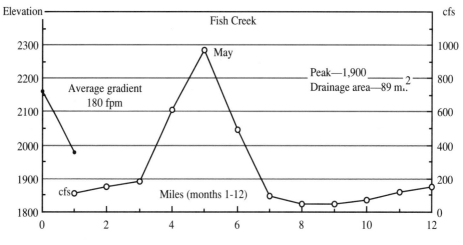

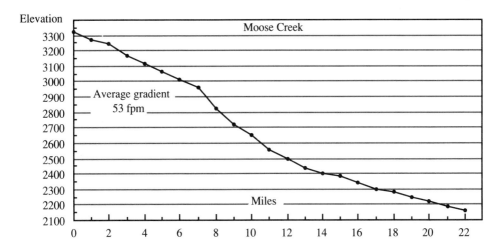

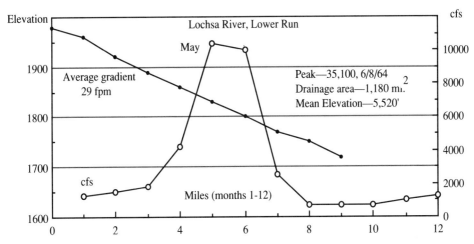

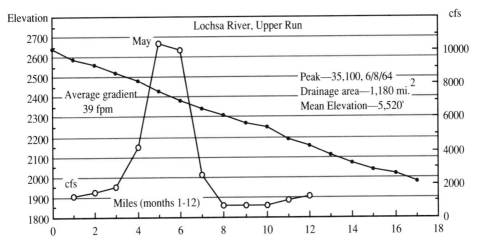

41

WHITE SAND CREEK, LOWER RUN

CLASS	LEVEL	LENGTH	GRADIENT	TIME
III-IV	600-1,500 cfs	12 miles	70 fpm	3-4 hours
IV	1,500-2,500 cfs			

PUT-IN:	Colt Creek Cabin (4,260 ft.)
TAKE-OUT:	White Sand Campground (3,420 ft.)
SHUTTLE:	18 miles
CRAFT:	Kayak, raft
PORTAGES:	0
SEASON:	June
GAUGE:	No
PERMIT:	No
MAPS:	Savage R., Grave Pk., Rocky Pt., *Clearwater NF*
CHARACTER:	Technical, boulder-choked rapids, gorge, blind-corners, wilderness.

DESCRIPTION: The Lower White Sand is another discovery and first descent of the Missoula Trio of, Doug Ammons, Monty Morevec and Jim Traub. This run is atypical of their usual fare — it can be run by mere mortals. Well, by mortals that are solid kayakers. It can also be rafted, Lew Moore of Glacier Raft Company took a paddle raft down the run in 1989.

The run is a 12 mile mix of class II, III and IV whitewater. The first section is easy class IV and continuous. If you make a mistake the rapids will jump a level in difficulty. There are some tricky moves — done right they present no problem, done wrong things could get out of control quickly. At higher levels the rapids pack a punch. This is a wilderness run so be prepared. The last three miles of the run the river widens and is rocky at lower flows. It's a splashy class II ride to the take-out. This is one of the more pristine Lochsa tributaries, unfortunately the surrounding forest is part of a proposed timber sale.

A boaters gauge is painted on the bridge abutment at the take-out. On this gauge, at flows of three or less, the run rates a class III-IV and lacks any real push. Above three, the rapids pick up some power. The optimum flow correlates to the Lochsa, at the Lowell bridge, between 1.5 and 3 feet. The minimum correlates to about .75 on the Lochsa or about 600 cfs on the Lower White Sand. If the Lochsa is above 5 feet, the White Sand should be flowing between 2,500 and 3,000. See the upper for shuttle directions. D.A.

White Sand Creek

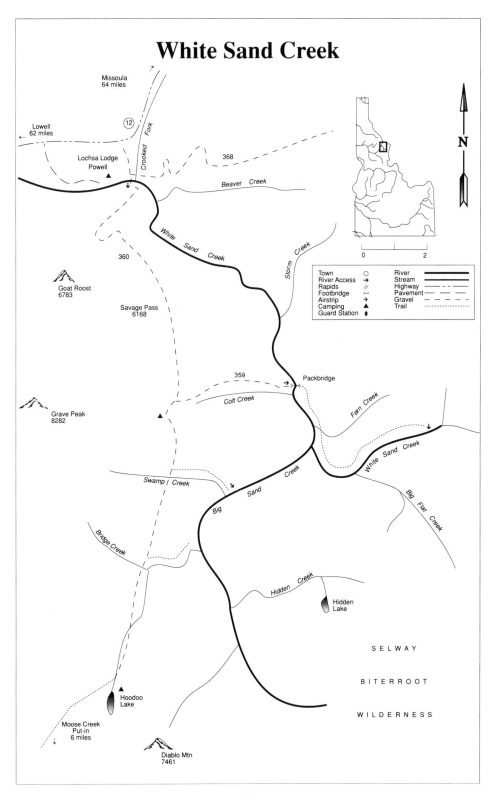

WHITE SAND CREEK, UPPER RUN

CLASS	LEVEL	LENGTH	GRADIENT	TIME
IV-V	250-700 cfs	4 miles	145 fpm	4 hours

PUT-IN:	Big Flat Creek (4,840 ft.)
TAKE-OUT:	Colt Creek Cabin (4,260 ft.)
SHUTTLE:	Hike 4 miles
CRAFT:	Kayak
PORTAGES:	1 (5 recommended)
SEASON:	June
GAUGE:	No
PERMIT:	No
MAPS:	Savage R., White Sand Lake, *Clearwater NF*
CHARACTER:	Extreme steep creek, boulder-choked rapids, gorge, blind-corners, wilderness, hike-in.

DESCRIPTION: This is an expert run. The four mile hike to the put-in should be enough to discourage all but the true devotees. If things get too hairy, the trail is multi-directional and you can walk back down. Of course, dragging a kayak around is a foolish way to wreck an otherwise beautiful walk.

Everything has been run on this stretch with the exception of the ledge towards the end that is blocked by two large logs. Logs shift and fall into the river each year so this can change. Just above the confluence with Big Sand Creek, the stream is constricted in a miniature gorge, with vertical granite walls, between 20 and 40 feet tall, rising straight out of the water. The gorge has all been run, but it is not recommended. It contains at least 20 consecutive drops of 4 to 8 feet. Broach, piton and pin possibilities abound and rescue would be next to impossible. Runs at any level, other than the optimal would be dangerous.

To get there turn off highway 12 onto Elk Summit Road one mile east of Powell Ranger station. Drive over the White Sand and Crooked Fork bridges to road 360. Continue approximately six miles to the ridge top where you can look down over a clear cut into the White Sand Drainage. Turn right up the Savage Pass Road, which heads directly up the ridge. Continue six miles to the Colt Creek Cabin Road 359. Turn left. Follow the switchbacks six miles down to the river and the take-out. Get out of your car, put your boat on your shoulder, hike four miles upstream to the put-in, about 2 hours. Enjoy.

D.A.

See graph page 46.

BIG SAND CREEK

CLASS	LEVEL	LENGTH	GRADIENT	TIME
IV-V	300-600 cfs	4.5 miles	160 fpm	5 hours

PUT-IN: Swamp Creek Trail (4,980 ft.)
TAKE-OUT: Colt Creek Cabin (4,260 ft.)
SHUTTLE: 7 miles
CRAFT: Kayak
PORTAGES: 4-8
SEASON: June
GAUGE: No
PERMIT: No
MAPS: Savage Ridge, *Clearwater NF*
CHARACTER: Extreme class V steep creek, sustained gradient, with severe single drops and continuous rock gardens, wilderness.

DESCRIPTION: Big Sand Creek is a steep wilderness run. It should only be attempted by expert boaters. The extreme gradient makes for outer limits kayaking and some mandatory portages. The middle section of the run is where the heat is. Don't get in over your head on this one. There is no trail along the creek. The middle section averages around 260 fpm. Each portage involves wrestling your kayak over uneven terrain and through dense brush. Portaging more than the minimum quickly becomes an ordeal.

The scenery is spectacular, towering granite bluffs border the stream, but the nature of the water demands one hundred percent concentration. After joining the White Sand, the volume increases and about two-thirds of a mile of extremely good class IV water, one long class V and a short portage around a log-blocked ledge remain. The last three quarters of a mile down to the Colt Creek Pack Bridge is class II-III whitewater. See the White Sand description for shuttle details to find the take-out. The put-in is another three miles up the Savage Pass Road to the Swamp Creek Trail. It's marked with a forest service sign and a small parking area. The put-in is a little over two miles down the trail where it meets the creek. D.A.

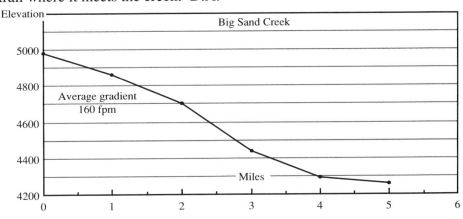

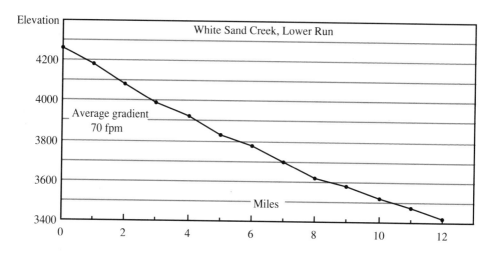

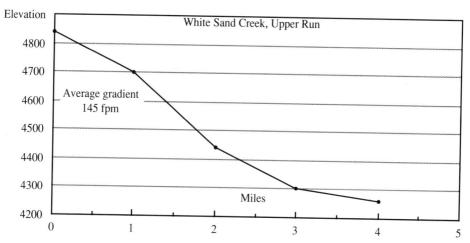

46

Monte Morevec ski-jumping on Big Sand Creek. Photo: Jim Traub

BRUSHY FORK

CLASS	LEVEL	LENGTH	GRADIENT	TIME
IV-VI	500-600 cfs	9 miles	95 fpm	5-6 hours

PUT-IN:	Elk Meadows (5,960 ft.)
TAKE-OUT:	Crooked Fork (3,900 ft.)
SHUTTLE:	18 miles
CRAFT:	Kayak
PORTAGES:	Logs
SEASON:	May, June
GAUGE:	No
PERMIT:	No
MAPS:	Dick Cr., W. Fk. Btt., Roundtop, Ranger Peak, *Clearwater NF*
CHARACTER:	Extreme steep-creek, boulder-choked rapids, gorge, blind corners, wilderness.

DESCRIPTION: Brushy Fork is another technical, wilderness steep-creek. Experts only. Everything, with the exception of logjams, has been run. There are two box canyons on the run, each with several blind corners and lots of drops. The steepest mile is a combination of boulders and ledges pouring down the side of the mountain. This run should only be attempted by experienced groups of class-V boaters.

To find the put-in, take the Elk Meadows Road east at the top of Lolo Pass and drive 13 miles until the road crosses the Brushy Fork (at this point, a meandering stream). To get to the take-out, return to highway 12. Go west and down to the Brushy Fork Confluence with the Crooked Fork.

D.A.

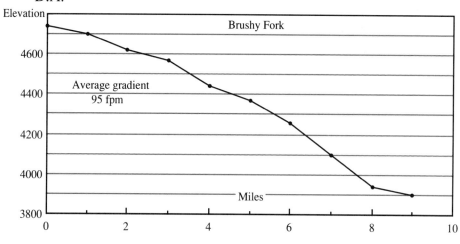

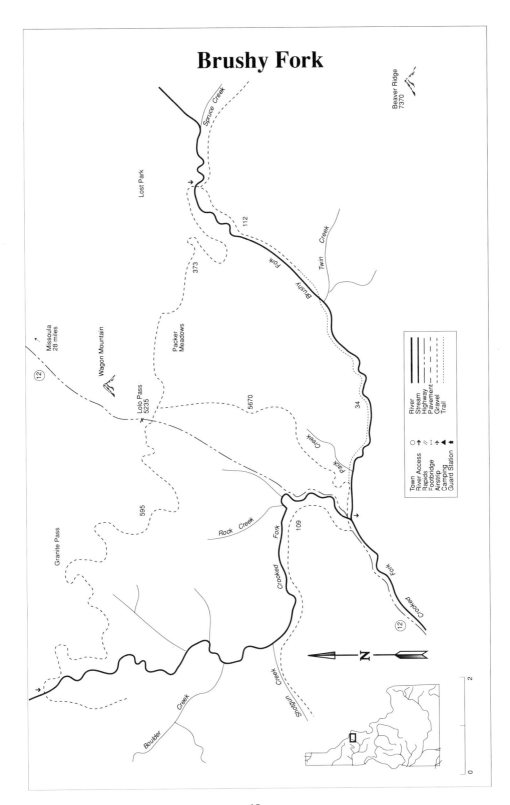

Brushy Fork

CROOKED FORK

CLASS	LEVEL	LENGTH	GRADIENT	TIME
III-IV (V)	200-600 cfs	12 miles	114 fpm	5 hours

PUT-IN: Hopeful Creek (4,980 ft.)
TAKE-OUT: Brushy Fork (4,260 ft.)
SHUTTLE: 17 miles
CRAFT: Kayak
PORTAGES: 10-15 logs
SEASON: June
GAUGE: No*
PERMIT: No
MAPS: Savage Ridge, *Clearwater NF*
CHARACTER: Moderate steep creek with a mixture of boulder-choked rapids changing to granite bedrock, ledges, gorge, numerous logs.

DESCRIPTION: The number of logjams and log portages on the Crooked Fork above Boulder Creek will discourage all but the most optimistic paddlers. Keep going. The rapids downstream make the portages worthwhile. After a couple miles, the stream picks up gradient and cascades down several smooth bedrock waterslides that will put a big smile on your face.

There are also several complicated, steep rapids that should be scouted. A little more than three miles down from the put-in the river runs over what looks to be a relatively simple five-foot ledge directly below a downed tree spanning the stream. Portage this drop or run it hard right, skittering as high as possible on the granite slab forming the right bank. Take this innocent looking drop seriously because in the backwash on the left side — just where you would want to ski-jump the ledge — there is a steel rod, driven into the river-bed, waiting to skewer you. This was found on the first descent when Doug Ammons made the mistake of running the drop without scouting. Committed to the ski jump at full speed, he caught sight of the steel rod just before he reached the lip of the ledge. Somehow, he managed to windmill several strokes, turn back to the right enough to avoid being skewered, and slam into a perfect vertical pin. Luckily, he was able to climb out of his boat and swim to shore.

At Boulder Creek, about four miles down, the volume doubles. The next two miles are the best part of the run. There are two miniature gorges with several difficult drops and one class V. After this stretch, the river flattens out and five miles of class II and III whitewater remain.

To find the put-in, take Granite Pass Road from the top of Lolo Pass, drive six miles to the top of Granite Pass. Stay on the main road, drive approximately six more miles to the bridge crossing the Crooked Fork just below the confluence of Hopeful Creek. The take out is at the Highway 12 bridge crossing the Crooked Fork at the bottom of the Lolo Pass Grade.

What's all the commotion? Ron Fry in the steep section of Moose Creek.
Photo: Rob Lesser

Photo: Glenn Oakley

Lower Salmon River Basin

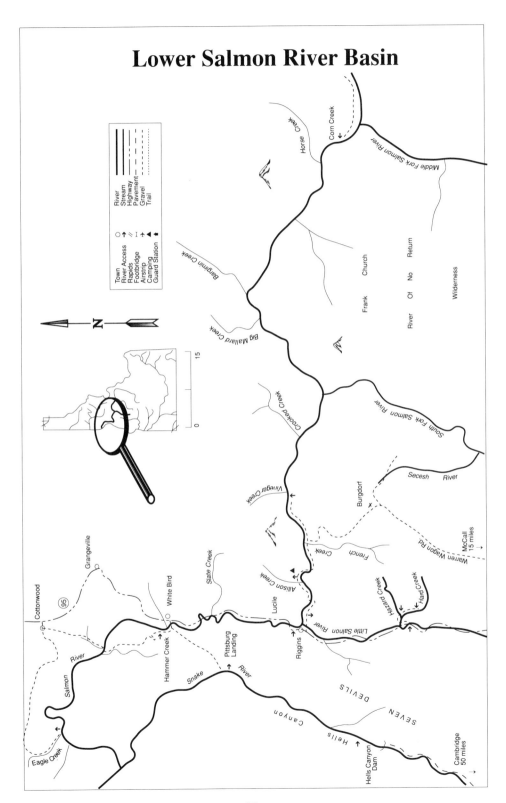

LOWER SALMON GORGE

CLASS	LEVEL	LENGTH	GRADIENT	TIME
II-III	3,000-12,000 cfs	40 miles	8 fpm	2 days
III-IV	12,000-30,000 cfs			
IV-V	> 30,000 cfs			

PUT-IN:	Hammer Creek (1,410 ft.)
TAKE-OUT:	Eagle Creek (1,080 ft.)
SHUTTLE:	70 miles
CRAFT:	Kayak, canoe, raft, jetboat
PORTAGES:	0
SEASON:	April, May, June, July, August, September
GAUGE:	Whitebird
PERMIT:	Yes
MAPS:	BLM "Lower Salmon River"
CHARACTER:	Big gentle river, beautiful canyon, big sandy beaches, wilderness.

DESCRIPTION: The lower Salmon is like the rest of the river, big and wide with a gentle gradient and a scenic canyon. The highlight of this stretch is its seclusion. The only evidence of man are the ruins left behind by miners and the pictographs of the Indians, the river traffic is minimal.

The canyon cuts through dry grass-covered mountains, which lack the pines found on the Upper Salmon. This is the place to get away from it all. Most of the trip is a scenic float, however there are several good drops mixed in, particularly at high water. The biggest rapids are Snow Hole, China Bar and Slide. Snow Hole is at the start of the big oxbow and China is about half-way around the bend. Slide is below Eagle Creek, near the confluence with the Snake, so unless you're going beyond Eagle Creek it isn't a problem. As flows approach 30,000 cfs the BLM recommends getting out at Graves Creek and most of the commercial outfitters cancel. At these flows Slide becomes a mandatory flip for rafts and dories.

The only easy access point to find on this river is the put-in at Hammer Creek. To get there, turn off highway 95 near milepost 232. There's a big sign marking the way. Head downstream, cross the bridge and follow the Salmon down a mile to the huge concrete boat ramp.

Graves Creek, 14 miles down from Hammer Creek can be used as an access point for a day run. To get to the Graves Creek/Rock Creek Road, go north on 95 from Whitebird to Cottonwood (31 miles), take the main street in Cottonwood south. This should then turn into the Graves Creek Road. Continue 10 miles to the river.

The other access point is down the Eagle Creek Road, 40 miles down the river. This road can be driven in a two-wheel drive vehicle, but don't take a nice car. The road is rocky and the overhanging brush is going to put lots of scratches in the paint. You will need a good map to find Eagle Creek, but you can drive in from either Cottonwood or Lewiston. Downstream of Eagle Creek, with the exception of Slide, the river is flat, on the Salmon 13 miles

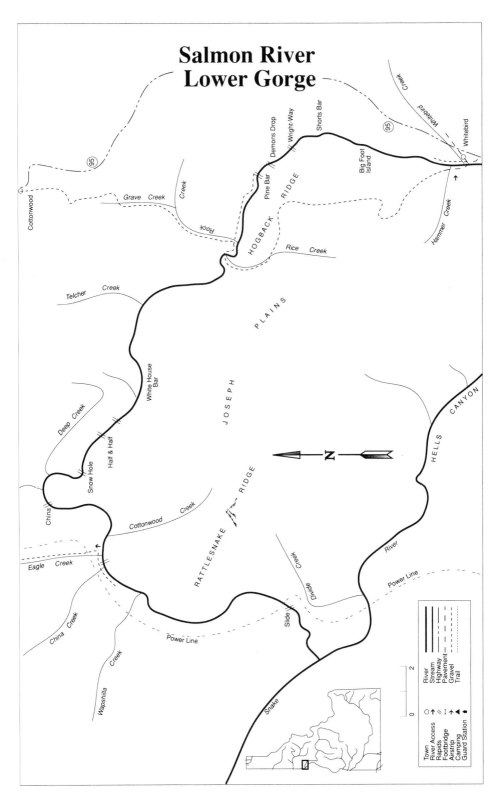

Salmon River
Lower Gorge

remain, on the Snake, another 20 until Heller Bar and the take-out.

Heller Bar is accessed through Lewiston 88 miles north of Whitebird on highway 95. From Lewiston cross the river into Clarkston Washington and go south 26 miles on highway 129 to Anatone. From Anatone go southeast 23 miles to the Grand Ronde take-out and Heller Bar. The take-out is at either the public boat ramp at the mouth of the Grande Ronde or the private ramp at Heller Bar. Shop around, because both charge a fee.

Permits are available for the asking. Basically, all you have to do is fill one out at Hammer Creek. There are campfire restrictions starting July first and running through mid-September. For all the details contact: BLM, Route 3, Box 181, Cottonwood, Id. 83522.

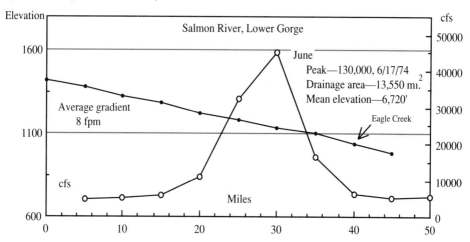

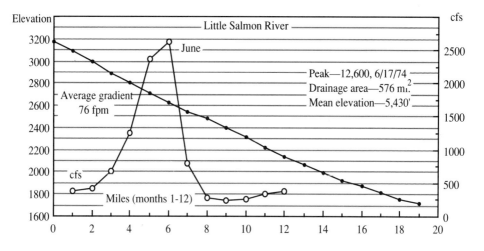

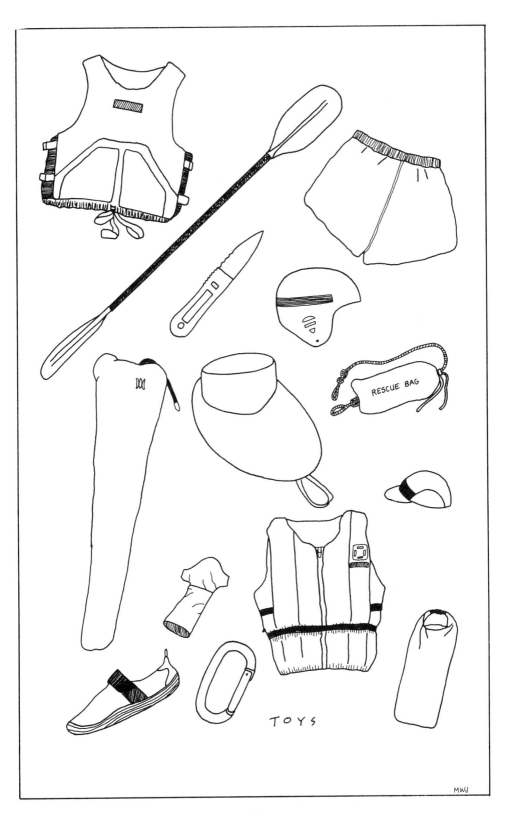

TOYS

LOWER SALMON, RIGGINS TO WHITEBIRD

CLASS	LEVEL	LENGTH	GRADIENT	TIME
II-III	3,000-12,000 cfs	34 miles	9 fpm	1 day
III-IV	12,000-30,000 cfs			

PUT-IN:	Riggins (1,720 ft.)
TAKE-OUT:	Hammer Creek (1,420 ft.)
SHUTTLE:	37 miles
CRAFT:	Kayak, canoe, raft, jetboat
PORTAGES:	0
SEASON:	April, May, June, July, August, September
GAUGE:	Whitebird
PERMIT:	No
MAPS:	BLM "Lower Salmon River"
CHARACTER:	Big gentle river, beautiful canyon, big sandy beaches, road.

DESCRIPTION: This run is a mix of long stretches of flat water with a few big rapids. The upper section from Riggins to Lucile contains three of the four named rapids: Time Zone, Chair Creek and Fiddle Creek. Below Lucile, with the exception of Blackhawk Rapid, the river is class II all the way to the take-out at Hammer Creek. All the rapids are wide open affairs with at least one clean line and a big pool (usually a mile or more) at the bottom. The sandy beaches along the river are good lunch or camping spots. The busy highway offers a vantage point for scouting, however it is also a major eyesore. If this was outstanding whitewater (it's not), the road wouldn't be an intrusion (it is). Enjoy the scenery and visualize the run while driving to the better whitewater and scenery to the north and south.

Kayakers will find some surf waves in this stretch. Unfortunately, most are one shot affairs that come and go with changes in the water level. Perhaps the best, or at least the best known, is the Machine Wave, located near the downstream end of Riggins at the base of the bluff.

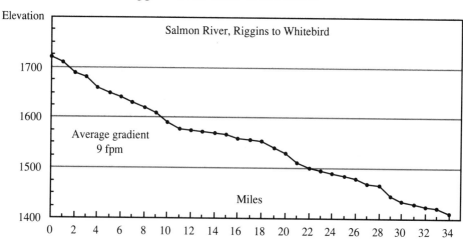

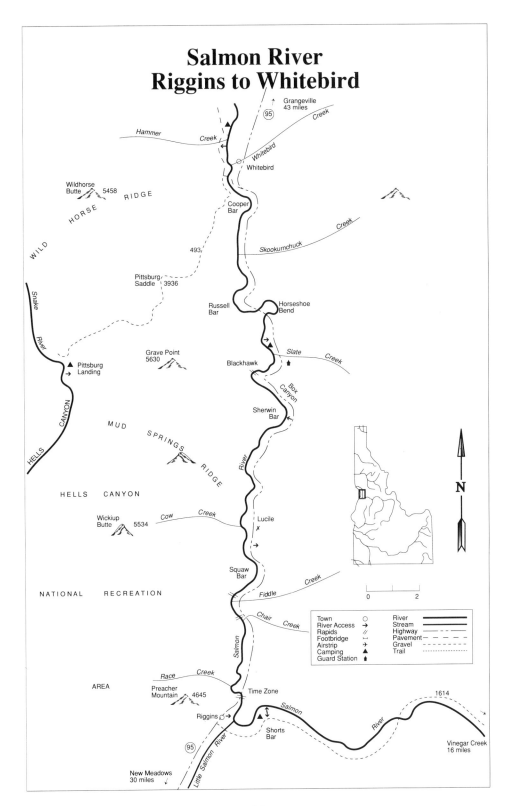

Salmon River
Riggins to Whitebird

LITTLE SALMON

CLASS	LEVEL	LENGTH	GRADIENT	TIME
III-IV	500-1,200 cfs	19 miles	76 fpm	5 hours
IV (V)	1,200-3,000 cfs			

PUT-IN:	Hazard Creek (3,170 ft.)
TAKE-OUT:	Riggins (1,720 ft.)
SHUTTLE:	19 miles
CRAFT:	Kayak, canoe, small raft
PORTAGES:	0 (1 recommended)
SEASON:	April, June
GAUGE:	Yes
PERMIT:	No
MAPS:	Indian Mtn.; Pollock; Riggins, *Payette NF*
CHARACTER:	Swift-water river, ledges, rock gardens, logs, brush, road.

DESCRIPTION: The Little Salmon is a great class III-IV day run. If the water is up, take the time to enjoy it. Most of the Little Salmon is continuous class II and III swift water, with some ledges, blind corners and rock gardens thrown in to keep things lively. When the water's high, the stand out rapid is a class V ledge drop called Amphitheater Hole. This is a simple pour-over into a large circular pool. It is located just below Boulder Creek.

One memorable day on the Little Salmon, we stopped to have lunch on the rocks by the edge of the pour-over at Amphitheater Hole. The river was high and the rapid looked unrunnable. We were consumed with nervous energy and we searched the stream banks for something to apply ourselves. We discovered it in the form of a 20 foot log precariously balanced near the lip of the rapid. With a collective heave-ho, we tumbled it into the river and watched it go over the drop. It plunged into the reversal, rose in a 20 foot endo and snapped in two. We were quite impressed — all the talk of ski-jumps and pancake landings was silenced and we portaged without another word.

The best camping is up Hazard Creek, providing there isn't any logging going on in the area. The huge sand beaches upstream of Riggins on the Salmon are good camping as well. Zim's Hot Springs, on the highway to the south is a step back into the '60s. For a fee you can plunge into your choice of two natural hot water swimming pools or take a shower from an endless supply of hot water.

See graph page 56.

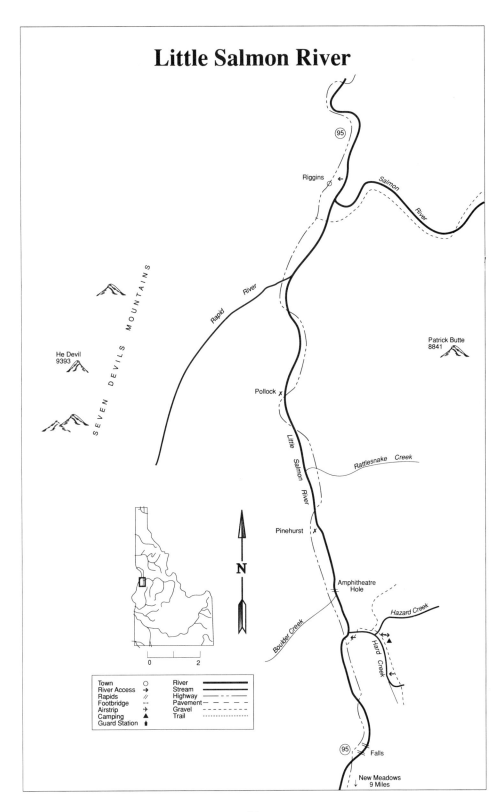

Little Salmon River

Riggins

Salmon River

95

Rapid River

SEVEN DEVILS MOUNTAINS

He Devil
9393

Patrick Butte
8841

Pollock

Little Salmon River

Rattlesnake Creek

Pinehurst

Amphitheatre
Hole

Hazard Creek

Boulder Creek

Hard Creek

N

0   2

Town	○	River	━━━
River Access	→	Stream	━━
Rapids	//	Highway	━·━·
Footbridge	⊢	Pavement	─ ─ ─
Airstrip	✈	Gravel	─ ─ ─
Camping	▲	Trail	·········
Guard Station	⚐		

95   Falls

New Meadows
9 Miles

HAZARD CREEK

CLASS	LEVEL	LENGTH	GRADIENT	TIME
III-IV	500-1000 cfs	1 mile	110 fpm	1 hour
IV	>1,000 cfs			

PUT-IN:	Hard Creek (3,280 ft.)
TAKE-OUT:	Little Salmon Confluence (3,170 ft.)
SHUTTLE:	1 mile
CRAFT:	Kayak
PORTAGES:	1 (log)
SEASON:	May, June
GAUGE:	No
PERMIT:	No
MAPS:	Indian Mtn.; *Payette NF*
CHARACTER:	Short steep creek, shear canyon walls, boulders, logs, road, secluded.

DESCRIPTION: Hazard Creek is another one of those fun, little, steep creeks that dot Idaho. It isn't much of a run by itself, because it's only a mile long. The gradient is constant, and the river flies along without pooling up. There is one good drop, it starts at the put-in and ends at the take-out. The rapids are steep rock gardens. A dangerous log just around the corner from the put-in must be portaged on the left. There's a great camp site at the put-in. Watch the Little Salmon flow for the Hazard Creek peak. The shuttle is along the river.

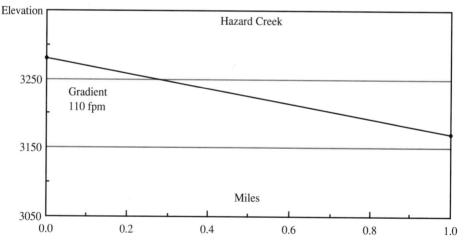

HARD CREEK

CLASS	LEVEL	LENGTH	GRADIENT	TIME
IV-V	200 cfs	2 miles	230 fpm	3 hours

PUT-IN:	Hard Creek (3,740 ft.)
TAKE-OUT:	Hazard Creek Confluence (3,280 ft.)
SHUTTLE:	3 miles
CRAFT:	Kayak
PORTAGES:	7 (5 logs)
SEASON:	May
GAUGE:	No
PERMIT:	No
MAPS:	Indian Mtn., *Payette NF*
CHARACTER:	Short steep creek, shear canyon walls, boulders, logs, road, falls, technical, secluded.

DESCRIPTION: The top of Hard Creek is a gentle stream. As the creek drops into the canyon, the whitewater picks up. The rapids are steep and choked with boulders. Be careful of broaching. Most of the lines involve skittering off some boulders. Expect to bash some boulders and make some dynamic rock pivots. Creek is the key word here. In places you can leap the creek in a single bound. There are five obvious logjams to be portaged and two rapids. One of the portages is around a beautiful boulder choked falls. Portaging is very difficult, so bring a rope to make things easier. Just above the falls, there is a long class V sluice box with a runnable four foot ledge at the end. It's a interesting move because of the difficult entry. After bombing around a tight corner and through 50 yards of ledges, you have to line up and ski jump off the four footer diagonally or you'll smash into a boulder that blocks most of the drop. The second rapid portage is a steep boulder-choked turn running into a cliff on the right. It can be quickly portaged on the left. With more than 200 cfs the number of portages may leap dramatically.

To find the put-in follow the road up Hazard Creek and continue along Hard Creek. If it's early in the spring bring a shovel. The road will climb up the canyon wall and then close back in on the creek. When you see the creek again, through the pines, and it looks easy, put in.

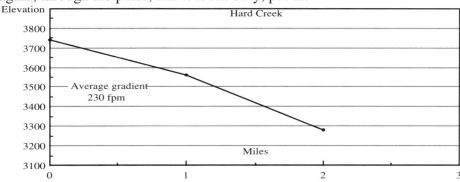

SALMON RIVER, VINEGAR CREEK RUN

CLASS	LEVEL	LENGTH	GRADIENT	TIME
III	1,000-20,000 cfs	25 miles	14 fpm	7 hours
III-IV	>20,000 cfs			

PUT-IN:	Vinegar Creek (1,960 ft.)
TAKE-OUT:	Riggins (1,720 ft.)
SHUTTLE:	26 miles
CRAFT:	Kayak, canoe, raft, jetboat
PORTAGES:	No
SEASON:	April, May, June, July, August, September
GAUGE:	Whitebird
PERMIT:	No
MAPS:	Burgdorf 15', Kelly Mtn., Riggins H.S., Riggins, *Payette NF*
CHARACTER:	Big gentle river, beautiful canyon, sandy beaches, road, heavy use.

DESCRIPTION: From Vinegar Creek to Riggins the Salmon River is big, broad and flat. There are some powerful rapids but, at all but high flows they are relatively straightforward, all you have to do is line up and ride them out. French Creek and Ruby are the standouts.

There are some good beaches on this stretch. A well maintained gravel road parallels the river, making access unlimited. In addition to the day use on this stretch, lots of people continue past Vinegar Creek after a trip on the Main. There are boat ramps at Vinegar Creek, Spring Bar and Riggins.

The camping is good, but the busy road detracts from the quality. This is the second deepest canyon in the States. (No, the Grand Canyon is not the deepest.) The deepest is covered in this book.

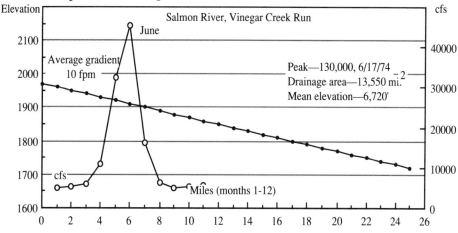

Salmon River, Vinegar Creek Run

Peak—130,000, 6/17/74
Drainage area—13,550 mi.^{2}
Mean elevation—6,720'

Average gradient 10 fpm

64

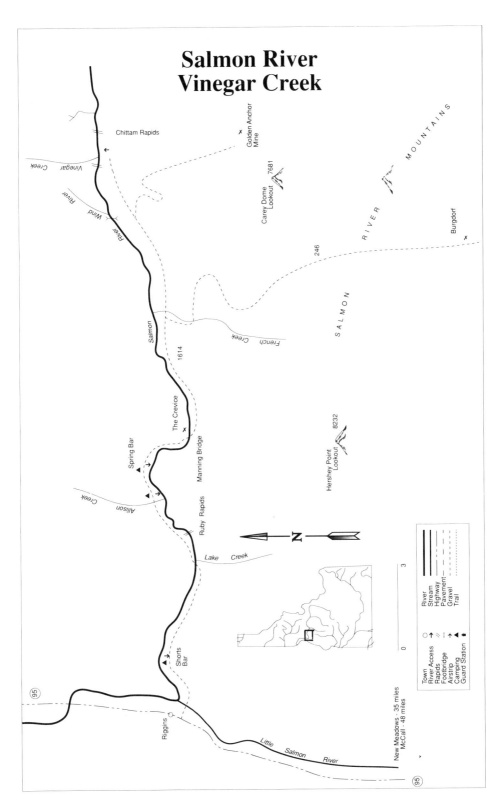

Salmon River
Vinegar Creek

SALMON RIVER, THE MAIN

CLASS	LEVEL	LENGTH	GRADIENT	TIME
III	<20,000 cfs	79 miles	12 fpm	3-8 days
III-IV	>20,000 cfs			
IV (V)	>50,000 cfs			

PUT-IN:	Corn Creek (2,920 ft.)
TAKE-OUT:	Vinegar Creek (1,960 ft.)
SHUTTLE:	400 miles
CRAFT:	Kayak, canoe, raft, jetboat
PORTAGES:	No
SEASON:	April, May, June, July, August, September
GAUGE:	Whitebird
PERMIT:	Yes
MAPS:	Forest Service: "River of No Return"
CHARACTER:	Wild and Scenic River, big waves, beautiful canyon and beaches, trail, wilderness, heavy use.

DESCRIPTION: This is the mighty "River of No Return," named by the local Indians and popularized by the Lewis and Clark Discovery Expedition. Unfortunately, Lewis and Clark portaged this stretch of the river, via Lolo Pass, a hundred miles to the north. They turned back at Shoup intimidated by the whitewater and the rugged canyon. Modern technology, including dynamite, has tamed this river. If whitewater is what you are after, at any but high flows you are going to be disappointed. Yes, there are rapids. Yes, some of them are extremely large, large enough to flip large rafts, but for most of the river the Salmon is a relaxing float through some incredible scenery. The clean sand beaches make wonderful camp sites. Try to select camps with side trails nearby, because the hiking in the Salmon Canyon is fantastic. The trails are well maintained and the forests are healthy.

At moderate flows, approximately 15,000 at Whitebird or 1.7 on the gauge at Corn Creek, the waves develop and the surfing for kayakers is incredible. The major rapids include: Salmon Falls, Split Rock, Big Mallard, Elk Horn, Whiplash or Groundhog Bar and Chittam. With the exception of Whiplash, most of the rapids wash out above 15,000 cfs, however, the waves are big and pushy, so if you're not used to big water it can be difficult.

The biggest rapid I've ever run is Whiplash at 86,000. The big rock outcrop on the right bank was a small island. Most of the river rushed down the center of the riverbed and crashed into the canyon wall in a series of huge waves. A boiling pool had formed at the bottom on the left. Between the pool and the canyon wall the river made a 90 degree turn in a mess of boiling water and giant waves. The pool would normally have been a welcome haven unfortunately, it was guarded by a marching eddy line about four feet tall. I think this eddy line is what astronomers have in mind when they talk about folds in space.

The movable eddy of despair had a range of about 10 yards. The trick was to enter the rapid while the eddy was at its maximum extension, then,

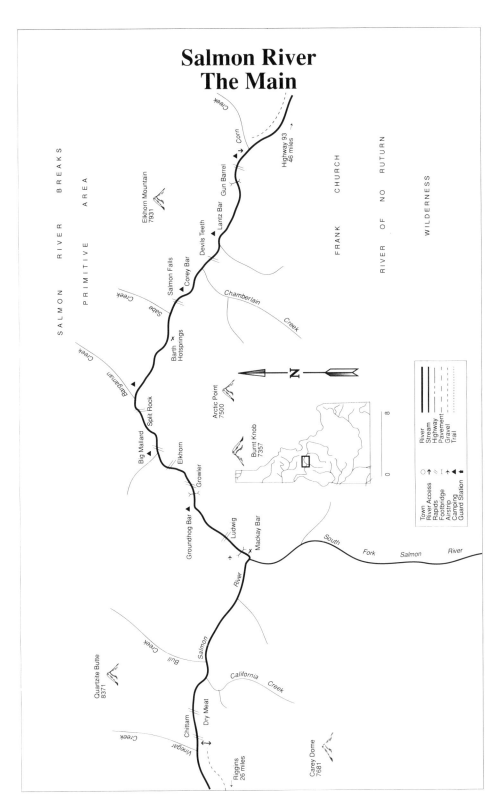

Salmon River
The Main

providing you didn't waste a lot of time inadvertently surfing a hole on the way in, it would be retreating as you passed. It went off without a hitch, but I was still a little nervous an hour later when we beached on the lawn at Mackay Bar to pick up some beer.

Unlike the Middle Fork, campsites along the Main are not designated, they are all first-come, first-served. During the permit season campsites can be tough to come by and late starts will leave you with the last choice of camping. It is a real bottleneck for the last 20 miles before take-out. There aren't a lot of campsites and there are scads of people. However, don't be discouraged. The beaches along the Main are some of the best anywhere, they are clean, big and sandy. For a really relaxing float and a nice tan aim for a late July start. For big water, June is best.

The shuttle is the longest in Idaho. The usual route is to the south on highway 95 through McCall and Cascade. At Banks go east through Lowman to Stanley. Then go north on 93 through Challis and Salmon to North Fork. Follow the river to the west to Corn Creek.

A plethora of information is available on this river, books movies and the Forest Service permit system. For a book, read Cort Conley's "River of No Return." For a movie, see Marilyn Monroe in "River of No Return." For a permit, contact the Forest Service, North Fork Ranger District, P.O. Box 780, North Fork, Idaho, 83466.

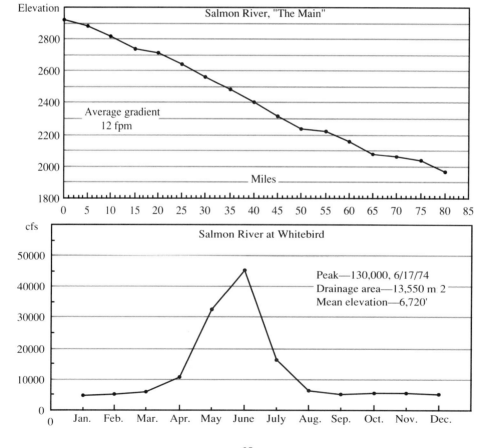

Threading the holes in Devil Creek. Photo: Rob Lesser

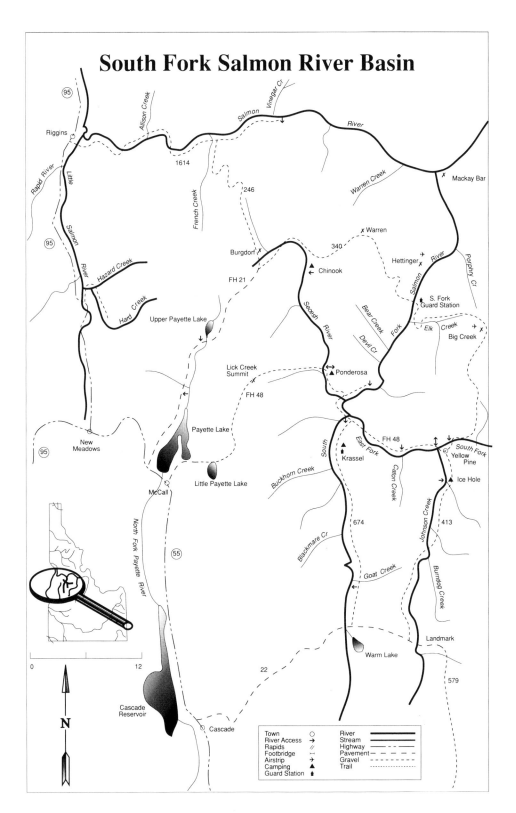

South Fork Salmon River Basin

95

Riggins

Rapid River

95

Little Salmon River

Allison Creek

Salmon River

Vinegar Cr

1614

French Creek

246

Hazard Creek

Hard Creek

Upper Payette Lake

Burgdorf

FH 21

Chinook

Lick Creek Summit

FH 48

Payette Lake

New Meadows

95

Little Payette Lake

McCall

North Fork Payette River

55

Cascade Reservoir

Cascade

Warren Creek

Mackay Bar

Warren

340

Hettinger

Salmon River

Porphy Cr

Seepah River

Bear Creek

Fork

S. Fork Guard Station

Elk Creek

Big Creek

Devil Cr

Ponderosa

FH 48

South

East Fork

Caton Creek

Krassel

Buckhorn Creek

South Fork Yellow Pine

Ice Hole

Blackmare Cr

674

413

Johnson Creek

Goat Creek

Burntlog Creek

Landmark

Warm Lake

22

579

0   12

N

Town	○	River	
River Access	→	Stream	
Rapids	//	Highway	
Footbridge	⊢	Pavement	
Airstrip	→	Gravel	
Camping	▲	Trail	
Guard Station	♠		

71

SOUTH FORK SALMON, CANYON

CLASS	LEVEL	LENGTH	GRADIENT	TIME
III+	<1.5'	52 (32) miles	42 fpm	2 days
III-IV	>1.5'			
IV-V	>4.2'			

PUT-IN: Road end (3,500 ft.)
TAKE-OUT: Vinegar Creek{(confl. 2,160 ft.) 1,960 ft.}
SHUTTLE: 101 miles
CRAFT: Kayak, canoe, raft
PORTAGES: No
SEASON: May, June, July
GAUGE: Krassel
PERMIT: No*
MAPS: Williams Pk., Parks Pk., Pilot Pk., Chicken Pk., Warren 15', *Payette NF*
CHARACTER: Steep mountain-river, boulder-choked rapids, limited access, trail, wilderness.

DESCRIPTION: There are good reasons the South Fork of the Salmon is becoming a popular whitewater run. It has the perfect mix of whitewater, scenery, and seclusion.

The rapids are a mix of long rock gardens and steep single drops. The South Fork has been kayaked and canoed when the flow was below 1'. The run loses most of the whitewater excitement at low flows, but remains a beautiful wilderness tour. When the water's high, the South Fork contains some challenging whitewater. Bruce Olson and Mike Lyons kayaked the entire 52 miles in a day by putting on when the water was high enough to entirely submerge the Krassel Gauge. The large flat rock below Hettenger is called Greyhound, because the hole that forms below the rock when the water's this high is, according to Lyons, big enough to surf a Greyhound bus.

The river runs through a beautiful granite canyon. The vegetation is a mix of thick forests and open mountain sides, much like the Middle Fork. The first named rapid is Devil Creek; a big boulder choked affair with a large hole on the left. You can sneak between the boulders at most flows. It's about five miles down from the put-in. The next big rapid is Surprise; a fun rock garden or a frightening minefield of deep holes, depending upon the water level. Elk Creek Rapid, formerly known as Teetering Log, can be identified by the tall cliff on the left and the steep drop at the base of the cliff. A teetering log, left by high water, used to be perched on the edge of this cliff. High water washed it off in '82. Don't go in the deep holes in the first part of this rapid. There's only a short recovery pool before the second part of the rapid.

At the South Fork Guard Station there is a bridge, some buildings and developed camping. A shuttle can drive here with camping gear if Profile Gap and Elk Summit are open to the east or Secesh and Warren Summit to the west. On the left bank, five miles downstream, Hettenger Ranch is on the left bank. Look for some buildings, an old incinerator and an airstrip. From the

South Fork Salmon River

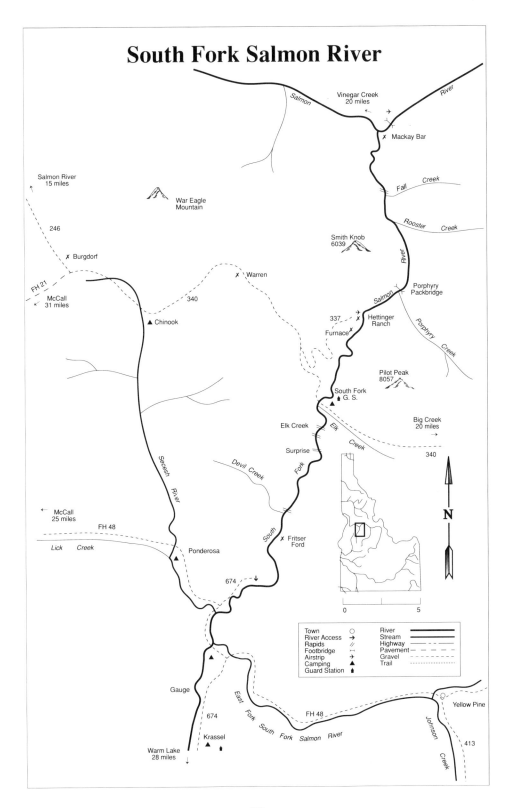

Salmon River

Vinegar Creek
20 miles

Mackay Bar

Fall Creek

Salmon River
15 miles

War Eagle
Mountain

Rooster Creek

246

Smith Knob
6039

Burgdorf

Warren

Porphyry
Packbridge

FH 21

340

Salmon

McCall
31 miles

337

Hettinger
Ranch

Porphyry Creek

Chinook

Furnace

Pilot Peak
8057

South Fork
G. S.

Elk Creek

Elk Creek

Big Creek
20 miles

Surprise

340

Devil Creek

South Fork

McCall
25 miles

FH 48

Secesh River

N

Lick Creek

Ponderosa

Fritser
Ford

674

Town   ○   River
River Access   →   Stream
Rapids   //   Highway
Footbridge   ⊢⊣   Pavement
Airstrip   →   Gravel
Camping   ▲   Trail
Guard Station   ♦

0   5

Gauge

Yellow Pine

674

East Fork South Fork Salmon River

FH 48

Johnson Creek

Krassel

413

Warm Lake
28 miles

73

river the ranch is out of sight . Equipment could be flown in and left at the airstrip if you want to live it up. Mackay Bar makes regular flights in here during the summer and cars can drive in here as well, but Secesh and Warren Summits must be open.

Fall Creek, the last rapid, is the biggest. A huge logjam on the right marks the rapid. At high water Fall Creek is a long series of steep chutes, deep holes and big waves. It's steep enough that you will probably want to scout it. As the flow drops, slow moving water develops between the first two drops and the rapid can be sectioned by kayaks.

Upstream of the South Fork's mouth, Mackay Bar, a back country guest ranch, is just a short hike up the river-left bank of the Main Salmon. To get there, stop when the trail on the right bank of the South Fork starts to climb away from the river, because at the mouth, there is a large bluff that's difficult to get around. With reservations, there are cabins and hot meals available at Mackay Bar. Beer and candy can be bought without reservations but, the price is reflective of American Economic Theory.

Don't camp along the Main Salmon unless you have a permit. Paddling out is recommended. This part of the Salmon is known as "Salmon Lake." There are two rapids in 20 miles; paddle don't float.

The gauge at Krassel is used to determine flows on the South Fork, but if you are going to use this gauge there are a couple things you should be aware of. Unfortunately, the Krassel gauge is located upstream from the confluence with the East Fork of the South Fork, which is equal to, or bigger than the South Fork at this point. The Secesh adds at least another 1000 cfs as well. There used to be a gauge located at the put-in (1932-1943). The records from this gauge show the river peaking in May. The Krassel gauge shows a June peak. Therefore a Krassel reading in May should indicate a higher flow in the canyon than a June reading.

The shuttle is long and difficult. Starting in McCall, go east on the main street along the lake. Where the main road turns south towards Boise, follow the Lick Creek Road 34 miles to the confluence with the South Fork. Then turn left and drive to the end of the road. If the Lick Creek Road is closed, go south of McCall to Cascade. Just north of Cascade take the Warm Lake Road to the east. Drive to the South Fork Road, and turn north. Follow the South Fork past the Secesh to the end of the road. The take-out is east of Riggins up the Salmon 26 miles at Vinegar Creek. McCall can also be reached from the take-out on the French Creek Road, if it's open. Most of the passes in this area open in June depending upon the snowpack. Call the McCall Ranger District for details. Shuttle drivers can be arranged at the sporting goods shops in McCall.

*To float out on the Main Salmon you need a permit. People have been stopped and fined coming off the South Fork.

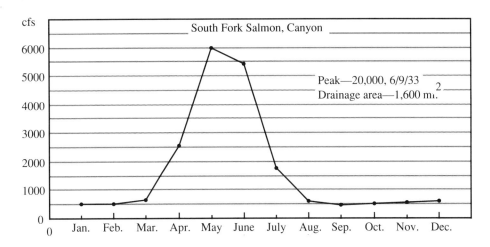

cfs — South Fork Salmon, Canyon

Peak—20,000, 6/9/33
Drainage area—1,600 mi.²

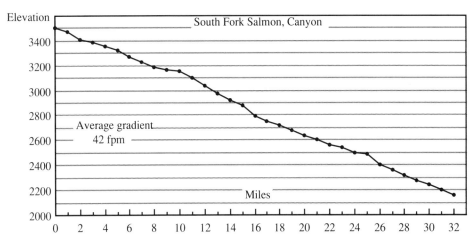

Elevation — South Fork Salmon, Canyon

Average gradient
42 fpm

Miles

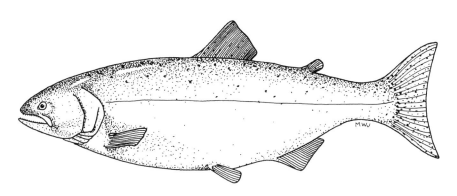

CHINOOK SALMON
Oncorhynchus tshawytscha

SOUTH FORK SALMON, GOAT CREEK RUN

CLASS	LEVEL	LENGTH	GRADIENT	TIME
IV-V	3'-4,5'	6 miles	83 fpm	3 hours
V	>4.5'			

PUT-IN:	Goat Creek, mile 8.9 (4,680 ft.)
TAKE-OUT:	Poverty Flats, mile 14 (4,180 ft.)
SHUTTLE:	7 miles
CRAFT:	Kayak, canoe
PORTAGES:	Logs
SEASON:	May, June
GAUGE:	Krassel
PERMIT:	No
MAPS:	White Rock Pk.
CHARACTER:	Swift mountain river, ledge drops and rock gardens, logjams, removed road, remote.

DESCRIPTION: The Goat Creek run on the South Fork of the Salmon is a great class IV day run. There are at least 20 good drops including one class V ledge. The run is extremely secluded and the water cold. The road climbs up away from the river at the put-in and doesn't return until the take-out.

You may have seen the high water put in technique for this run in a Rocky Rossi video. It's very shallow and rocky below the pipe. If you can see the rocks, walk down the steep hill and avoid the theatrics.

About half way down this run, logs start to show up. A sharp, but open, corner to the right signals the start of the bigger drops. There is a huge log in the eddy at the top on the left. You can't miss the obvious horizon downstream. The next drop is a class V series of ledges known as Double Drop. Keep your nose up. Pitons are common here. There's an easy portage on the right, put in either mid-way or at the bottom.

The class II riffle just below has an innocuous, but dangerous under-cut rock right in the middle. On one cold spring morning, I was eddied out in the pool below this drop watching Clinton LaTourrette float down. Suddenly, he literally disappeared from the river's surface, pulled down by the undercut. As I jumped out of my boat, his yellow helmet rose up and broke out of the water in the same place he had gone under. His face was out of the water and he could breath, but he was pinned to the bottom. Our eyes locked and I remember mentally going through a hundred rescue techniques in about five seconds. Then I could see he was moving forward in the water. He had reached down, put his hands on the rock and bottom and pulled forward and free. His kayak breached out of the water like a surfacing submarine.

Two more significant rapids remain, both are steep ledges dropping into reversals. The first is marked by a log bridging the river below the drop. As you come around the corner it looks like the log is sitting right on the water's surface, however at all but the highest flows there's plenty of clearance. If you're on this run and going under this log is a tight squeeze, you don't need a guidebook. There are lots of logs and sweepers on the this run as well and

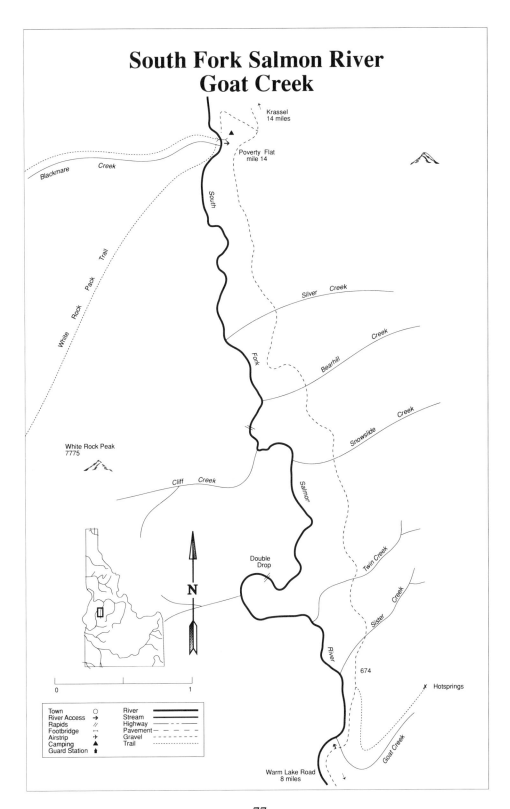

South Fork Salmon River
Goat Creek

Krassel
14 miles

Poverty Flat
mile 14

Blackmare Creek

South

White Rock Pack Trail

Silver Creek

Fork

Bearhill Creek

Snowslide Creek

White Rock Peak
7775

Cliff Creek

Salmon

Double
Drop

Twin Creek

Sister Creek

N

River

674

Hotsprings

Goat Creek

0   1

Town	○	River	———
River Access	→	Stream	——
Rapids	//	Highway	——
Footbridge	⊢	Pavement	– –
Airstrip	✈	Gravel	– – –
Camping	▲	Trail	·····
Guard Station	⬥		

Warm Lake Road
8 miles

several must be portaged depending on the water level. The river mellows out about a half mile above Poverty Flats, the take-out. A mile-and-a-half downstream, Teapot Hot Springs are on the right bank. There's a little gorge in this stretch, which makes the run to Teapot worthwhile. From the road Teapot Hotsprings are close to milepost 16, but if the flow is 6.4' or higher they'll be under water. The gauge is located about a mile downstream from the Krassel Ranger Station on the right bank.

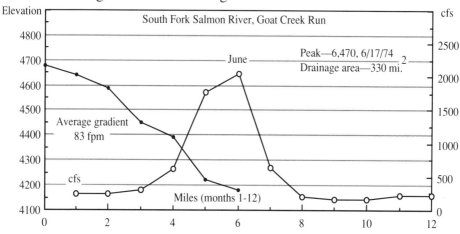

South Fork Salmon River, Goat Creek Run

Peak—6,470, 6/17/74
Drainage area—330 mi.^{2}

June

Average gradient 83 fpm

cfs

Miles (months 1-12)

Plenty of clearance. Bruce Olsen dropping into the Swimming Hole.

The famous Teetering Log. Photo: Rob Lesser

SECESH RIVER, LOWER RUN

CLASS	LEVEL	LENGTH	GRADIENT	TIME
IV	1,500 cfs	5 miles	80 fpm	1-2 hours

PUT-IN: Ponderosa Campground (4,000 ft.)
TAKE-OUT: South Fork Salmon Confluence (3,600 ft.)
SHUTTLE: 5 miles
CRAFT: Kayak
PORTAGES: 0
SEASON: May, June
GAUGE: No
PERMIT: No
MAPS: Enos Lake, Williams Pk., *Payette NF*
CHARACTER: Swift steep-creek, sustained gradient, road, remote.

DESCRIPTION: The last five miles of the Secesh River run along the Lick Creek Road to the confluence with the South Fork of the Salmon River. This is a good little section of whitewater.

Because it runs along the road, most of the run can be road scouted. Some of the river is obscured behind trees or is just too far away to see. In these places use the *numero uno* road scout's rule of thumb: if you can't see it from the road — it's easy. Logs try to sneak down this stretch from year to year, so don't be too cavalier. From Ponderosa the run starts with a good drop and then flattens out a bit. It is continuous class II-III water for about two miles. The best whitewater is in the last mile before the confluence with the South Fork of the Salmon. This is a non-stop class III-IV rapid. To run it correctly proceed downstream for two paddle strokes, then . . . who cares? Look for yourself as you drive up the road.

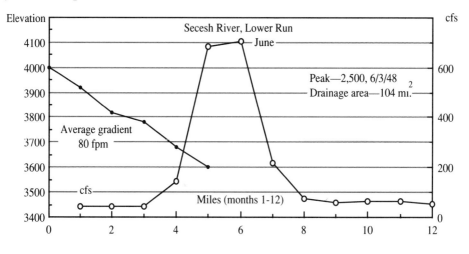

Secesh River, Lower Run

Peak—2,500, 6/3/48
Drainage area—104 mi.^{2}

Average gradient 80 fpm

Miles (months 1-12)

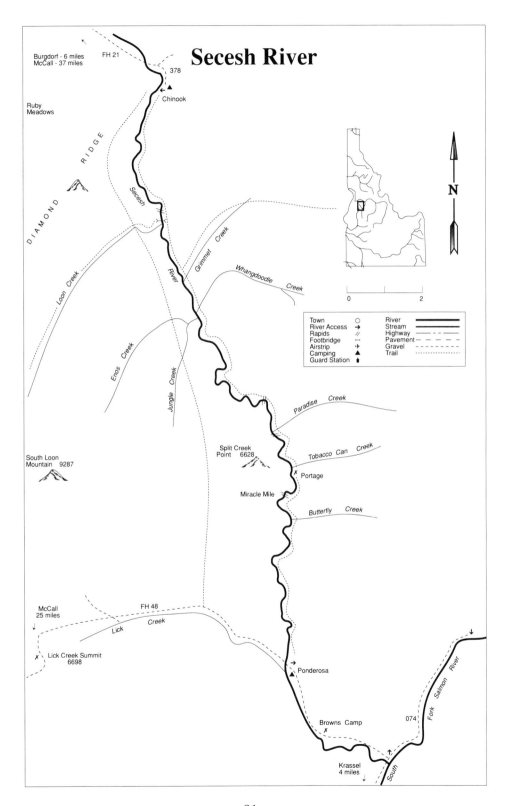

Secesh River

Burgdorf - 6 miles
McCall - 37 miles

FH 21

378

Chinook

Ruby
Meadows

D I A M O N D   R I D G E

Secesh

River

Loon Creek

Grimmet Creek

Whangdoodle Creek

Enos Creek

Jungle Creek

Paradise Creek

Split Creek
Point   6628

Tobacco Can Creek

Portage

South Loon
Mountain   9287

Miracle Mile

Butterfly Creek

McCall
25 miles

FH 48

Lick Creek

Lick Creek Summit
6698

Ponderosa

Browns Camp

074

South Fork Salmon River

Krassel
4 miles

Town	○	River
River Access	→	Stream
Rapids	//	Highway
Footbridge	⊢	Pavement
Airstrip	✈	Gravel
Camping	▲	Trail
Guard Station	♦	

N

0   2

SECESH RIVER CANYON

CLASS	LEVEL	LENGTH	GRADIENT	TIME
IV-V	1,000 cfs	15 miles	111 fpm	6-8 hours
V+	>1,500 cfs			

PUT-IN:	Chinook Campground (5,670 ft.)
TAKE-OUT:	Ponderosa Campground (4,000 ft.)
SHUTTLE:	70 miles
CRAFT:	Kayak
PORTAGES:	1
SEASON:	May, June
GAUGE:	Krassel
PERMIT:	No
MAPS:	Loon Lake, Enos Lake, *Payette NF*
CHARACTER:	Extreme steep-creek, narrow river bed,boulder choked rapids, logjams,trail, wilderness.

DESCRIPTION: If the traditional naming style of Idaho had been applied to the Secesh, it would be known as the West Fork of The South Fork of the Salmon River. The Secesh gets its name from the Secessionist miners who worked the river during the civil war. Kayaking history buffs will recall the Secessionists lost, however, lucky for us they did end up with a winner of a river.

The Secesh is a demanding class V day-run. There are several big drops, a portage and miles of swift water. There are lots of logs and sweepers as well. In 1988 a kayaker died on a sweeper in The Miracle Mile, the big rapid below the portage.

The river starts out gentle and swift. A trail follows the river on the left bank for its entire length. The banks are lined with logs, felled and cabled to the river bank in an attempt to reduce stream-bank erosion and improve the salmon spawning beds. The Secesh is a steep, swift and shallow river. At all but high flows, rocks, pins, and pitons are a hazard.

Be careful of high water on the Secesh. Mark Fraas, Mike Lyons and a couple of friends (who will remain unnamed) made a high water descent in 1982. After five miles of wipeouts, everyone but Fraas and Lyons decided to portage — the rest of the river — over 10 miles. Fraas and Lyons spent so much time scouting, the portage crew almost beat them to the take-out.

The first rapid is less than two miles below the put-in. When the canyon closes in and river fills it from wall to wall, brace yourself for some whitewater. The action starts above the Loon Creek Pack Bridge, about three miles down. It's a little more than a mile and one tight rock garden to the next major tributary, Whangdoodle Creek, which comes in from the left. Several more miles and rapids will bring you to the next major tributary, Blue Lake Creek. The rapids take a leap in difficulty above here and continue to climb the whitewater scale the further downstream you go. The next major tributary, Paradise Creek, again from the left, is just upstream of a long complicated rapid which dumps into a series of pools.

The portage is at is at the end of these pools. The river enters a small class II rapid and then disappears under the horizon. Tobacco Can Creek forms a shoestring waterfall which runs down the left side of the canyon wall and a big gravel bar on the right forces the river into a narrow channel on the left. The portage is on the left and it's a long one. Even with the trail, you'll find it difficult to get back to the river. Things heat up from here down. The first rapid after the portage is the Miracle Mile. The crux move is a difficult and powerful chute about half-way down The Miracle Mile. The seam below the boulder will test your bracing ability. If you're worried about rolling here — portage. In the last two miles the canyon opens up and the river stretches its banks, it's swift and full of logs.

This is a long involved shuttle. To reach the put-in, drive north from Lardos in McCall on Warren Wagon Road 36 miles to Chinook Camp-ground and the put-in.

To find the take-out from McCall, go east on the main street along the lake. Where the main road turns south towards Boise, follow the Lick Creek Road 29 miles to Ponderosa Campground and the take-out. If the Lick Creek Road is closed, go south of McCall to Cascade. Just north of Cascade take the Warm Lake Road to the east. Drive to the South Fork Road, and turn north. Drive 35 miles to the Secesh. Go up the Secesh five miles to Ponderosa Campground.

The camping at the put-in and the take-out is good. I like to warm up the night before any Secesh run in the hotsprings pool at Burgdorf. Camping along the Secesh is limited due to the steep canyon walls. There are a couple outfitters' camps in the top stretch that could be used and some good spots right above the portage. Because the river is extremely shallow and swift, stowed equipment should be avoided or kept to a bare minimum.

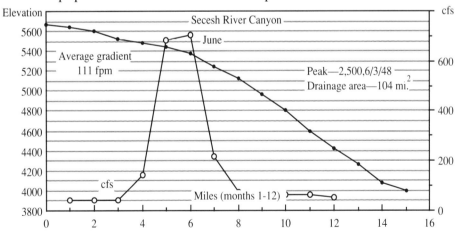

EAST FORK SOUTH FORK SALMON RIVER, LOWER

CLASS	LEVEL	LENGTH	GRADIENT	TIME
III-V	1,000 cfs	15 miles	67 fpm	5-8 hours
IV-V+	>1,500 cfs			

PUT IN:	Johnson Creek (4,650 ft.)
TAKE OUT:	Indian Point (3,640 ft.)
SHUTTLE:	15 miles
CRAFT:	Kayak
PORTAGES:	No
SEASON:	May, June
GAUGE:	No*
PERMIT:	No
MAPS:	Williams Pk., Parks Pk., Pilot Pk., Chicken Pk., Warren 15, *Payette NF*
CHARACTER:	Small mountain river, high gradient, continuous boulder-choked rapids, logs, road, secluded.

DESCRIPTION: This is an outstanding whitewater run. It is full of class IV drops with the most difficult rapids at the top. At most levels the river is full of big holes and even if you've scouted and planned out a line, you can count on falling into a couple of them over the course of the run; boat scouting will put you in a lot more.

Below the short flat water warm-up, the river drops directly into two back-to-back class V rapids. The first one has a fairly clean line, but you will still have to take on a few holes towards the bottom. We call this Flight Simulator. While scouting this rapid one morning, Tony Brennan and I kept looking towards the sky to find the jet plane we were hearing. As we scrambled down the bank we realized the jet sound was coming from the rapid. The second rapid doesn't have a clean line. It has lots of nasty rocks, hydraulics and a log or two as well. Above 1,600 cfs on the Johnson Creek gauge consider the Caton Creek put-in.

Take the time to road scout this run while setting up the shuttle. If you start at the bottom and things are looking pretty big to you by the time you reach Caton Creek — go no further. Things only get tougher upstream and Caton Creek is a common alternative put-in. This will cut out most of the class V, but you'll still be crashing through some river wide holes and dodging some adrenaline focus points. At lower flows the rapids become technical as the rocks emerge and the eddies take on some definition. The East Fork South Fork can be a fun day at low water, but be careful of broaching or pinning.

There are good camp sites at both the put-in and the take-out. Food and drink as well as gas and groceries can be found a mile up from the start in the little mining town of Yellow Pine.

*A stick gauge is located 100 yards up Johnson Creek on the right bank. Because Johnson Creek is the major source of water for the East Fork, this gauge can be used to judge the flows for this run. See the appendix for the rating table.

East Fork
South Fork Salmon River

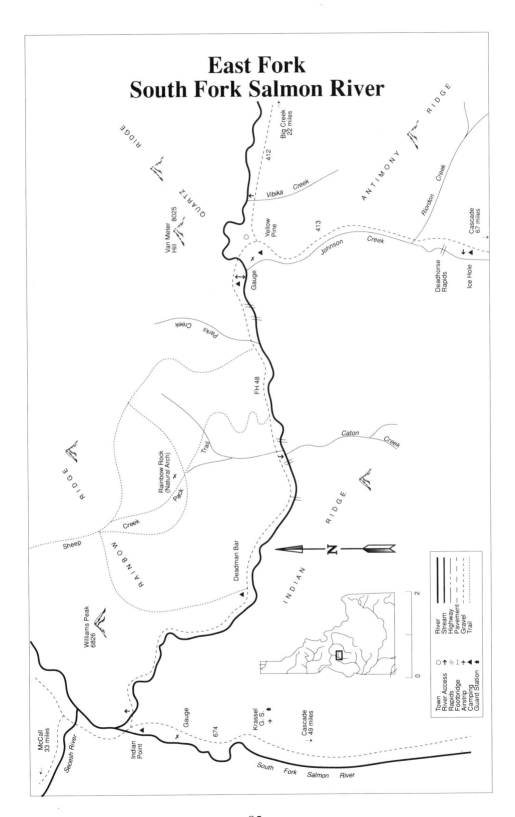

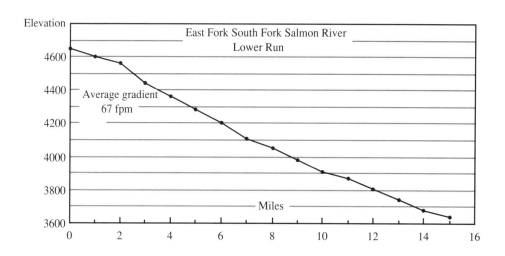

East Fork South Fork Salmon River
Lower Run

Average gradient
67 fpm

Elevation

Doctor Stoener taking off on the East Fork of the South Fork.

EAST FORK SOUTH FORK SALMON RIVER, UPPER

CLASS	LEVEL	LENGTH	GRADIENT	TIME
III-IV	250 cfs	3 miles	123 fpm	1-2 hours

PUT IN:	Vibika Creek (5,020 ft.)
TAKE OUT:	Johnson Creek (4,650 ft.)
SHUTTLE:	3 miles
CRAFT:	Kayak
PORTAGES:	No
SEASON:	May, June
GAUGE:	Near Stibnite
PERMIT:	No
MAPS:	Yellow Pine, *Payette NF*
CHARACTER:	Steep creek, continuous, technical, logs, road, secluded.

DESCRIPTION: If you like catching eddies and flying down steep chutes, you'll like this run. This is a little creek, with lots of technical rock gardens and a couple of steep chutes. Some of the chutes may require scouting simply because the bottom is hidden under the horizon. At higher flows these ledges could change into powerful reversals. There are two good rapids at the end of the run. The first is just upstream from the East Fork Road Bridge and the second is at the confluence with Johnson Creek. The stretch that can't be seen from the road is basically the same as the rest of the run.

There is an operating gauge seven miles upstream from the put-in. The hydrograph is based on the old gauge, located upstream of the confluence. Though this gauge is no longer operating, the data is more accurate for judging the season and actual volume of this run.

The put-in is east of Yellow Pine three miles on road 412.

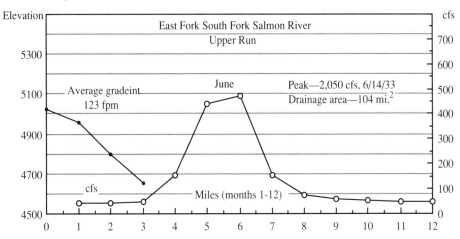

JOHNSON CREEK

CLASS	LEVEL	LENGTH	GRADIENT	TIME
II-V	600 cfs	6 miles	53 fpm	3 hours

PUT-IN: Ice Hole Campground (5,600 ft.)
TAKE-OUT: Yellow Pine Campground (4,650 ft.)
SHUTTLE: 6 miles
CRAFT: Kayak
PORTAGES: 0
SEASON: May, June
GAUGE: Yellow Pine
PERMIT: No
MAPS: Log Mtn., Caton Lake, Yellow Pine, *Boise NF*
CHARACTER: Steep creek, rock gardens, logjams, road, secluded.

DESCRIPTION: There are two outstanding rapids on this run. The first is right at the start, the second at the end. In between, there are four miles of class II and III busy water.

If you start at Ice Hole Campground, Deadhorse Rapid is around the corner following a hundred yards of class II-III; not much of a warm up for what follows. Deadhorse starts off with a long rock garden. After crashing down a series of ledges, the river is pinched between two boulders in a slot ten feet across dropping six feet onto a boulder in the center of the current. Depending on the level, you're either going to hit the boulder, surf an ugly cushion or, if you've been living right, you might squeak through clean. Then the river takes a sharp turn to the left. The outside is choked with sweepers, don't go out here. The turn leads into a fantastic rock garden that ends in a great play hole. From here down to the confluence with the East-Fork South-Fork you can relax and reflect on your fast start. The last rapid is a steep boiling mess due to the mixing currents of the two rivers. At this point, Johnson Creek is about twice as large as the East Fork South Fork. There's a stick gauge on Johnson Creek about 100 yards up from the confluence. See the appendix for the rating table.

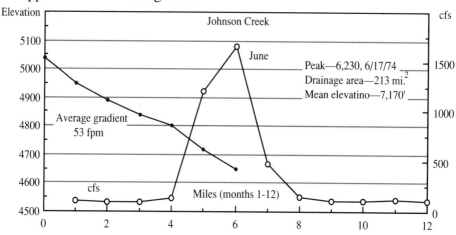

The crux of the Miracle Mile. Photo: Tom Schibig

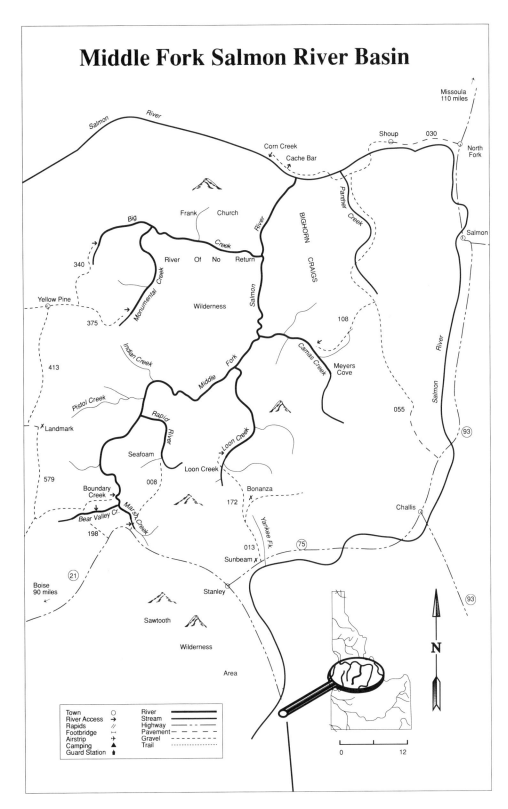

Middle Fork Salmon River Basin

THE MIDDLE FORK OF THE SALMON

CLASS	LEVEL	LENGTH	GRADIENT	TIME
III	1'-3'	100 (96) miles	28 fpm	2-8 days
IV	3'-6'			
IV+	>6'			

PUT-IN:	Boundary Creek (5,640 ft.)
TAKE-OUT:	Cache Bar (3,000 ft.)
SHUTTLE:	270 miles
CRAFT:	Kayak, canoe, raft, driftboat
PORTAGES:	No
SEASON:	April, May, June, July, August, September
GAUGE:	Middle Fork Lodge
PERMIT:	Yes
MAPS:	Forest Service: The Middle Fork of the Salmon
CHARACTER:	Wild and Scenic River, gravel bed changing to rock gardens, gorge, wilderness, trail.

DESCRIPTION: One hundred miles of wilderness boating — the Middle Fork is a river trip worth doing. It is a wonderful mix of history, scenery and whitewater. Do not go expecting a giant whitewater thrill. You will be disappointed. Go expecting some incredible fishing, amazing scenery, hot hot-pots and some good whitewater. Expect a Forest Service bureaucracy, get a permit.

The Middle Fork starts off as a tight alpine stream. Then riverbed is narrow and the canyon walls are covered with a lush pine forest. At low water some of the maneuvers along the upper stretch can be tricky. Velvet Falls and Pistol Creek are good rapids. After Indian Creek, the whitewater backs off and the river becomes wide and gentle. At Marble Creek the canyon opens up and the vegetation changes from pine trees to dry grasslands. The whitewater picks back up at Tappen Ranch, backs off again more or less until Big Creek and the Impassable Canyon (named because the trail leaves the river, not because of the whitewater). However, most of the whitewater on the Middle Fork is in the Impassable Canyon: Redside, Weber, and Rubber are in this stretch. When the water's high (>5'), the surfing is fantastic in the canyon. Plan your last day to take advantage of this. The scenery is some of the best as well with the river cutting through the shadows of towering granite spires and barren cliffs.

For the entire story read Cort Conley's "The Middle Fork and the Sheepeater War." For a permit application and an excellent map, contact the Middle Fork Ranger District, P.O. Box 750, Challis Idaho, 83226. Apply between December first and January 31st. It costs $5.00.

The Middle Fork can be run on a first-come, first-served basis if you show up before June first, opening day of the permit season. Parties using this approach will still be required to register and fulfil all the requirements: firepan, toilet, 24 people to a party, no littering, etc. There are seven launches allowed on the Middle Fork each day, including three outfitters.

Middle Fork Salmon River

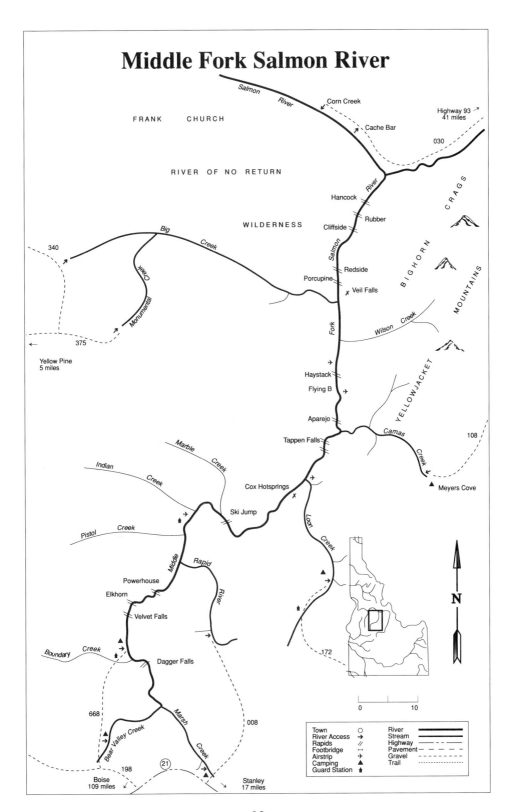

Preseason access is also limited by the road into Boundary Creek. In big snowpack years the road doesn't always open until well into permit season. If the Capehorn Road is closed, Marsh Creek can be floated, right from the highway 21 bridge, to access the Middle Fork. If you float in Marsh Creek, you're probably going to end up portaging Dagger Falls (see Marsh Creek for details).

There are a few other tricks that will help make a Middle Fork trip more enjoyable. First, show up the evening before your launch date. If it's not crowded you can rig and launch your boats the night before your launch date. Middle Fork campgrounds are designated. This means you have to sit down with the ranger and hash out where you are going to camp. Each party is allowed one hotsprings campground. If another party wants the campground, you want, you may have to flip a coin for it. Almost all the camp spots on the Middle Fork are nice. Avoid Stoddard and Tumble Creek: big hikes up the bank. Unfortunately on the lower end of the river, the canyon is steep and camping is limited, you may be forced to take one of these. Lightening Strike, Parrot Placer and Otters are the best down here. Everybody else thinks so too: they always seem to be taken. Look for places from where you can hike to hotsprings or other places of interest. Remember, you don't have to camp at a hot springs to use them.

The river can be managed by experienced boaters at almost any level. I've run the Middle Fork at over nine feet without mishap nor undue stress, other than having to share the river with countless migrating logs. At flows below 2' flying into Indian Creek avoids the shallow gravel bars and narrow chutes upstream. However, flying to Indian Creek can be expensive, prices are around $180 for a plane capable of carrying five people (without gear).

I've run from Boundary Creek as low as 1.7 in a canoe. I hit more rocks in that week than I do in a normal year. A commercial outfitter was there as well, with folks paying $100 a day to push a large rubber raft down a little stream. Above Indian Creek during low water runs beware of Sulfur Slide, The Chutes and everywhere else. Downstream look out for Devils Tooth, not because they're difficult, don't be silly, because they're shallow.

The shuttle is long, but straight forward. To get to the put in, turn off highway 21 at mile 110, go nine miles to Bruce Meadows and turn right. It's 10 miles more to Boundary Creek. From the put-in go back to 21, east 19 miles to Stanley. Go north, 116 miles through Salmon to North Fork. Go west 41 miles to Cache Bar.

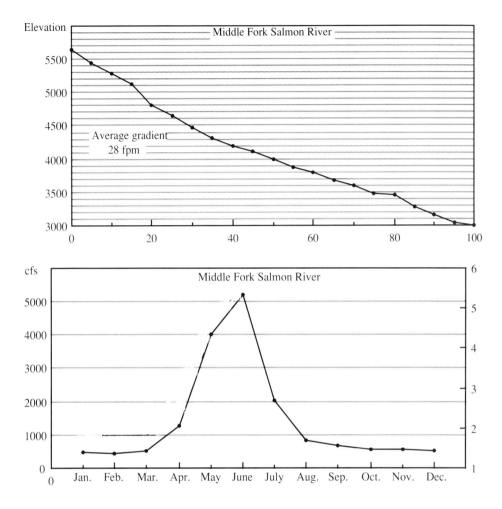

BIG CREEK

CLASS	LEVEL	LENGTH	GRADIENT	TIME
III-IV	700-1,000 cfs	54 (34) miles	61 fpm	2 days
IV	1,000-2,000 cfs			

PUT-IN:	Big Creek Air Strip (5,440 ft.)
TAKE-OUT:	Cache Bar {(confl. 3,380 ft.) 3,000 ft.}
SHUTTLE:	3rd longest
CRAFT:	Kayak
PORTAGES:	6 logs
SEASON:	June, July
GAUGE:	No
PERMIT:	Yes*
MAPS:	Big Creek, Bismark Mtn., Acorn Btt., Vinegar Hill, Mormon Mtn., Dave Lewis, Puddin Mtn., *FCRONRW*
CHARACTER:	Beautiful, pristine mountain stream, swift water, gorge, trail, wilderness.

DESCRIPTION: Big Creek has always been a special whitewater adventure due to the areas isolation and the unusual shuttle logistics of timing the run. When the flows on Big Creek are high enough to run, the road to the put-in is usually closed due to snow. Therefore, access to the Big Creek put-in is usually by air, which makes the shuttle short, but expensive. The airstrip at Big Creek is long enough to accommodate fairly large aircraft. So you don't have to fold your boat or go through any contortion other than paying about $180 for a plane. A Cessna 207 can handle three kayakers and all their gear.

The top of Big Creek is a tight little swift-water stream. As the river continues on its path, it grows in size. There are several logjams that must be portaged in the first 10 miles. The middle section of the river flattens out. Below Coxey Bar a bunch of huge boulders form a big class IV rapid. The best whitewater is in the Big Creek Gorge at the river's end. At high flows this is a fantastic five mile rapid. The action starts close to Soldier Bar and continues in a class III-IV blaze all the way to the Middle Fork.

Kayakers running the Middle Fork of the Salmon can drag their boats up the trail a mile to the first pack bridge and get a good sample of the best Big Creek rapids. Big Creek boaters coming into the Middle Fork will get to sample its best whitewater.

The scenery at the top is beautiful, consisting of a mix of brush and pine forest. As the river gets closer to the Middle Fork ,it drops into a gorge of barren mountains. There is good camping all along the river and the canyon is relatively untouched by man.

Starting in Salmon is the shortest shuttle. Leave a car at Cache Bar, the Middle Fork take-out, drive 60 miles to the Salmon Airfield, fly to Big Creek. Wilderness Aviation in Salmon is the least expensive air taxi I could find. If you're really cheap you can drive into Monumental Creek year-round and float/walk down to Big Creek. Read the Monumental Creek description for all the details.

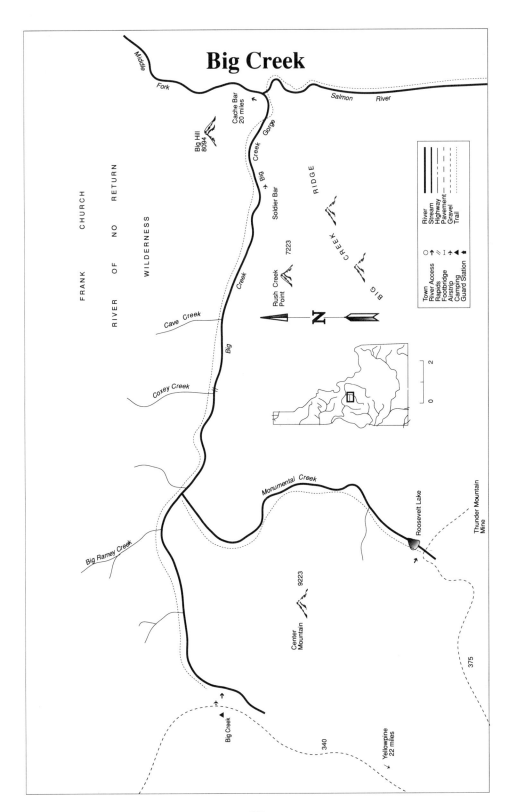

Big Creek

If Profile Summit is open (7606') (usually late June), you too can drive one of the world's longest shuttle. Phone the McCall Ranger District, (208) 634-8151 for road conditions. From Cascade, drive just north of town on highway 55, go east on the Warm Lake Road (37 miles). Then, north on the Johnson Creek Road (25 miles). Just south of Yellow Pine turn east and drive six miles to the Profile Creek Road, go north (18 miles) up Profile Creek to Big Creek. If the road's open, the lodge is usually open and you can get a good meal there. The shuttle driver will then drive back to highway 55. South, to Banks. East, to Stanley. North, to North Fork. West, to Cache Bar and the take-out. Roughly, 400 miles one way and the better part of two days. There is a gravel short cut for people with rugged vehicles and good tires. At the Johnson Creek/Warm Lake Road junction, go east on the Warm Lake Road (579) and follow this south over Deadwood Summit, then east through Deer Flat, Elk Creek, Bruce Meadows and down to highway 21 west of Stanley.

*To Float out on the Middle Fork you need a permit.

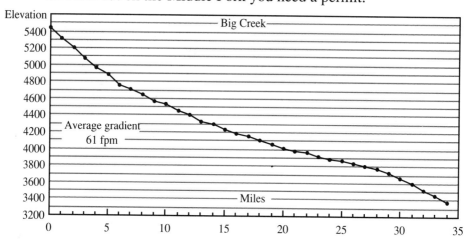

Lincoln Williams in the lower half of Coxey Rapid.

MONUMENTAL CREEK

CLASS	LEVEL	LENGTH	GRADIENT	TIME
III-IV	500 cfs	60 (18) miles	92 fpm	2 days

PUT-IN:	Upper Monumental Campground (6,160 ft.)
TAKE-OUT:	Cache Bar {(confl. 4,500 ft.) 3,000 ft.}
SHUTTLE:	World's 2nd longest
CRAFT:	Kayak
PORTAGES:	27 logs
SEASON:	June, July
GAUGE:	No
PERMIT:	Yes*
MAPS:	Big Creek, Bismark Mtn., Acorn Btt., Vinegar Hill, Mormon Mtn., Dave Lewis, Puddin Mtn., *FCRONRW*
CHARACTER:	Beautiful, pristine mountain stream, swift water, gorge, trail, wilderness.

DESCRIPTION: This is the poor man's approach to Big Creek. The road to Thunder Mountain is plowed all year so you don't have to pay to fly into Big Creek Airstrip. You will miss the joy of flying and some good whitewater on the top of Big Creek. And like the poor man, your burden will be a heavy one; in the form of 27 portages. You won't be portaging any gnarly whitewater, just an endless procession of logs and logjams. You may also have to portage a cabin in Roosevelt Lake depending on which of the little streams you choose to follow. Try the left, we went right and were boxed in by a cabin. In 1909 a landslide crashed down the mountain side and dammed Monumental Creek, the backwaters formed by the landslide inundated the mining town of Roosevelt. The remnants of the town still poke their tops out of the water and silt of the lake.

Lincoln Williams, Slater Crosby and I made the first and probably the last descent in the spring of 1989. For the first five miles Monumental Creek is a non-stop portage binge. After about number ten, I stopped putting on my sprayskirt for the little stretches of splashy water between the walks. After the West Fork comes in, the creek begins to behave with a couple of half-mile portage-free stretches. The first rapid is about 7 miles down near Milk Creek. Look for a bend to the left with a bare and eroded bank on the right: class III. The last five miles of the run, to the confluence with Big Creek, are a non-stop class II rapid. Several portages remain. Don't get lazy about the portaging. It's easy to lose your focus on safety after indulging in 10 or more portages.

One of the positive aspects of running Monumental is experience of starting on a little creek, small enough to leap without getting your feet wet and finishing, only 60 miles downstream, on a river large enough to float an ocean liner. The scenery and wildlife made up for some of the portaging as well. We saw three moose, a golden eagle, the watery ruins of Roosevelt and the famous monument that lends the creek its name, but if I ever want to see this stuff again I'm going to hike on the nice forest service trail and hike back out the same way.

To get to the put-in and take-out, follow the Big Creek directions, except instead of turning up Profile Creek continue up over Monumental Summit and down into the Monumental drainage. Put in where the road crosses the creek for the second time or hike down 100 yards and cut the number of portages to 26.

*To float out on the Middle Fork you need a permit.

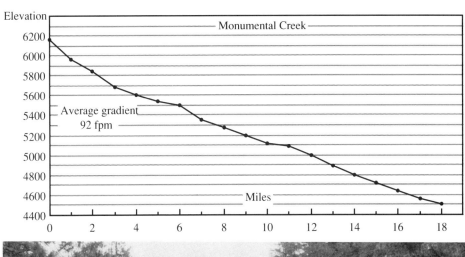

CAMAS CREEK

CLASS	LEVEL	LENGTH	GRADIENT	TIME
V	600 cfs	53 (13) miles	106 fpm	2 days

PUT-IN:	Duck Creek (5,150 ft.)
TAKE-OUT:	Cache Bar {(confl. 3,770 ft.) 3,000 ft.}
SHUTTLE:	69 miles
CRAFT:	Kayak
PORTAGES:	12 (11 logs)
SEASON:	June
GAUGE:	Middle Fork Lodge
PERMIT:	Yes*
MAPS:	Apparejo Pt., Yellowjacket Mtn., Meyers Cove, Meyers, *FCRONRW*
CHARACTER:	Extreme class-V steep creek, severe single drops and continuous rock gardens, logs, gorge, trail, wilderness.

DESCRIPTION: For class V boaters Camas Creek is the best of the Middle Fork tributaries. It's full of challenging rock gardens and steep boulder choked slots. There are at least 10 class IV drops on Camas Creek along with several class V drops. Once on the river, plan on doing lots of scouting and portaging.

Camas Creek starts out meandering through a meadow. Watch out for the fence in this stretch. After about three miles the creek goes into a steep constricted gorge. Camas Falls are the first significant rapid and the only rapid that hasn't been run. It's a long and complicated cascade. Almost all the rapids on Camas Creek should be scouted. The best stretch of the run is about three miles up from the confluence. The whitewater backs off after this, and some places for camping open up.

Camas Creek is only 13 miles long. The other 40 miles are on the Middle Fork, so you'll need a permit. The shuttle roads are kept in good shape. From the take-out at the Middle Fork, Main Salmon Confluence, drive upstream to Panther Creek. Go up Panther Creek 36 miles to Rooker Basin, and west on forest service road 108 for 17 miles to Meyers Cove. Start here or if the gate is unlocked, go to Duck Creek at the end of the road, another three miles downstream. From the north it is possible to drive in from Challis. North of Challis eight miles take forest service road 055 to the northwest and follow this 20 miles over the Morgan Creek Summit and another 24 miles to Meyers Cove. If you're going into the Salmon, travelling this road takes about the same amount of time as the oil road through North Fork. Call the Challis Ranger District, (208) 879-4321, for road conditions.

*To float out on the Middle Fork you need a permit.

Camas Creek

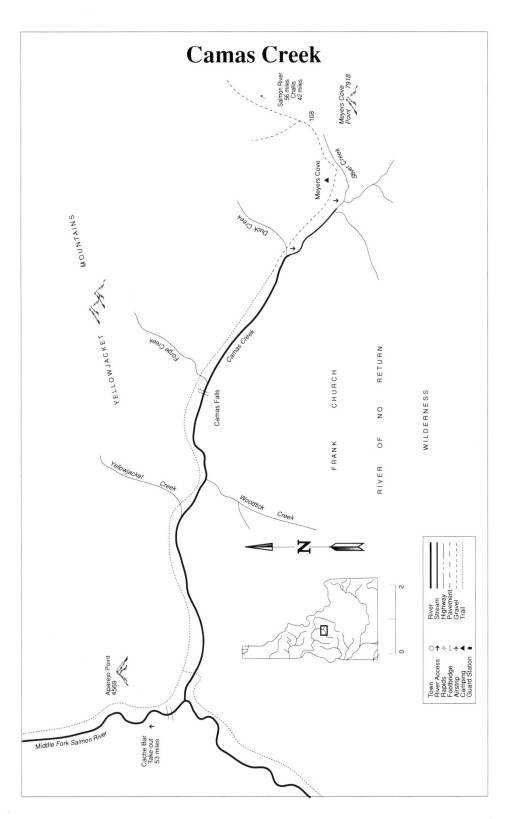

Salmon River
56 miles
Challis
42 miles

Meyers Cove
Point 7918

108

Meyers Cove

Sal Creek

Duck Creek

MOUNTAINS

YELLOWJACKET

Forge Creek

Camas Creek

Camas Falls

FRANK

CHURCH

Yellowjacket Creek

Woodtick Creek

RIVER OF NO RETURN

WILDERNESS

N

2

0

Town
River Access
Rapids
Footbridge
Airstrip
Camping
Guard Station

River
Stream
Highway
Pavement
Gravel
Trail

Aparejo Point
4569

Middle Fork Salmon River

Cache Bar
Take-out
53 miles

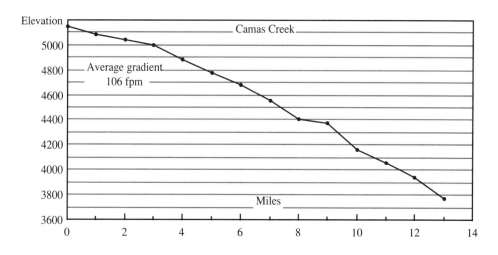

Looking up at Camas Falls. Photo: Jim Ciardelli

Tony Brennan lining up for another rock slot.

LOON CREEK

CLASS	LEVEL	LENGTH	GRADIENT	TIME
III-V	600 cfs	66 (20) miles	68 fpm	2 days

PUT-IN: Phillips Transfer Camp (5,360 ft.)
TAKE-OUT: Cache Bar {(confl. 4,000 ft.) 3,000 ft.}
SHUTTLE: 190 miles
CRAFT: Kayak
PORTAGES: 1 log
SEASON: June, July
GAUGE: No
PERMIT: Yes*
MAPS: Casto, Rock Cr., Falconberry Pk., Ramey Hill
CHARACTER: Steep mountain stream, constricted boulder gardens, shear drops, gorge, trail, wilderness.

DESCRIPTION: Every Middle Fork kayaker who has walked up Loon Creek to the hot springs must wonder if it has been run and what it is like. Yes, Loon Creek has been run — lots. It is one of the more beautiful streams in Idaho.

At the put-in the river is a tight, winding creek. There are two good ledge drops and a number of fun little rock gardens. About four miles down, some hot springs spill in from the right bank. The Falconberry Guard Station is about four miles further. After two more miles, the river passes the Biggs Ranch and the whitewater starts to pick up. Where the canyon closes in the good rapids start. A long class III-IV rock garden starts the action. The next rapid is a tight class V. You'll know you've found it when the river disappears downstream. At most flows the line winds through a couple of holes at the top and then drops down a tight slot on the right. There are several long rock gardens in this stretch as well. The next big rapid is a blind left turn.

The Bennett Creek Pack Bridge signals the start of the gorge. Loon Creek Hot Springs are only a mile below and the Middle Fork two. There are a couple of nice little ledge drops, followed by a not-so-nice big ledge drop. Most of the creek goes down the center into a hole, backed up by a boulder. The right bank is cut off by a boulder with a very thin cushion. Choose your line carefully.

The run is typically done in a day down to the Middle Fork and then out to a campsite. Camping is strictly regulated on the Middle Fork, so make sure you have a permit. Loon Creek Guard Station, upstream of the put-in, is manned and they are key to kayakers who try to sneak onto the Middle Fork. If you go tooling past here in your shuttle vehicle, you're sure to attract some attention. There are some nice campsites with river access upstream on Mayfield Creek.

To find the put-in from Stanley, drive 12 miles north on highway 75 to Sunbeam. Go 10 miles up the Yankee Fork past Bonanza, turn left careening at high speed for 21 miles, up and over Loon Creek Summit on Forest Service Road 172. Drive past Loon Creek Guard Station (be sure to wave), and down

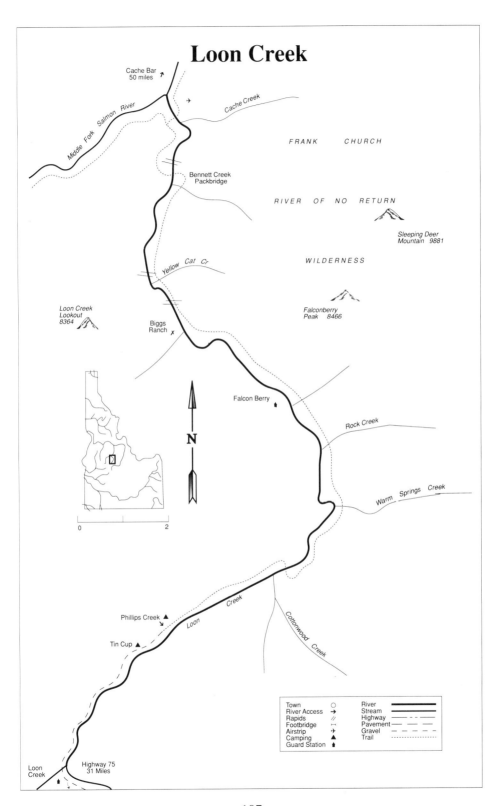

Loon Creek

Cache Bar
50 miles

Cache Creek

Middle Fork Salmon River

FRANK   CHURCH

Bennett Creek
Packbridge

RIVER   OF   NO   RETURN

Sleeping Deer
Mountain 9881

Yellow Cat Cr

WILDERNESS

Loon Creek
Lookout
8364

Falconberry
Peak   8466

Biggs
Ranch

N

Falcon Berry

Rock Creek

Warm Springs Creek

0   2

Loon   Creek

Phillips Creek ▲

Cottonwood Creek

Tin Cup ▲

Town	○	River	▬▬▬
River Access	→	Stream	—·—·
Rapids	//	Highway	
Footbridge	⊢⊣	Pavement	— —
Airstrip	✈	Gravel	– – –
Camping	▲	Trail	··········
Guard Station	♠		

Loon
Creek

Highway 75
31 Miles

Loon Creek to the end of the road at Phillips Transfer Camp. See the Middle Fork of the Salmon for directions to the take-out.

*To float out on the Middle Fork you need a permit.

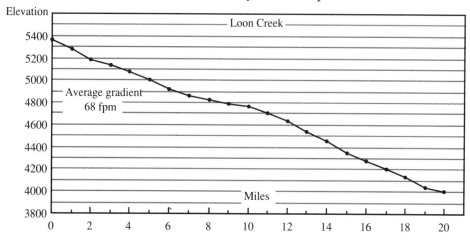

The first big rapid on Loon Creek. Photo: Jim Ciardelli

Jim Ciardelli on Loon Creek.

RAPID RIVER

CLASS	LEVEL	LENGTH	GRADIENT	TIME
IV	4' *	90 (13)miles	85 fpm	2 days

PUT-IN: Below Seafoam G.S. end of road (6,000 ft.)
TAKE-OUT: Cache Bar {(confl. 4,890 ft.) 3,000 ft.}
SHUTTLE: 270 miles
CRAFT: Kayak
PORTAGES: 4-8
SEASON: June
GAUGE: Middle Fork Lodge
PERMIT: Yes**
MAPS: Greyhound Ridge 15'
CHARACTER: Steep creek, extreme gradient, jumbled rock streambed, logjams, trail, wilderness.

DESCRIPTION: This is a class V wilderness steep creek. The gradient is severe and like many wilderness runs, Rapid River has lots of logs in the water. There are several blind corners where the current literally sweeps right into a logjam. Prior to putting on, a quick check from an airplane would be a good idea.

Besides the portaging and dangerous logjams there are several logistical obstacles to running Rapid River. First, is the brief window. The road to Seafoam is usually snowed in until the river is too low to run. Second, you need a permit to float out on the Middle Fork. Finally, even if the road is open, it doesn't lead all the way to the put-in — hiking in is required.

This could be considered an alternate put-in for Middle Fork permit holders, 77 of the 90 miles are on the Middle Fork. The scenery is nice but not spectacular. Much of it has been burnt over.

The shuttle to the put-in is almost the same as Marsh Creek. Instead of turning left down Marsh Creek, continue across the bridge, following the road to the left (forest service 008) 14 miles to Seafoam, then hike in until there's enough water to float your boat.

*The level refers to the Middle Fork gauge.
**To float out on the Middle Fork you need a permit.

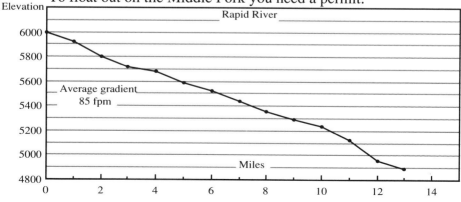

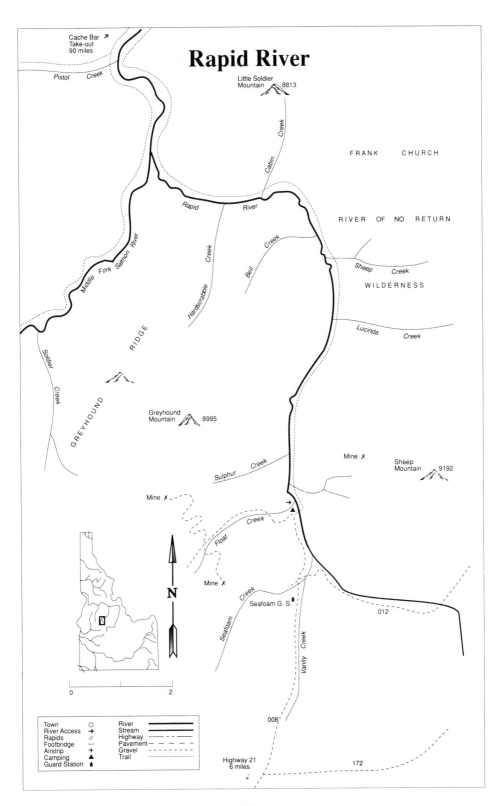

Rapid River

Cache Bar ↗
Take-out
90 miles

Pistol Creek

Little Soldier
Mountain 8813

Cabin Creek

FRANK CHURCH

Rapid River

RIVER OF NO RETURN

Hardscrabble Creek

Bell Creek

Sheep Creek

WILDERNESS

Middle Fork Salmon River

RIDGE

Lucinda Creek

Soldier Creek

GREYHOUND

Greyhound
Mountain 8995

Mine ✗

Sheep
Mountain 9192

Sulphur Creek

Mine ✗

Float Creek

▲

Mine ✗

012

Seafoam Creek

Seafoam G. S.

Vanity Creek

0   2

N

008

Highway 21
6 miles

172

Town	○	River	▬
River Access	→	Stream	—
Rapids	//	Highway	– · –
Footbridge	)(	Pavement	– –
Airstrip	✈	Gravel	- - -
Camping	▲	Trail	····
Guard Station	⚑		

MARSH CREEK

CLASS	LEVEL	LENGTH	GRADIENT	TIME
III	2.8'-4'	14 miles	54 fpm	8 hours
III-IV	4'-6'			
IV	>6'			

PUT-IN: Marsh Creek Transfer Camp (6,440 ft.)
TAKE-OUT: Dagger Falls Bridge (5,680 ft.)
SHUTTLE: 21 miles
CRAFT: Kayak, canoe, raft
PORTAGES: No
SEASON: May, June, July, August
GAUGE: No
PERMIT: No
MAPS: Capehorn, Greyhound Rg. 15', Chinook Mtn. 15'
Frank Church RONRW
CHARACTER: Mountain stream, gravel bed, logjams, wilderness, trail.

DESCRIPTION: Marsh Creek offers one of the best opportunities to follow the growth of a river from its headwaters to its end. At the put-in you may have trouble floating a raft. Seven miles downstream Marsh Creek joins Bear Valley Creek to become the Middle Fork of the Salmon. At this point, it's no more than a stream. If you continue all the way to the Main Salmon, 100 miles downstream it's a very big river.

Marsh Creek is also the only early season access to the Middle Fork. The Cape Horn Road to Boundary Creek is often closed until the middle of June and the only access to the Middle Fork is down Marsh Creek. Of course, if the road is closed, you're committed to the entire 114 miles to Cache Bar, unless you're flying out at one of the airstrips below the snowline.

Marsh Creek is a continuous swift-water stream. Geologically it is young, coursing over a gravel bed, in an undefined speed run. There are lots of logs in the river and several logjams. Most of the logjams occur where the river rounds a blind corner and is divided into two channels by an island. I use the old rule of always sticking to the inside and I've yet to portage, of course this could change any time. At high flows a low pack bridge one mile down from the put-in could be a problem for rafts. When the flow is below 5', Dagger Falls, a nasty dynamite-altered class V, is a problem for any type of craft. Above 5' it's big and intimating, but the rocks are covered and the chute on the left is manageable. For a raft, portaging is an ordeal. For others, the portage is obvious, or just take out at the bridge.

Most of the rapids on Marsh Creek are below the confluence with Bear Valley Creek, so they're really on the Middle Fork. If the Middle Fork is below 3', Marsh Creek is going to be rocky.

The put-in is just off highway 21 at about mile 113. Drive down alongside Marsh Creek to the end of the road or put in at the little bridge right next to the highway. See the M. F. Salmon for directions to the take-out.

See graph page 115.

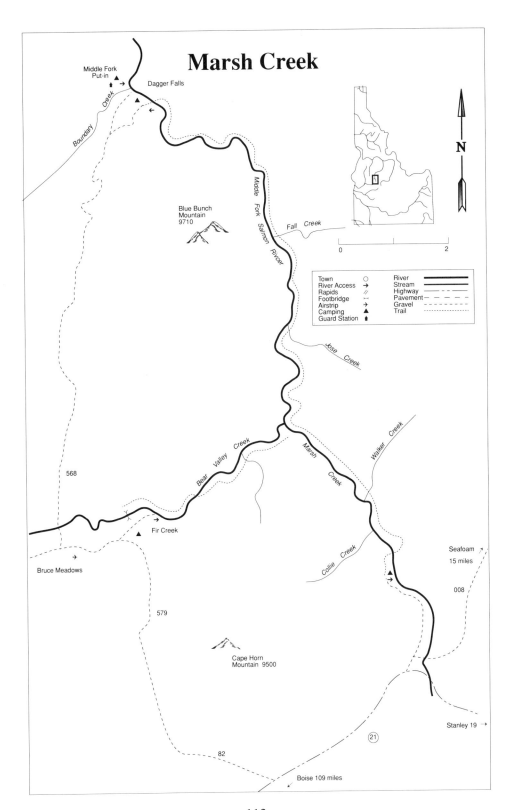

Marsh Creek

Middle Fork Put-in

Dagger Falls

Boundary Creek

Blue Bunch Mountain 9710

Middle Fork Salmon River

Fall Creek

N

0   2

Town	○	River	
River Access	→	Stream	
Rapids	//	Highway	
Footbridge	⊢⊣	Pavement	
Airstrip	↗	Gravel	
Camping	▲	Trail	
Guard Station	♦		

Jose Creek

Bear Valley Creek

Marsh Creek

Walker Creek

568

Fir Creek

Bruce Meadows

579

Collie Creek

Seafoam 15 miles

008

Cape Horn Mountain 9500

82

21

Stanley 19 →

Boise 109 miles

113

BEAR VALLEY CREEK

CLASS	LEVEL	LENGTH	GRADIENT	TIME
II-III	3'-6'	14 (7) miles	46 fpm	6 hours

PUT-IN:	Fir Creek Campground (6,320 ft.)
TAKE-OUT:	Dagger Falls Bridge (5,680 ft.)
SHUTTLE:	11 miles
CRAFT:	Kayak, canoe, small raft
PORTAGES:	No
SEASON:	June, July
GAUGE:	No
PERMIT:	No
MAPS:	Blue Bunch Mtn., *Frank Church RONRW*
CHARACTER:	Beautiful mountain canyon, sustained-gradient, hot springs, trail, wilderness.

DESCRIPTION: Bear Valley and Marsh Creek are the headwaters of the Middle Fork of the Salmon. Bear Valley Creek starts as a small stream in a wide alpine valley. Elk, deer and a variety of wildlife live along the banks of this stream. Around the corner from the put-in, the creek drops into a pine covered canyon. The whitewater is gentle and for most of the run, straightforward. Watch out for logs. Marsh Creek comes in from the right seven miles downstream. The hot springs on the right bank just up from the confluence are worth a stop. The whitewater picks up at this point and several good class III rapids are spread out between here and the take-out.

This run doesn't get much use because Marsh Creek has better access and rapids. Later in the summer, usually close to the end of July, salmon will be making their way up Bear Valley Creek. The spawning beds upstream of Fir Creek Campground are still productive. The camping in this area is fantastic.

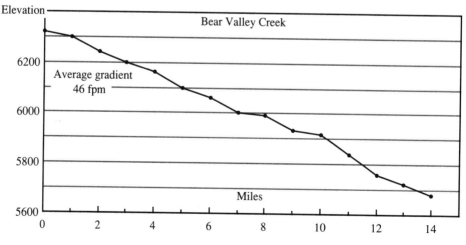

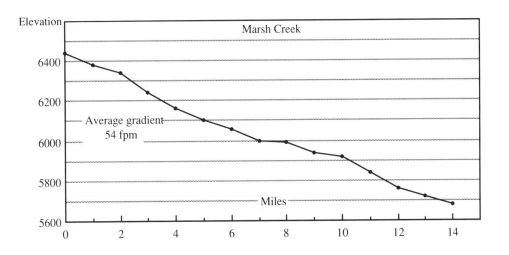

Photo: Glenn Oakley

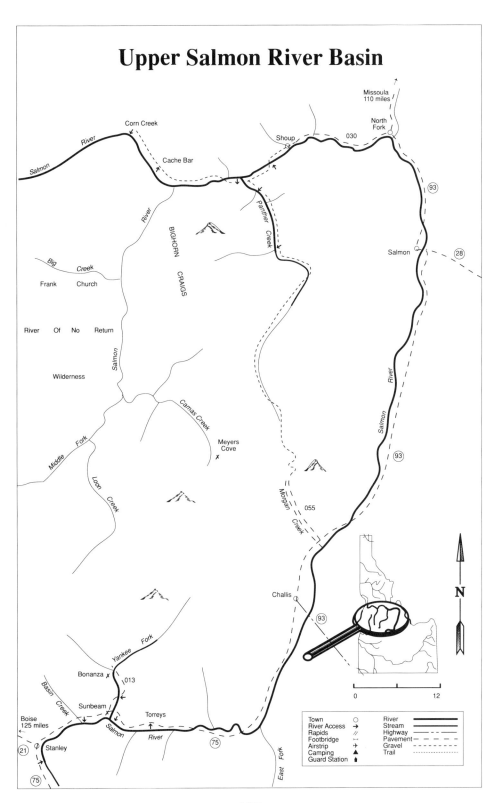

Upper Salmon River Basin

Missoula
110 miles

North
Fork

Corn Creek

Shoup

030

93

Salmon River

Cache Bar

Salmon

28

Panther Creek

BIGHORN

CRAIGS

Big Creek

Frank Church

River Of No Return

Salmon River

Wilderness

Salmon

93

Camas Creek

Meyers
Cove

Middle Fork

Morgan Creek

055

Loon Creek

93

Challis

93

Yankee Fork

Bonanza

013

Basin Creek

Sunbeam

Torreys

Boise
125 miles

21

Stanley

Salmon River

75

East Fork

75

Town	○	River	
River Access	→	Stream	
Rapids	//	Highway	
Footbridge	⊢	Pavement	
Airstrip	→	Gravel	
Camping	▲	Trail	
Guard Station	♦		

0   12

N

SALMON RIVER, PINE CREEK RUN

CLASS	LEVEL	LENGTH	GRADIENT	TIME
III	600-6000 cfs	7 miles	21 fpm	2 hours

PUT-IN:	Pine Creek (3,320 ft.)
TAKE-OUT:	Panther Creek (3,170 ft.)
SHUTTLE:	7 miles
CRAFT:	Kayak, canoe, raft
PORTAGES:	No
SEASON:	May, June, July, August
GAUGE:	Yes
PERMIT:	No
MAPS:	Shoup 15'
CHARACTER:	Swift mountain river, steep canyon, gravel beds and rock gardens, road, moderate use.

DESCRIPTION: This is a interesting day run that can be done on the way into the Main or out from the Middle Fork. It is a short stretch mixing rock gardens and swift turns. The road runs along the river, so the shuttle and scouting are a breeze. There are several good play spots for kayaks on this stretch. Pine Creek Rapid downstream of the bridge and Dutch Oven, a mile up from the take-out, are two of the better rapids. As the water rises most of the rapids wash-out and lose their character.

The best camping in the area is up Panther Creek. Some of the best hot springs in Idaho are a four miles up Panther Creek and several more up the east side of the canyon. See the Panther Creek description for the specifics.

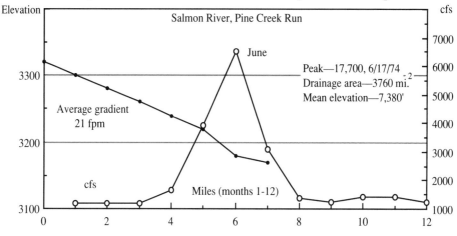

118

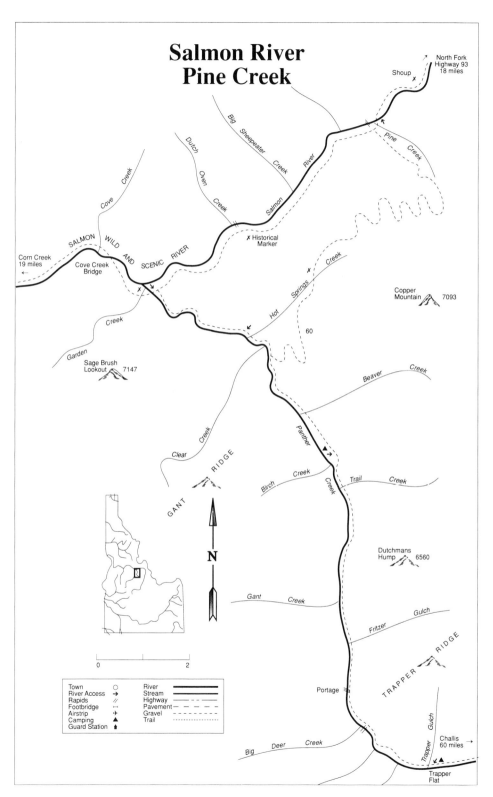

Salmon River
Pine Creek

PANTHER CREEK, LOWER RUN

CLASS	LEVEL	LENGTH	GRADIENT	TIME
III	600 cfs	4 miles	50 fpm	1 hour

PUT-IN:	Clear Creek (3,400 ft.)
TAKE-OUT:	Salmon Confluence (3,200 ft.)
SHUTTLE:	4 miles
CRAFT:	Kayak
PORTAGES:	1 log
SEASON:	May, June
GAUGE:	1955-1977
PERMIT:	No
MAPS:	Long Tom, Bighorn, Gant Mtn., *FCRONRW*
CHARACTER:	Steep creek, rocky, shallow, logs, brush, road, secluded.

DESCRIPTION: The last couple of miles of Panther Creek are a fun little swift-water run. Most of the run is class II-III busy water. At the put-in the creek is swift and undefined. The best whitewater is close to the end. All the rapids are shallow and rocky. As the water drops, the rocks become exposed and difficult to avoid. There is a snag all the way across the river just up from the Salmon confluence. Look to see if it has washed out and if it is still there, find a safe take-out upstream.

The gauge is no longer in existence so you will have to estimate flows for yourself. The season can be determined using the graph.

The shuttle is along the road. Scout and look for logs on the drive to the put-in. Just upstream from the put-in, forest service road 60 climbs the east side of the canyon to some good hot springs and camping.

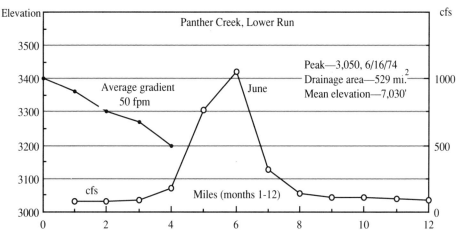

PANTHER CREEK, UPPER RUN

CLASS	LEVEL	LENGTH	GRADIENT	TIME
III-V	600 cfs	8 miles	108 fpm	2 hours

PUT-IN:	Trapper Flat Campground (4,400 ft.)
TAKE-OUT:	Birch Creek Campground (3,540 ft.)
SHUTTLE:	8 miles
CRAFT:	Kayak
PORTAGES:	2
SEASON:	May, June
GAUGE:	1955-1977
PERMIT:	No
MAPS:	Long Tom, Bighorn, Gant Mtn., *FCRONRW*
CHARACTER:	Steep creek, Continuous rock gardens, technical, shallow, logs, road, secluded.

DESCRIPTION: The upper run on Panther Creek has an altogether different character from the lower run. Up here it's tough and technical whitewater. With the exception of a brief flat water warm up below the put-in, the run is continuous from top to bottom.

There are at least eight good rapids in this stretch. One of these is an obvious portage and another contains a must-make move above a dangerous log. The remaining rapids are long, complicated and rocky. The first rapid is a short III-IV rock garden, a long tight rapid follows. The gradient backs off briefly, then picks back up with a easy rock garden leading into the top of a tight class V. Be careful, because following several powerful hydraulics the current pushes into a sweeper. The run-out is long and technical. Just downstream, the top of the portage is marked by several large boulders on the left. You should have no trouble identifying this rapid, it is a steep boulder sieve filled with logs and can easily be portaged on the road. A couple of mile-long rapids remain. Like all the other rapids on this run, they are mazes of rocks. Be careful of broaching or pinning.

Take out at the undeveloped campground below Birch Creek or continue through the two miles of flat water to the start of the lower run and take out at the confluence with the Salmon.

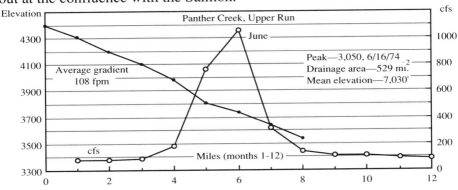

Panther Creek, Upper Run

Peak—3,050, 6/16/74
Drainage area—529 mi.²
Mean elevation—7,030'

Average gradient 108 fpm

121

SALMON RIVER, SUNBEAM RUN

CLASS	LEVEL	LENGTH	GRADIENT	TIME
II-III	500-1,500 cfs	13 miles	28 fpm	5 hours
III	1,500-3,000 cfs			
III-IV	>3,000 cfs			

PUT-IN:	Basin Creek (6,065 ft.)
TAKE-OUT:	Torreys Hole (5,700 ft.)
SHUTTLE:	13 miles
CRAFT:	Kayak, canoe, raft
PORTAGES:	No
SEASON:	May, June, July
GAUGE:	Clayton
PERMIT:	No
MAPS:	E. Basin Cr., Sunbeam, Thompson Cr.
CHARACTER:	Swift mountain river, steep canyon, gravel beds and rock-gardens, road, moderate use.

DESCRIPTION: The best whitewater on the upper Salmon is between Basin Creek and Torreys Hole There is an easier run upstream from Sunny Gulch Campground to Basin Creek where the river is wide and swift and the scenery provided by the Sawtooth Mountains outshines the whitewater.

At Basin Creek the canyon closes in and the whitewater picks up. The first rapid is a baby called Rough Creek, marked by the Rough Creek Bridge. Between here and Sunbeam is Shotgun Rapid, made famous by Old Milwaukee Beer and media hyperbole (Don't look for Shotgun Rapid at the base of Mount Heyburn where the Hollywood wizards have placed it). The hot springs along this stretch are developed and busy, so you shouldn't have any trouble finding them. The old Sunbeam Dam, dynamited to let the salmon continue upstream, can be tricky at high flows. Watch out for rebar at any level. There are several good access points downstream of Sunbeam. One of the best being Piece-of-Cake Rapid. In addition, Warm Springs Gorge has some whitewater in it. Below Torreys Hole the river flattens out and remains flat all the way to Pine Creek, 160 miles downstream. Everything can be scouted from the road.

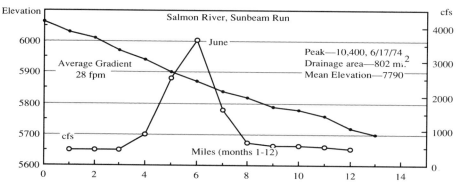

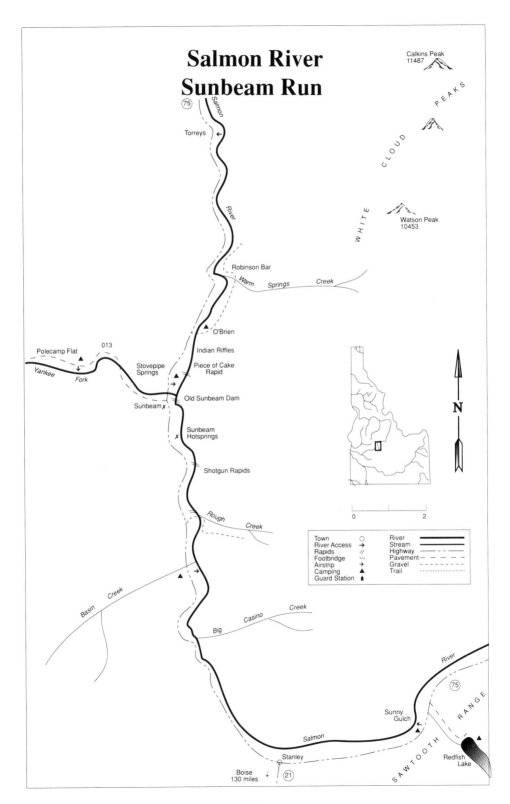

Salmon River
Sunbeam Run

YANKEE FORK

CLASS	LEVEL	LENGTH	GRADIENT	TIME
III-IV	300-1500 cfs	3 miles	87 fpm	1 hour

PUT-IN:	Polecamp Flat (6,160 ft.)
TAKE-OUT:	Sunbeam (5,900 ft.)
SHUTTLE:	3 miles
CRAFT:	Kayak, canoe
PORTAGES:	1 log
SEASON:	May, June
GAUGE:	No
PERMIT:	No
MAPS:	Sunbeam
CHARACTER:	Swift mountain stream, constricted river-bed, blind corners, logs, road, secluded.

DESCRIPTION: During the Civil War Idaho gold miners staged their own war of words in naming the Yankee Fork and the Secesh River. In spite of the superior whitewater on the Secesh, the North was victorious. However, the Yankee Fork should not be overlooked due to one's political beliefs. It is a steep little river with lots of blind corners and some good drops. Several good rapids are spread out along the run, though none of them are outstanding. The river winds through a beautiful dark hollow. Later in the year, the water is a beautiful cobalt blue.

The miners on the Yankee Fork left lots of evidence of their efforts. At the rivers mouth are the remains of the Sunbeam Dam, built to supply power for the mines stamp mills. Upstream from the put-in, seven miles, the old Yankee Fork Dredge rests in a shallow dredge pond. Dredges similar to this one dug up Mores and Grimes Creek with the same disastrous results.

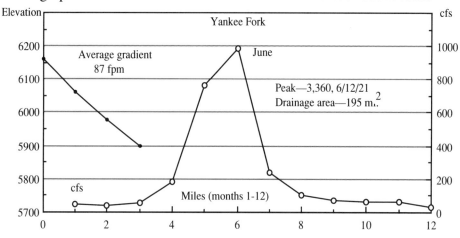

Photo: Glenn Oakley

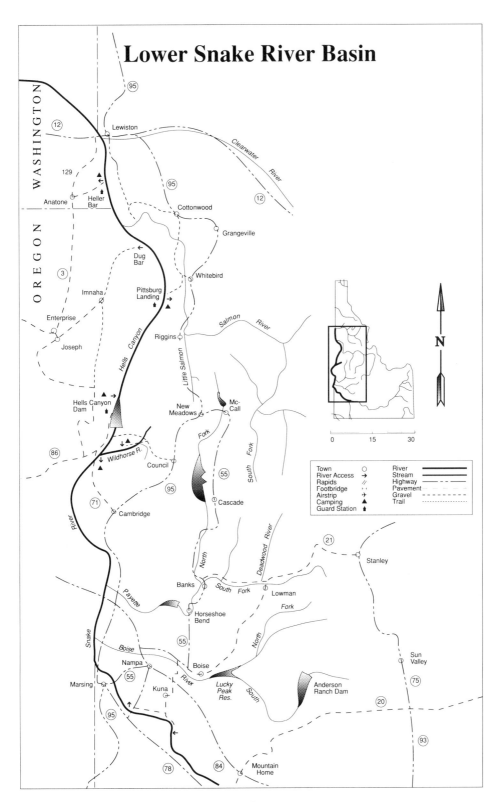

Lower Snake River Basin

WASHINGTON
OREGON

95

12
Lewiston

129

Clearwater River

95

12

Anatone
Heller Bar

Cottonwood

Grangeville

3

Dug Bar

Whitebird

Imnaha
Pittsburg Landing

Enterprise

Joseph

Salmon River

Riggins

Little Salmon

Hells Canyon

Hells Canyon Dam

New Meadows

Mc-Call

86

Wildhorse R.

Council

South Fork

Fork

71

95

Cascade

55

Cambridge

North

Deadwood River

21

Stanley

River

Payette

Banks

South Fork

Lowman

Fork

Horseshoe Bend

North

55

Snake

Boise

Boise

Sun Valley

Nampa

River

75

Marsing

55

Kuna

Lucky Peak Res.

South

Anderson Ranch Dam

20

93

95

78

84

Mountain Home

Town	○	River	
River Access	→	Stream	
Rapids	//	Highway	
Footbridge	··	Pavement	
Airstrip	↗	Gravel	
Camping	▲	Trail	
Guard Station	↟		

0   15   30

N

SNAKE RIVER, HELLS CANYON

CLASS	LEVEL	LENGTH	GRADIENT	TIME
III-IV	10,000-30,000 cfs	30 miles	12 fpm	1-2 days
IV	30,000-80,000 cfs			

PUT-IN:	Hells Canyon Dam (1,475 ft.)
TAKE-OUT:	Pittsburg Landing (1,120 ft.)
SHUTTLE:	183 miles
CRAFT:	Kayak, canoe, raft, jetboat
PORTAGES:	No
SEASON:	April, May, June, July, August, September, October
GAUGE:	Hells Canyon (208) 743-2297
PERMIT:	Yes
MAPS:	Cuprum, He Devil, Kernan Pt. (all 15'), Grave Pt. Kirkwood Cr., *Hells Canyon Nat. Rec. Area*
CHARACTER:	Wild and Scenic River, low gradient, big waves and rapids, stark rocky canyon, trail, wilderness.

DESCRIPTION: There's more to Hells Canyon than what's covered here, but it's beyond the scope of this book to describe it all. Below Pittsburg Landing there are another 50 miles of flat water, a pleasant float with a few rapids— if the wind's blowing you'll be floating upstream. The best rapids on Hells Canyon are described here as well as a considerable amount of flat water.

Hells Canyon is a big river: big water, big scenery, big canyon. The canyon is big enough to be the deepest in North America. It averages over 5,500 ft. in depth for over 40 miles, but in places it reaches 7,900 feet, two thousand feet deeper than the Grand Canyon. The scenery is outstanding, with huge cliffs towering up out of the river. The Seven Devil's Wilderness is on the east and the Wallowa Mountains are on the west.

The good whitewater is between the put-in and Sheep Creek. You should expect early summer flows of around 30,000. Below 10,000 cfs the rapids take on a different character and kayakers can find some good play waves. During the summer the water level fluctuates as much as three feet in a day due to hydroelectric demand. Make sure you tie up your boats and leave all your equipment well above the waterline.

At all but the lowest levels the waves in Hells Canyon are big enough that you have to paddle up, up, up, then down, down, down. Wild Sheep, mile six, and Granite, mile eight, are the standout rapids. Both are big class III-IV rapids simply because of their size. There's not much to do, other than line up and hurl yourself over the edge. Don't be too cavalier, these rapids do more flipping than the pancake cook at Denny's. Beginners, with a roll, can run Hells Canyon by portaging Granite and Wild Sheep. Advanced kayakers should encourage beginners and intermediates to make this trip. When you get to the rapids, point out the hazards and offer to run up the bank after your run and paddle their boat down. As the water drops, Waterspout becomes somewhat tricky and intermediates may want to scout it.

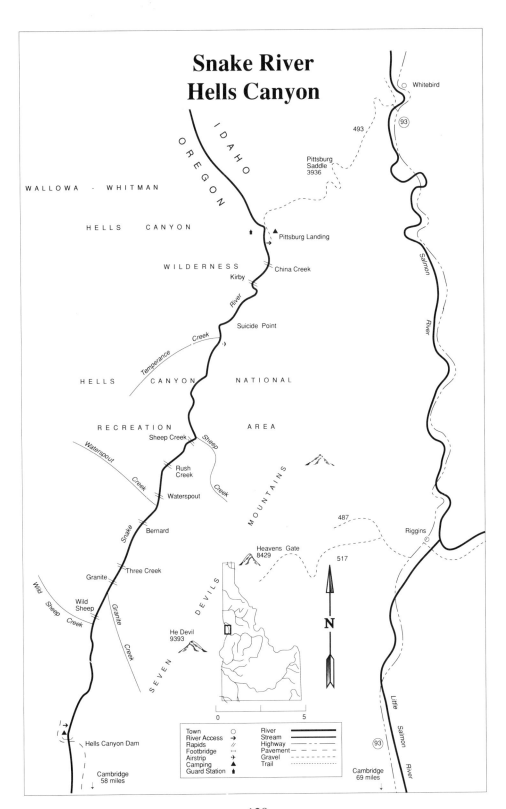

Snake River
Hells Canyon

I recommend taking out at Pittsburg Landing; downstream the river is no longer officially "Wild and Scenic" — just "Scenic."

Float boaters should try to get on the river early, particularly on weekends. The campgrounds fill up early with upstream campers (jet-boaters). Saddle Creek on the right above Granite, Battle Creek on the left above Waterspout and Salt Creek are good campsites.

Lots of float boaters are choosing to do the shuttle on Hells Canyon by jet boat. Rather than deal with the long overland shuttle, plan ahead and charter a jetboat for the jet-back upriver to the put-in. Another option is to start at the take-out, jet-back to Hells Canyon Dam and float back to your cars. For large groups jet-back prices can beat the cost of having your cars shuttled, and the ride is considerably more exciting. The prices vary considerably depending on things as simple as time of day. For more information call Hells Canyon Adventures, 1-800-422-3568, or call the Idaho Outfitters and Guides, (208) 376-5680, for a complete list of jetboat operators on Hells Canyon.

Shuttles for Hells Canyon could fill a book. There are four access points: Hells Canyon Dam, Pittsburg Landing, Dug Bar and Grand Ronde/Heller Bar. From Cambridge, Idaho, Hells Canyon Dam is 60 miles northwest on highway 71 and along the banks of the Snake. Pittsburg landing is 183 miles from here. To run this shuttle, go back through Cambridge, then north on highway 95 to Whitebird. Get off highway 95 near milepost 232. There's a big sign marking the way. Cross the Salmon on the old bridge and drive upstream on the other side of the river. Pittsburg Landing is 17 miles over the hill on forest service road 493.

To get to Dug Bar from the put-in, take highway 86 out of the canyon at Copperfield, after seven miles, turn right on the Wallowa Mountain Loop, FS road 36. Follow the pavement 70 miles to Joseph, Oregon. Imnaha, Oregon is another 30 miles along 350. From here take The Dug Bar road 25 miles down into the canyon (The last 20 miles are dirt).

Heller Bar is best approached through Idaho, follow the directions to Pittsburg Landing, then continue to Lewiston, 88 miles north of Whitebird, on highway 95. From Lewiston cross the river into Clarkston, Washington and go south 26 miles on highway 129 to Anatone. From Anatone go southeast 23 miles to the Grand Ronde take-out and Heller Bar.

The Forest Service produces an excellent river guide, "The Wild and Scenic Snake River." A good map for navigating the shuttle is "Hells Canyon National Recreation Area." Write: Hells Canyon National Recreation Area, Wallowa-Whitman National Forest, 3620-B Snake River Ave., Lewiston, ID 83501. (208) 743-2297. For all the details, see Cort Conley's "Snake River."

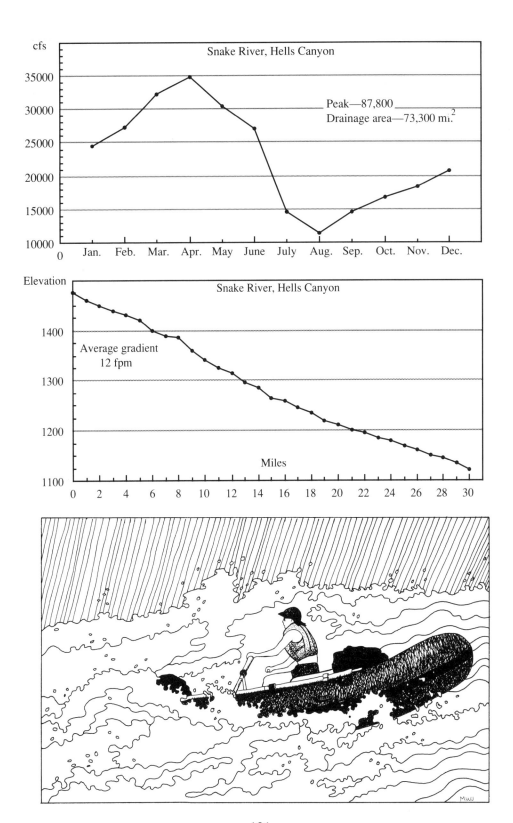

cfs

Snake River, Hells Canyon

35000

30000

Peak—87,800
Drainage area—73,300 mi.^{2}

25000

20000

15000

10000

0   Jan.   Feb.   Mar.   Apr.   May   June   July   Aug.   Sep.   Oct.   Nov.   Dec.

Elevation

Snake River, Hells Canyon

1400

Average gradient
12 fpm

1300

1200

Miles

1100

0   2   4   6   8   10   12   14   16   18   20   22   24   26   28   30

WILDHORSE RIVER

CLASS	LEVEL	LENGTH	GRADIENT	TIME
III-IV	500 cfs	14 miles	108 fpm	5 hours

PUT-IN:	Bear Creek Bridge (3,350 ft.)
TAKE-OUT:	McCormick Campground (1,840 ft.)
SHUTTLE:	43 miles
CRAFT:	Kayak
PORTAGES:	3 (2 logs, 1 bridge)
SEASON:	March, April, May
GAUGE:	Wildhorse River
PERMIT:	No
MAPS:	Copperfield, Rocky Comfort Flat, *Payette NF*
CHARACTER:	Steep mountain stream, blind corners, overhanging trees and brush, logjams, wilderness.

DESCRIPTION: One spring morning, Eric Straubhar and I dragged our boats down through the snow and launched on the South Fork of the Payette for the millionth time. I walked down the familiar path, launched from the same old rock, went through the same routine of stretches, caught the same little warm-up eddies; Bronco Billy, Dog Leg, surf, surf, surf. Another day at the whitewater office, business good, but dull. It rained like hell, and all the side streams were bank full and rising. Something snapped in my brain. "What are you doing tomorrow?"

"Tomorrow's Easter. The family's getting together for a big Easter dinner," Eric replied.

I could tell by the tone of his voice he'd rather kayak so I went to work. "I know a great little steep creek."

"What's it like?"

"It looks good on the map." The wrong thing to say. I've led Eric on more than a few wild goose chases.

"We can go next week," he countered.

"No, it won't be high enough. You've got to catch the peak."

"I don't know. My wife would be really mad."

I upped the ante. "Well, let's see," I said as if wondering aloud, "I'll bet Tony can go if you can't." Tony was out of town, but Eric didn't know this.

At seven, Easter Morning, Eric and I were searching for a shuttle bunny instead of the Easter Bunny. In Idaho most people take Easter seriously; two hours later, Eric and I, without a shuttle driver, were setting up a two-car shuttle. We left a car in the sunshine at the take-out and climbed up the Kleinschmidt Grade out of Hells Canyon. Up on the canyon rim we were surrounded by snow. The road was snow on mud; a real mess. We passed Bear River, one of the Wildhorse tributaries — 200 cfs meandering between patches of snow, beaver dams and willows. The other tributary, Crooked Creek, was even more discouraging — 100 cfs, at least 200 fpm and covered by a canopy of willows. We rounded a corner and there was a bridge — it crossed a river and it was big enough to kayak!

Wildhorse River

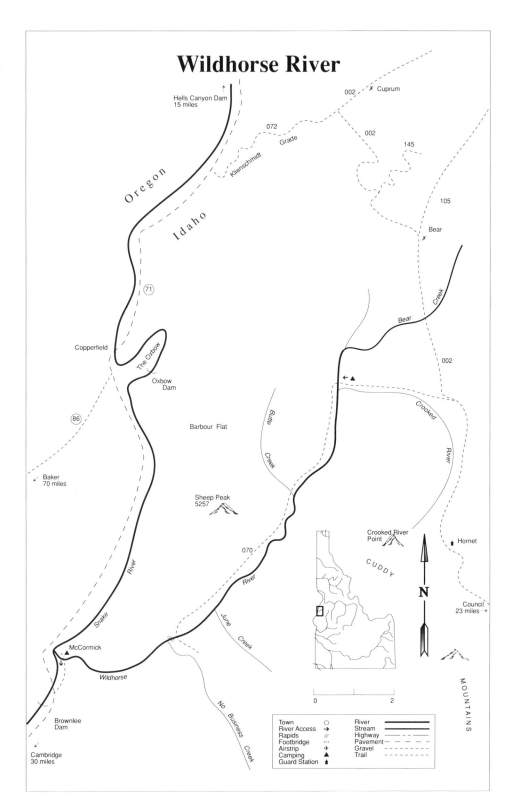

Hells Canyon Dam
15 miles

002 ✗ Cuprum

072

Grade

Klienschmidt

002

145

105

Oregon

Idaho

Bear ✗

Bear

Creek

71

Copperfield

The Oxbow

Oxbow
Dam

Crooked

River

002

Barbour Flat

Butte

Creek

86

Baker
70 miles

Sheep Peak
5257

Crooked River
Point

Hornet

070

CUDDY

River

N

Snake

River

June

Creek

Council
23 miles →

McCormick

Wildhorse

No Business Creek

MOUNTAINS

Brownlee
Dam

Cambridge
30 miles

Town	○	River	
River Access	→	Stream	
Rapids	//	Highway	
Footbridge	⊣⊢	Pavement	
Airstrip	→	Gravel	
Camping	▲	Trail	
Guard Station	⬥		

0   2

The first five miles are shallow class I swift water flowing over an undefined gravel bed. The trees and willows in the water make it dangerous. On the second corner we avoided having to portage by slipping over the edge of a logjam. A hundred yards further, a second logjam forced a portage. The next five miles consisted of class II water and class V willows. At the second ranch (the blue one) the river picks up some speed. The largest rapid on the river, a good class IV is marked by a large pinnacle of rock on the right bank and the overpowering smell of hot springs sulphur. On the left bank is the last ranch and the road climbs up out of the canyon. Unfortunately, midway through this rapid an old bridge has fallen into the river and must be portaged. Portage on the right bank and be careful. For the rest of the run, the river never lets up. All the corners are blind with every sign hinting at logjams. Four miles of non-stop class III fun remain. The power lines from Oxbow Dam signal the run's end.

Take a four-wheel drive for the shuttle. The shortest route is over the Kleinschmidt Grade to Cuprum if it's open (ask the cowboys who live at McCormick). From McCormick drive down, along the Snake, 17 miles to the Kleinschmidt Grade (road 050). Go up the hill nine miles to the Speropulos Ranch and turn right on road 002. Less than a mile from here, the road forks, stay right. Continue on this road another six miles, over the Bear River to the Crooked River. Turn right (road 070) and follow the Crooked River four miles to the confluence with Bear River. Start here or follow the road down and put in at leisure.

If the Kleinschmidt Road is closed, return to Cambridge, go north on 95 to Council. Where 95 turns to the right in Council, turn to the left. This is the other end of road 002. Follow it to the Crooked River.

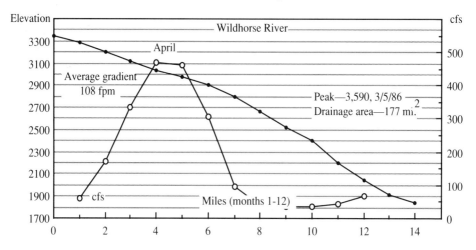

Eric Straubhar below the end of the road on the Wildhorse River.

SNAKE RIVER, BIRDS OF PREY NATURAL AREA

CLASS	LEVEL	LENGTH	GRADIENT	TIME
II	10,000-20,000 cfs	15 miles	3 fpm	1 day

PUT-IN: Swan Falls Dam (2,290 ft.)
TAKE-OUT: Walters Ferry (2,245 ft.)
SHUTTLE: 19 miles
CRAFT: Kayak, canoe, raft
PORTAGES: No
SEASON: April, May, June, July, August, September, October
GAUGE: Swan Falls
PERMIT: No
MAPS: Initial Pt., Sinker Pt., Walters Btt.
CHARACTER: Scenic float, low gradient, farmland, road.

DESCRIPTION: This is one of the few flat water runs included in this book. It deserves a mention due to the unique nature of the surrounding area. From Grand View to Walters Ferry the Snake runs through the Birds of Prey Natural Area. The stark cliffs of the Snake River canyon provide vital nesting habitat for at least 14 species of raptors. The surrounding desert and farm land provide the necessary hunting grounds. Eagles, falcons, ospreys and owls can be seen from the river. Golden eagles and prairie falcons are the most abundant raptors in the area. Bring your binoculars, lunch and a Peterson's.

As for whitewater, the only real hazard is a diversion by the island, below the first bridge. There is a clear and safe run down the left side as well as the left channel. However, most of the current flows into the canal, and if you should fall asleep you might be swept over the dam. Otherwise, there are a few riffles, some strong current, and many large birds.

Hydroelectric demands on Swan Falls Dam cause the water levels to fluctuate daily, so if you're going for a hike tie up your boat or leave it well above the water line. Swan Falls Dam was the first dam in the Snake River Basin to stop salmon and steelhead runs.

The Birds of Prey Natural Area is reached from highway 84 west of Boise. Get off the highway at exit 44 and go south eight miles to Kuna. Then follow the Swan Falls Road 18 miles south to the put-in. If you have time visit the Kuna Cave on the way. It's about four miles south of Kuna on the Swan Falls Road.

A new marina with a boat-ramp, parking and toilets has been developed at the end of Can-Ada Road. Most people are using the marina as a take-out and cutting the run in two. From Swan Falls, go back on Swan Falls Road about six miles to Victory Lane. Go west on Victory for two miles, turn north and drive one mile. Then turn to the west on the Warren Spur Road to Can-Ada Road and head south to the marina. Or, to find Walters Ferry, continue on Warren Spur another two miles. As it winds around to the north, take the first road to the west, Ferry Road and follow it a little over a mile until you can see the bridge.

Snake River
Birds of Prey Run

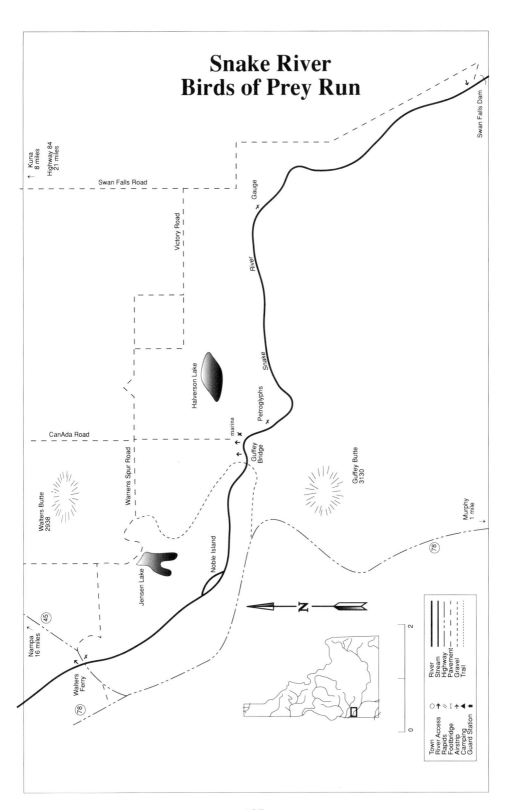

Kuna
8 miles
Highway 84
21 miles

Swan Falls Road

Victory Road

Gauge

River

Snake

Petroglyphs

Halverson Lake

marina

CanAda Road

Warrens Spur Road

Guffey
Bridge

Walters Butte
2938

Guffey Butte
3130

Murphy
1 mile

Noble Island

Jensen Lake

Nampa
16 miles

45

Walters
Ferry

78

78

Swan Falls Dam

N

2

0

Town
River Access
Rapids
Footbridge
Airstrip
Camping
Guard Station

River
Stream
Highway
Pavement
Gravel
Trail

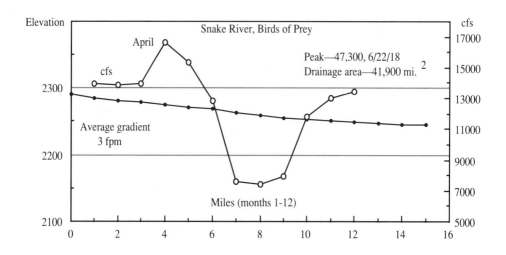

Snake River, Birds of Prey

Elevation

cfs

April

cfs

Peak—47,300, 6/22/18
Drainage area—41,900 mi. [2]

2300

Average gradient
3 fpm

2200

Miles (months 1-12)

2100

17000

15000

13000

11000

9000

7000

5000

0   2   4   6   8   10   12   14   16

Osprey

Golden Eagle

Bald Eagle

MWJ

138

Running Big Falls. Photo: Jack Weinberg

Clinton LaTourrette making the rock drop look easy.

Doug Ammons — Sunnyside up at Jake's Place.

Payette River Basin

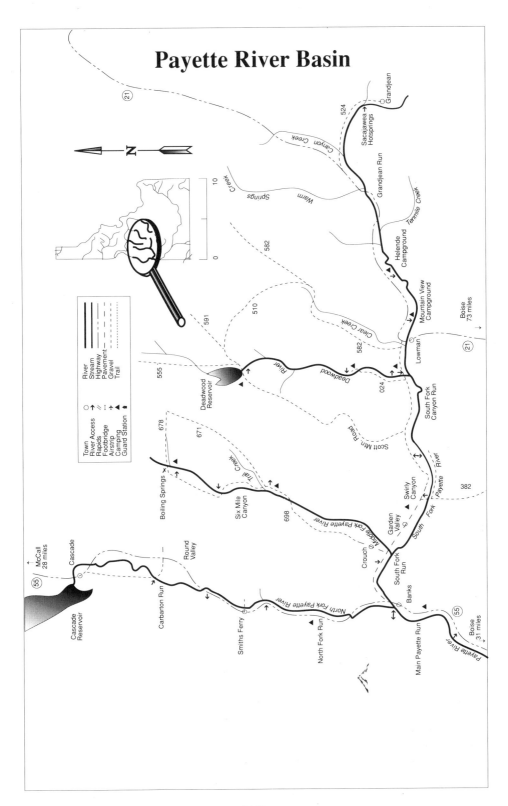

PAYETTE RIVER, THE MAIN

CLASS	LEVEL	LENGTH	GRADIENT	TIME
I-III	600-4,000 cfs	7 miles	13 fpm	3 hours
III+	>4,000 cfs			

PUT-IN:	Banks (2,790 ft.)
TAKE-OUT:	Beehive, Bend, > mile 71 (2,700 ft.)
SHUTTLE:	7 miles
CRAFT:	Kayak, canoe, raft
PORTAGES:	No
SEASON:	April, May, June, July, August, September, October
GAUGE:	Horseshoe Bend
PERMIT:	No
MAPS:	Dry Buck Mtn., Banks, *Boise NF*
CHARACTER:	Gentle river, low gradient, pool-drop, road, heavy use, dam.

DESCRIPTION: The Mighty Main; this is probably the most popular whitewater run in Idaho. It's easy. It's roadside. It's close to the big city, and it's littered with stupid names.

The Main Payette is one of the best beginner runs around. There are four good class III rapids and two excellent surf-waves. The rapids can't be missed. A pair of unnamed class II rapids lie just around the corner from the put-in. This is where most first-time kayakers learn to swim. I can't force myself to write down their "names." The bigger rapids start with Bennetts Rock — a big rock down the hill from Banks Two (not to be confused with Banks One). Downstream, Mikes Hole, the only rapid with a sensible name, is the trickiest move on the river. At some flows, there's a chicken route for kayakers down the left. Mixmaster and AMF follow. Both are full of big waves, but otherwise are straightforward. The jet-boaters call AMF, Turnout. I side with the gear-heads on this one.

Look for the first surf-wave, aptly called The Main Surf Wave, in the S-turn below the big sandy beach at the Banks Campground. From the road, it's upstream of mile post 78, marked by a little turnout 100 yards upstream from the Boise National Forest sign.

The other wave is a big sheet of laminar glass about three-quarters of a mile below Banks Two. This is a relatively new addition and still lacks a name. It was created a couple years ago by the landslide upstream.

There is an access point about half way down the run above all the rapids except Mikes Hole and Chief Parrish. From the river look for a set of stone stairs leading up the bank to a large tree-covered meadow. It was once a nice campsite until the BLM put a gate on the road and made it an official "Day Use Area. No Overnight Camping." From milepost 74 on the road look for a quaint, but large BLM gate and a small white sign designating Chief Parrish Lane. Until about 1983 Chief Parrish lived on this bar with a large German Shepherd, which barked at all the river runners. Hence, the name, thanks to

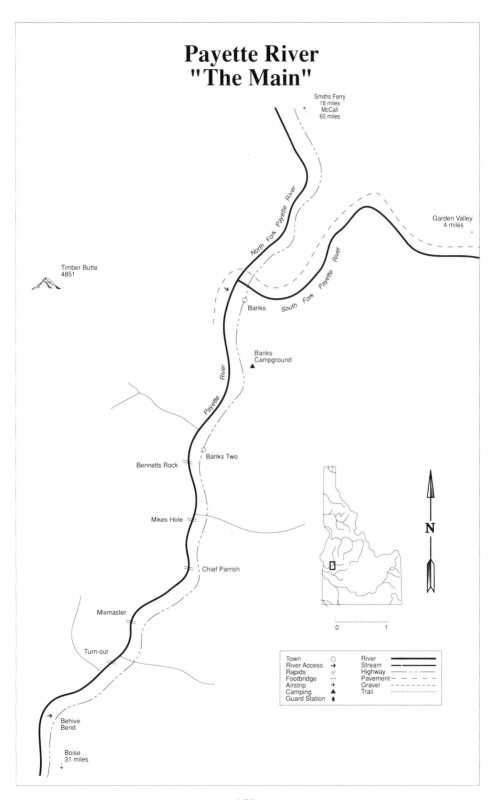

Payette River
"The Main"

the creative touch of Eric Straubhar: Barking Dog Rapid.

The put-in and the take-out are both crowded. The take-out used to be a real problem. It was nothing more than a wide spot on a very busy highway.

The Payette River Task Force (a formidable name), an organization created to deal with river running problems like the old take-out, scored a river runner's victory by moving the take-out downstream of The Pipe to Beehive Bend (alliteration: the lowest form of naming).

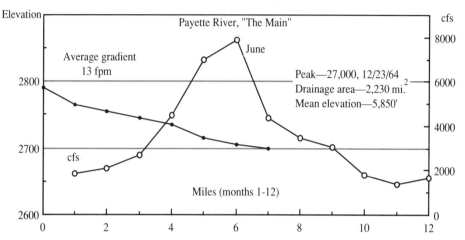

Stan Colby on the Main surf wave.

NORTH FORK PAYETTE RIVER , "THE NORTH FORK"

CLASS	LEVEL	LENGTH	GRADIENT	TIME
IV-V	1,000-1,700 cfs	16 miles	106 fpm	3-6 hours
V	1,700-3,000 cfs			
V-VI	>3,000 cfs			

PUT-IN:	Below Smiths Ferry (4,490 ft.)
TAKE-OUT:	Banks (2,790 ft.)
SHUTTLE:	16 miles
CRAFT:	Kayak
PORTAGES:	No
SEASON:	May, July, August, September
GAUGE:	Cascade Reservoir
PERMIT:	No
MAPS:	Banks, Packer John Mtn. Smiths Ferry, *Boise NF*
CHARACTER:	Constricted mountain river, congested boulder filled streambed, road, railroad, heavy bank use, dam.

DESCRIPTION: The North Fork is, without a doubt, some of the best whitewater in Idaho. It offers the rare combination of extreme gradient, warm water and access. For me the key is the warm water and the late season. Like any other river, the North Fork has its freezing spring runoff, but this is the time to explore the rest of the state. Later in the summer, irrigation flows provide all the power you'll need — imagine class V whitewater in the middle of summer with water temperatures hovering in the high 70s.

In only 16 miles the North Fork has over 20 named drops. At least twenty more rapids remain, unnamed but distinct. These are the stomping grounds of the Old Guard of Whitewater. A host of Idaho boaters tested parts of the North Fork starting in the mid '70s. There are some old super 8 clips of Blackadar bombing down the lower rapids. Bob McDougall made this his summer home for years. In 1987 McDougall kayaked a vertical mile by making three top to bottom runs in a day. The 48 miles of horizontal class V whitewater are a milestone as well.

Boaters have over the years informally divided the river into three sections. Highway 55 runs the length of the river, providing access and doubling as a welcome safety valve. The lower third, Hounds Tooth to Banks, is considered less difficult. The middle section, Swinging Bridge to Hounds Tooth, is big and tight. The river feeds naturally into some very big and hard to see holes. The top is full of steep drops and long run-outs.

The put-in for the top is three miles down from Smiths Ferry, just short of milepost 95. The only identifying marks are a small turnout, a "Watch for stock" sign if you're driving north and a "Watch for rock" sign if you're driving south. An easy path leads down to a pine-filled meadow bordering the river's last calm stretch. Murray Creek is across the river. There is about a mile

North Fork Payette River

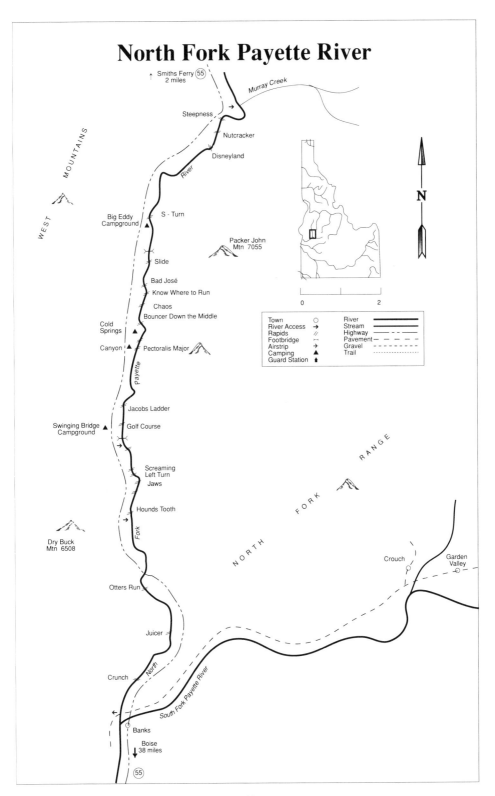

Smiths Ferry (55)
2 miles

Murray Creek

Steepness

Nutcracker

Disneyland

River

WEST MOUNTAINS

Big Eddy
Campground

S - Turn

Packer John
Mtn 7055

Slide

Bad José

Know Where to Run

Chaos

Bouncer Down the Middle

Cold
Springs

Canyon

Pectoralis Major

Payette

Jacobs Ladder

Swinging Bridge
Campground

Golf Course

Screaming
Left Turn

Jaws

Hounds Tooth

Fork

Dry Buck
Mtn 6508

NORTH FORK RANGE

Crouch

Garden
Valley

Otters Run

Juicer

North

Crunch

South Fork Payette River

Banks

Boise
38 miles

(55)

Town	○	River	━━━
River Access	→	Stream	━━━
Rapids	//	Highway	━·━·
Footbridge	⊢	Pavement	━ ━
Airstrip	→	Gravel	‑ ‑ ‑
Camping	▲	Trail	·····
Guard Station	◨		

N

0   2

of class III-IV whitewater before the first named rapid: Steepness.

Mile 93 marks Nutcracker, one of the more difficult runs on the river. Disneyland and S-Turn are just downstream. After Big Eddy (you can't miss it) there is a cable footbridge followed by a long narrow rapid called Slide. The pool at the top is a convenient put-in for a total whitewater blast, although starting here puts you right into some very big water with virtually no warm up. I don't recommend it.

Bad José starts off, turning left, directly into Know-Where-to-Run. There are six big rapids between here and Swinging Bridge. All of these require a plan and some forethought. In every one, the river seems to feed blindly into some sort of trouble. The standouts are: Bouncer-Down-the-Middle, Pectoralis Major, Jacobs Ladder and Golf Course.

Jacobs Ladder is the most difficult rapid on the run. Lots of people take the right line — the one next to the highway. The approach for this route involves getting out of your boat, hiking up the bank and dragging your boat along the road. There are three crucial moves necessary to avoid eating at Jake's. The first and third should be obvious. If they aren't, leave your car at the top and take out there. The second is one of the best moves in kayaking. Your goal is to ski-jump off the flume of water created by the large rock, river left, and pancake in the eddy downstream. One hint: I've never seen anyone go off this rock drop too high or too fast (don't hit the rock). If you should miss this move (you won't be the first) prepare yourself for a whitewater ordeal. You have about three seconds until you enter Taffy Puller, the third move. This should flush you, or if the water's low slam you, into the most critical move in Golf Course as well. Enjoy, only a mile of technical and powerful class V whitewater remains.

Below Golf Course is Swinging Bridge, another convenient put-in or take-out. It provides a great warm-up with two unnamed class III rapids. Back Nine starts the mapped action, pitching into Screaming Left Turn.

The Jaws are next. They are actually one long rapid. The holes are numbered for ease of reference in recalling your adventures. Jaws One is worth having someone lead who is familiar with the drop. It is the classic unavoidable hole that feeds into a rock, that feeds back into the hole and so on . . . . There is an eddy on the right bank, just at the lip of the drop. From here you can safely peer down into the hole. The problem with this eddy is it is so close to the hole, when you peel out there isn't much room in which to build up speed.

In 1988 Tony Brennan and I were showing open-canoeist, Nolan Whitesell, the "line" through Jaws One. The three of us pulled into the small eddy at the lip. With a canoe in there it's really small. There was quite a bit of bumping and pushing going on. We were all a little jumpy, Tony volunteered to show the way. Because of the canoe, he was forced to peel out lower than usual. The reversal totally buried him. He surfaced downstream in a towering back-endo.

"Holy shit!" Nolan was envisioning a back-ender in his canoe. I started laughing. He turned around, smiled and said, "He did that on purpose!" All I could say was, "I hope so."

Hounds Tooth to Banks, is the usual fare for sampling the North Fork.

There is no missing the aptly named drop and large turnout for the put-in, close to milepost 84. Some choose to start just below the Tooth due to the lack of warm up. On the other hand, there is a convenient pool, behind a large boulder, just at the top of the rapid. If you are into big adrenaline surges, this is the place to start.

All the rapids on the lower part, with the exception of Otters Run, can be seen from the road. Otters is just down from where the road crosses the river. The gauge is on the right bank, below the bridge and above Otters. The last two rapids, Juicer and Crunch, provide a grand finale of huge waves and steep drops that will leave you cheering. The take-out is, of-course, on the sandy beach across from Banks. Beer is four bucks a six-pack at the little store. But, hey, you deserve one.

There are some developed campsites along the river, but they are a little noisy due to the road. A favorite camping spot for river runners is up the South Fork of the Payette about 12 miles at Hot Springs Campground. There is a fee.

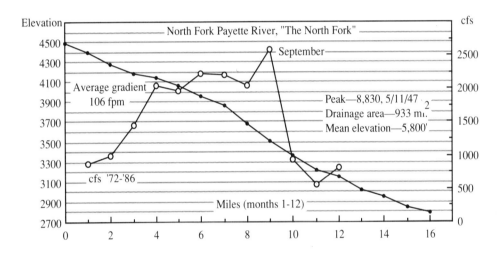

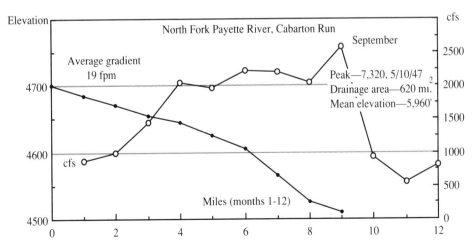

NORTH FORK PAYETTE RIVER, CABARTON RUN

CLASS	LEVEL	LENGTH	GRADIENT	TIME
I-III	1,000-3,000 cfs	9 miles	21 fpm	3 hours

PUT-IN:	Cabarton Bridge (4,700 ft.)
TAKE-OUT:	Above Smiths Ferry (4,510 ft.)
SHUTTLE:	11 miles
CRAFT:	Kayak, canoe, raft
PORTAGES:	No
SEASON:	May, June, July, August, September, October
GAUGE:	Cascade Reservoir outflow
PERMIT:	No
MAPS:	Cascade 15', Smiths Ferry 15', *Boise NF*
CHARACTER:	Low gradient mountain river, rock gardens, rail road, some road, secluded, dam.

DESCRIPTION: This stretch of the Payette is a popular intermediate run. For most of the run the river is in a canyon away from the road. It has a good mix of rapids and pools making it fun for intermediates and within the limits of beginners. The crowd of rafts, canoes and kayaks on summer weekends attests to its popularity.

The rapids are easy and straight-forward. There are two good class III rapids on the run. The first one starts just above the railroad trestle (guess what its name is). The second big drop, Howards Plunge, is the last on the run and dumps into the mile of flat water above Smiths Ferry.

This stretch is named after a Boise Cascade tree farm near the put-in. It is the contraction of the name of a Boise Cascade employee, C. A. Barton.

The take-out is the large pine covered bar between the road and the river upstream of Smiths Ferry , near milepost 98. To get to the put-in drive north on 55 to the Clear Creek Road, near milepost 107. Keep your eyes peeled, there is nothing to mark the road other than a little store. Go west about two miles to where the road crosses the river. This is the put-in.

The best camping in the area is a long ways from the river. Sage Hen Reservoir, six miles west and up the hill from Smiths Ferry is my favorite. People do camp at both the put-in and the take-out, neither are outstanding. There are some developed sites downstream along the North Fork, but their proximity to the road makes them a little noisy. If you're going north there is some nice camping on the northwest side of Cascade Lake.

See graph page 163.

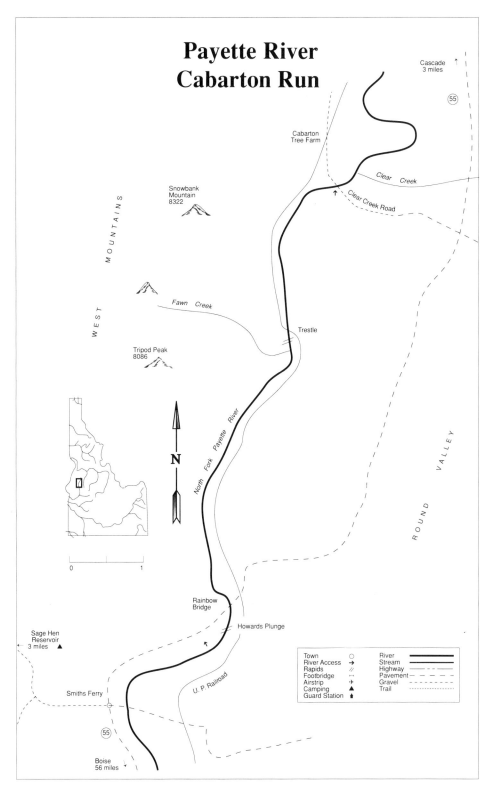

Payette River
Cabarton Run

Cascade
3 miles

55

Cabarton
Tree Farm

Clear Creek

Clear Creek Road

M O U N T A I N S

Snowbank
Mountain
8322

Fawn Creek

Trestle

W E S T

Tripod Peak
8086

North Fork Payette River

N

R O U N D   V A L L E Y

0   1

Rainbow
Bridge

Howards Plunge

Sage Hen
Reservoir
3 miles ▲

Town	○	River	
River Access	→	Stream	
Rapids	//	Highway	
Footbridge	⊢	Pavement	
Airstrip	✈	Gravel	
Camping	▲	Trail	
Guard Station	♠		

U. P. Railroad

Smiths Ferry

55

Boise
56 miles

165

NORTH FORK PAYETTE RIVER, WARREN WAGON RUN

CLASS	LEVEL	LENGTH	GRADIENT	TIME
III-IV	500-800 cfs	5 miles	106 fpm	2 hours
IV	>800 cfs			

PUT-IN:	Below Upper Payette Lake (5,550 ft.)
TAKE-OUT:	Fisher Creek (5,020 ft.)
SHUTTLE:	5
CRAFT:	Kayak
PORTAGES:	No
SEASON:	May, June
GAUGE:	No
PERMIT:	No
MAPS:	Granite Lake, *Payette NF*
CHARACTER:	Steep mountain stream, rock gardens, road, secluded.

DESCRIPTION: On the way to the Secesh put-in the road runs along the Upper North Fork of the Payette. This is a rocky stretch of whitewater. The gradient is continuous and the river bed is choked with boulders. Most of the run is continuous class III-IV whitewater. At low flows there isn't a clean line because of all the boulders. As the water rises the boulders are covered and the run washes out a little and so do the eddies. Don't underestimate this run while you're road scouting, it's deceptive. At Pearl Creek there is a big constricted rapid. Take out at Fisher Creek, or a mile upstream where the whitewater becomes easier. Put in below Upper Payette Lake where the road crosses the river.

Camping in this part of the state is some of the best. There are lots of developed and undeveloped sites. The commercial hot springs at Burgdorf are worth the fee.

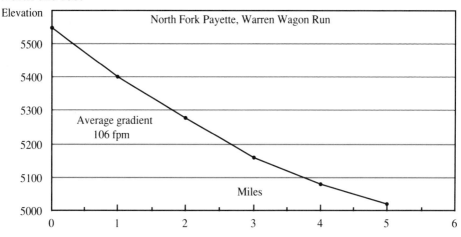

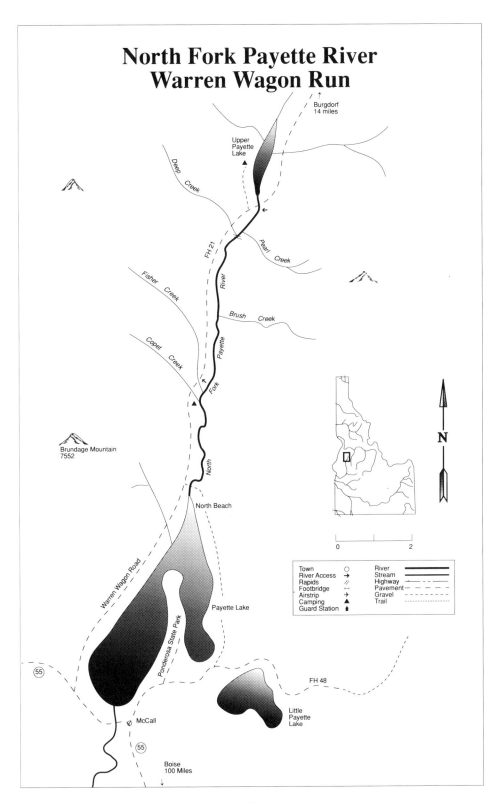

North Fork Payette River
Warren Wagon Run

Burgdorf
14 miles

Upper
Payette
Lake

Deep Creek

FH 21

Pearl Creek

Fisher Creek

River

Brush Creek

Copet Creek

Payette

Fork

Brundage Mountain
7552

North

North Beach

Warren Wagon Road

Ponderosa State Park

Payette Lake

Town	○	River	■■■
River Access	→	Stream	—
Rapids	//	Highway	—·—
Footbridge	⊢⊣	Pavement	—
Airstrip	✈	Gravel	– – –
Camping	▲	Trail	········
Guard Station	⬧		

N

0   2

FH 48

55

McCall

Little
Payette
Lake

55

Boise
100 Miles

167

SOUTH FORK PAYETTE RIVER, STAIRCASE RUN

CLASS	LEVEL	LENGTH	GRADIENT	TIME
III	200-800 cfs	5 miles	32 fpm	3 hours
III-IV	800-1,800 cfs			
IV	>1,800 cfs			

PUT-IN: Deer Creek Turnout (2,950 ft.)
TAKE-OUT: Banks (2,790 ft.)
SHUTTLE: 5 miles
CRAFT: Kayak, canoe, raft
PORTAGES: No
SEASON: April, May, June, July, August, September
GAUGE: Lowman
PERMIT: No
MAPS: Banks , *Boise NF*
CHARACTER: Beautiful mountain river, rock gardens, road, moderate use.

DESCRIPTION: The South Fork of the Payette is one of the most popular runs in Idaho. It offers the great combination of whitewater, scenery, surfing and access. Because of its proximity to Boise, less than an hour's drive on highway 55, the South Fork attracts a big weekend crowd.

The whitewater is a mix of sharp turns and rock gardens. In this short five mile stretch there are five good rapids and many fun easy ones. The put-in is at the turn out about 100 yards downstream from the former Deer Creek bridge (A victim of the Idaho guard flexing its demolition muscles).

The first big rapid is Bronco Billy, marked by the hot springs coming in from a rock outcrop on the right bank at the top (don't bother, they're too hot). The hole at the bottom of Bronco Billy, at the right levels (high), is great side-surfing (experts only). Great, but very sticky. Many people choose to swim out of this hole and lots of rafts get munched as well.

Dog Leg is the next rapid, and the name should tell you what to expect. The famous South Fork Surf Wave is just downstream. It can be identified by all the kayakers queued up in the eddies and a twisted pine tree growing out of the small cliff on river left. Its name is The South Fork Surf Wave — or simply: The Wave. It has been erroneously called "the pretty little beach wave" in a whitewater video. This has been the site of the Payette Whitewater Roundup since the Ultimate-Play-Wave washed out. Below 1,200 (at Lowman) the surfing is strictly head on, but the endos are good. Around 1,600 a break develops and you can side surf and spin. Above 2,000 the wave becomes steep and green.

Staircase, a long class IV, is less than a mile downstream. The rapid is close to a quarter mile in length and the most difficult move is right at the entrance. The clean run is to slice between the holes moving from the center to the right, however through the course of time and a process of trial and error, (mostly error) people have discovered that you can go just about anywhere

South Fork Payette River
Staircase Run

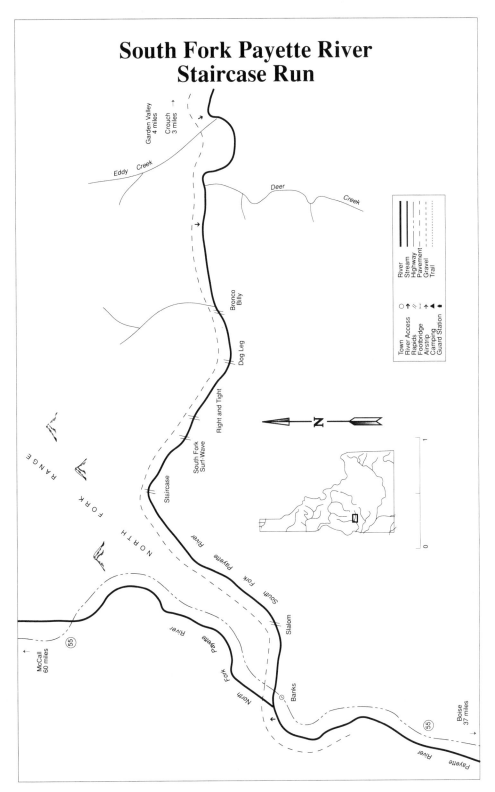

and survive. Be careful, because it's shallow here and if you should tip or swim you might bump a rock. The big rocks in the middle of the rapid are called the Whale Rocks. When the river peaks, they are usually covered. After Staircase, the river is mellow for about a mile until Slalom Rapid.

A half-mile of flat water leads to Banks. If you have a shuttle, continue under the bridge where the South Fork joins the North Fork. In the summer the water temperature difference is startling with the South Fork painfully cold and the North Fork a tepid bathtubby 70 degrees. The take-out is on the big sandy beach. Hitchhiking is fairly easy if you get out before going under the South Fork Bridge and use your kayaks as visual aids. Camping is fair, see the North Fork description for details.

The USGS gauge on the South Fork is 34 miles upstream at Lowman. Between Lowman and the Deer Creek put-in the Deadwood and the Middle Fork add a considerable amount of water. The flows listed above refer to the Lowman gauge. To figure the flow on the South Fork at Banks, subtract the North Fork flow from the Horseshoe Bend flow. The remainder is roughly the flow in the South Fork.

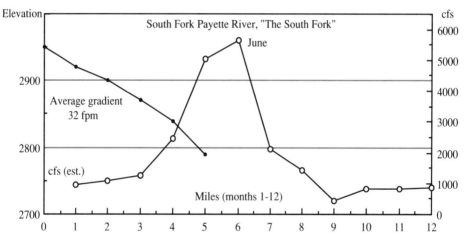

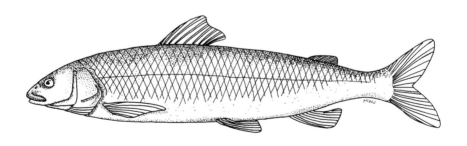

MOUNTAIN WHITEFISH
Prosopium williamsoni

170

SOUTH FORK PAYETTE RIVER, SWIRLY CANYON

CLASS	LEVEL	LENGTH	GRADIENT	TIME
II	500-1,000 cfs	9 miles	21 fpm	2 hours
II+	> 1,000 cfs			

PUT-IN:	Danskin Station (3,240 ft.)
TAKE-OUT:	Alder Creek Bridge (3,050 ft)
SHUTTLE:	10 miles
CRAFT:	Kayak, canoe, raft
PORTAGES:	0
SEASON:	May, June, July, August
GAUGE:	Lowman
PERMIT:	No
MAPS:	Garden Valley, Grimes Pass, *Boise NF*
CHARACTER:	Low gradient, undefined streambed, swirly eddies, gorge, secluded.

DESCRIPTION: Squirty Canyon might be a better name for Swirly Canyon. There are no big rapids along this stretch, just some tight turns in a narrow canyon. The resulting eddies give the canyon its name. The Ultimate Play Wave, created by the remains of the Grimes Pass Dam, is in this stretch as well. The spring runoff of '86 washed out some pilings and altered the shape of the wave. A more accurate name today would be the Penultimate Play Wave. Squirt boaters and endo seekers will still find it exciting. The eddy lines provide big stretches of down time. During high water be careful, the pilings, which are pincushions of nails and spikes, become covered with water and are dangerous.

Swirly Canyon starts and ends with a mile or two of undefined swift water. The actual canyon stretch is short, so make the most of it. The road is up and away for the river for the entire run.

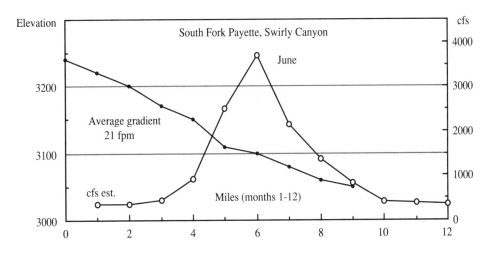

SOUTH FORK PAYETTE RIVER, THE CANYON

CLASS	LEVEL	LENGTH	GRADIENT	TIME
III	500-1,000 cfs	10 miles	39 fpm	4-8 hours
III-IV	1,000-2,000 cfs			
IV	>2,000 cfs			

PUT-IN:	Deadwood Confluence (3,670 ft.)
TAKE-OUT:	Upstream from Little Gallagher Creek (3,280 ft.)
SHUTTLE:	10 miles
CRAFT:	Kayak, canoe, raft
PORTAGES:	1
SEASON:	May, June, July, August
GAUGE:	Lowman
PERMIT:	No
MAPS:	Lowman, Pine Flat, Grimes Pass, *Boise NF*
CHARACTER:	Beautiful mountain river, rock gardens, pool-drop, secluded.

DESCRIPTION: The South Fork Canyon is a small technical river with good scenery and good rapids. The sheer canyon walls keep the road up and away from the river and give the river a wilderness character.

Some of the best hot springs in Idaho are on this stretch. Pine Flats Hot Springs are on the right bank at the downstream end of Pine Flats Campground. Pine Flats can also be used as an access point, however, the hill is steep and brushy.

Big Falls, at mile six, has only been run once and is still considered a mandatory portage. The trail is on the left and rudimentary, so keep equipment to the minimum. Rafters should bring lots of rope. The commercial outfitters work this portage by trading danger for hard work. They pitch the boats into the cleft at the bottom of the the last drop and haul them out with a rope. To date roughly 15 people have made it through Big Falls, one way or another: In 1983 Salt Lake kayaker Larry Dunn, blindly paddled into the top and swam out the bottom, in 1988 twelve people in two rafts flushed through and Craig Martin of Boise gets top honors for being knocked into last drop while portaging. Luckily no one has been hurt. However Big Falls still remained unrun in the sense of a intentional and successful (i.e. still in your boat) run.

Then in the Summer of 1989 while sitting on the lunch rocks below Big Falls I looked up to see cataraft lined up and entering the falls, unfortunately it was unmanned. The owner had forgotten to tie it to shore. The raft plunged over the first drop and exited the hole in a perfect tail stand, it remained upright and almost ski jumped the second drop. The third and forth drops didn't even give it a splash. If someone would have simply gone along for the ride, they wouldn't have even gotten their hair wet. After it surged free, and we got it to shore it suddenly dawned on me that it was only a matter of time until someone made the rational decision to run Big Falls.

I called Chris and Al (both known for trying just about anything in a

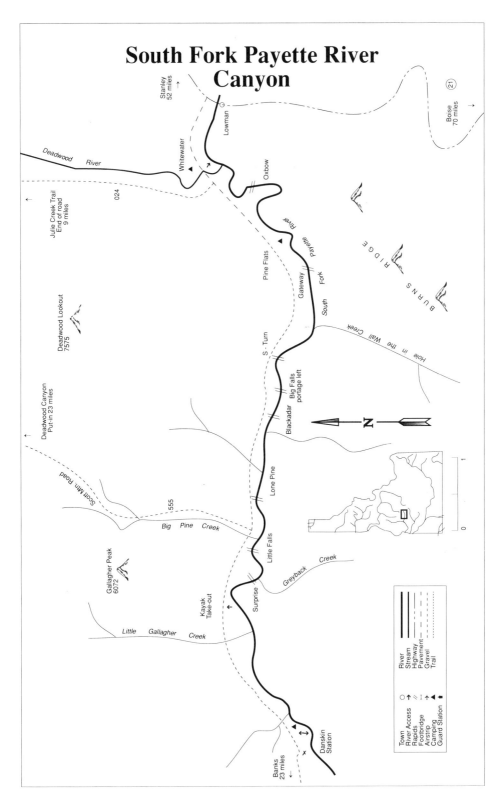

South Fork Payette River Canyon

Stanley
52 miles

Lowman

Boise
70 miles

21

Deadwood   River

Whitewater

Oxbow

Julie Creek Trail
End of road
9 miles

024

Pine Flats

Payette   River

Gateway

South   Fork

Deadwood Lookout
7575

BURNS RIDGE

Hole in the Wall Creek

Deadwood Canyon
Put-in 23 miles

S - Turn

Big Falls
portage left

Blackadar

N

Scott Mtn. Road

Lone Pine

1

555

Big   Pine   Creek

Gallagher Peak
6072

Little Falls

Greyback   Creek

0

Kayak
Take-out

Surprise

Little   Gallagher   Creek

Danskin
Station

Banks
23 miles

Town
River Access
Rapids
Footbridge
Airstrip
Camping
Guard Station

River
Stream
Highway
Pavement
Gravel
Trail

173

cataraft) at Argo Inflatables, but they failed to rise to the bait. I was working for Cascade Raft Company at the time as a "safety" boater (an oxymoron of incredible dimension) and every time we portaged the falls I would run this movie of the cataraft through my imagination. As the water level dropped I reasoned I could make the moves and punch the hydraulics. When dropping flows approach 600 cfs, the contours of the river bed begin to emerge and Big Falls takes on a completely different character. For saftey's sake (?) I waited until the South Fork was running at a low 400 cfs. At 400 cfs Big falls still drops at least 35 feet. I broke it down into five drops and three must make eddies. The lines were tight and a mistake would probably put me in the last hole sideways.

I had a little trouble with the second move, but managed to stab the eddy. The third and fourth drops were the crunch, because they had to be run together. I was buried in the hole at the bottom and when I could see again it was obvious I had missed the eddy I was aiming for. I had to opt for eddy B, which worked out fine, because it lined me up for the last drop with a good diagonal line and a big head of steam. The next thing I knew I was sitting in the calm water by the lunch rocks with a big grin on my face.

Above Big Falls there are several good drops: Oxbow, Gateway and S-turn. At the top of Oxbow, on the right, there is a small tunnel leading into the mountain. Miners used this tunnel to divert the water and expose the streambed for placer mining. Downstream, on the opposite side of the oxbow the water reenters the canyon from a cleft on the right. Currently, there is a plan to dam the Payette at the tunnel's mouth and place a power plant at the downstream end. A venture capital dream: most of the work, the tunnel, has been done, just put in the plugs and a turbine and man's progress continues.

Just below Big Falls is Blackadar or Walts Drop. There is a brass plaque on the large boulder on the right sticking out into the pool above the drop. It's hard to see, so keep your eyes peeled. Blackadar died on a strainer here (long since dynamited) in May of 1978. He is buried in the Garden Valley Pioneer Cemetery.

The next significant drop is close to a mile downstream. Lone Pine is formed by several large boulders and a ledge in the riverbed. At high water the hole takes on epic proportions.

At Big Pine Creek the river takes a sharp bend to the right. This is a good take-out, or at least the only easy one for rafts. Just downstream is Little Falls, formed by a resistant ledge about four feet tall. Jump left or bounce right, stay out of the center. Right below Little Falls is the last easy take-out, around the bend, the river drops into Surprise Canyon and from here on it's a steep climb back to the road. One more big rapid remains: Surprise. The next take-out for kayaks is on the right bank, just below the island, it's steep here so rafters should continue down two miles past another big island, just above Danskin Station. It's steep here as well. Be careful of the log stuck between the boulder island and the cliff in this stretch.

The shuttle is a simple matter of following the road. The take-out is hard to spot because most people refuse to believe there isn't an easier place to climb out — there isn't. Driving from the west, a mile above Danskin Station, look for Little Gallagher Creek. It's marked by a little forest service sign, after

174

another mile, the road turns to the left and the river comes into sight. Pull over and look for an island in the river. If you see one you've found the take-out. Camping is good at the put-in, but better at Pine Flats, downstream, because of the great hot springs.

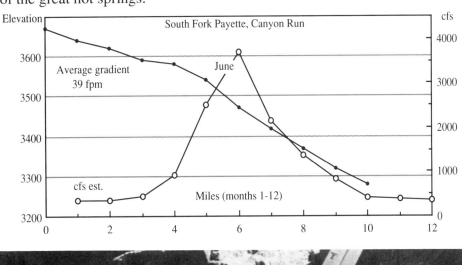

Name that rapid! Karen Watenmaker on the South Fork Payette.

PAYETTE RIVER, GRANDJEAN RUN

CLASS	LEVEL	LENGTH	GRADIENT	TIME
III	550-1,400 cfs	30 miles	40 fpm	8 hours
III-IV	1,400-2,600 cfs			

PUT-IN:	Sacajawea Hot Springs (5,000 ft.)
TAKE-OUT:	Mountain View Campground (3,800 ft.)
SHUTTLE:	30 miles
CRAFT:	Kayak, canoe, raft
PORTAGES:	No
SEASON:	May, June
GAUGE:	Lowman
PERMIT:	No
MAPS:	Grandjean, Eight Mile Creek, Tyee Mtn., Jackson Pk., Lowman, *Boise NF*
CHARACTER:	Mountain river, gravel bed, blind corners, gorge, road, secluded.

DESCRIPTION: Because of all the other good whitewater runs in the area, this stretch doesn't get the use it should. The scenery is good and the water swift and clear. The gradient is constant and the streambed, for most of the run, undefined. Most of the rapids are wide-open rock gardens.

Perhaps the best feature of this run are the hot springs along the river. Sacajawea Hot Springs are at the put-in. From Sacajawea to Canyon Creek the run is swift water and jammed with logs. The logs are more of a hazard to your peace of mind than your life. To avoid most of them, start above Canyon Creek Rapid. Approximately nine miles down from the put-in, Warm Springs Creek enters from the right and Bonneville Hot Springs are upstream less than a mile. You could take out here, but you'd miss a good rapid about 300 yards below the highway bridge. It's a rock choked affair caused by a flash flood that washed out the road and flushed Chapman Creek into the Payette. Low water floaters will find an interesting rock slot here.

Another nine miles downstream, Helende Campground offers good river access and is probably the most popular put-in for this entire stretch. The best rapids are between here and Mountain View Campground, the take-out. After the river goes under a bridge, it follows a big oxbow to the south. As the river heads back to the north, Emma Creek dumps in from the left bank and signals Wake-Up Rapid. The hole that gives this rapid its name deserves some respect. There's another little rapid at Whangdoodle Creek and then the mighty Kirkham Gorge. The bridge should cue you in on the start of the rapid and the hot springs will mark the end. These are the best and the most popular hot springs on this stretch, so don't expect a secluded soak. The gorge can be jammed with logs, make sure it's clear while setting up the shuttle. Pine Flat Hot Springs and campground are downstream from Lowman, on the South Fork, several miles. Both the hot springs and camping are excellent.

The most difficult part of this shuttle is making the turn to the put-in. It's

South Fork Payette River
Grandjean

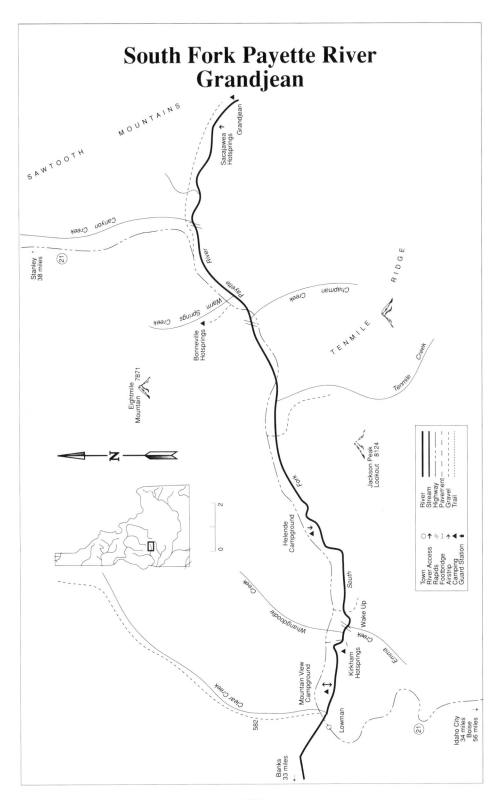

no more than a wide spot in the trees and the sign is so small it might as well be unmarked. It's near milepost 94.

Camping is good at the put-in and Bonneville. It's fair at Helende and Mountain View because of the 1989 Lowman fire.

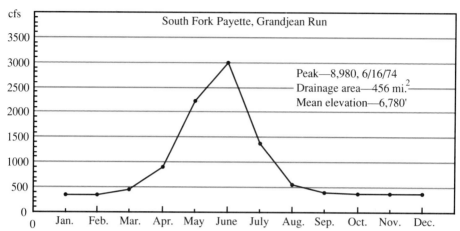

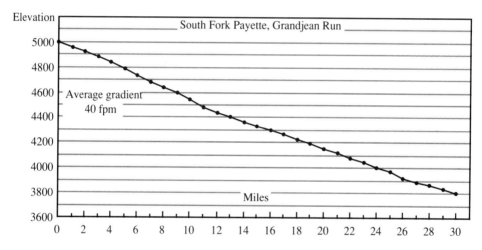

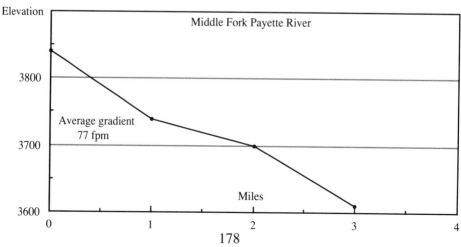

Big Falls Launch. Photo: Clinton LaTourrette

MIDDLE FORK PAYETTE RIVER

CLASS	LEVEL	LENGTH	GRADIENT	TIME
IV	300-500 cfs	3 miles	77 fpm	2-4 hours

PUT-IN: West Fork Bridge (3,860 ft.)
TAKE-OUT: Upstream of Trail Creek (3,650)
SHUTTLE: 3 miles
CRAFT: Kayak
PORTAGES: 2 logs
SEASON: June
GAUGE: No
PERMIT: No
MAPS: Six Mile Point, *Boise NF*
CHARACTER: Steep-creek, technical, ledges, logjams, road, secluded.

DESCRIPTION: The Middle Fork of the Payette is a fantastic little class IV run. It remained unexplored for years because the number of logjams and the flat or falls character of the riverbed. Without a doubt some of the rapids were runnable. In addition, Six Mile Canyon keeps a mile of the river out of sight of the road. The first time I drove up the Middle Fork, I stopped at the gorge; from the top of the cliffs I could only glimpse little pieces of whitewater — just enough to get the adrenaline going, no more.

The character of the Middle Fork is distinctly different from the other runs in the area. The rapids in this stretch are pool-drop boulder choked ledges; more like a California steep-creek than the typical Idaho rock garden. If you've been boating in the area for a week and need a change of pace, this might be the run for you.

To run the Middle Fork you should be skilled at spotting logs, running ledges and skittering off boulders. The run starts off with a couple steep little drops followed by two logjams that must be portaged. Things flatten out a bit until the river enters the gorge. There are six good drops in this stretch. The best is last; a small falls, run down the chute on the left, bouncing off the rock and landing in the plunge pool.

The put-in for this run is about 18 miles up the Middle Fork from Crouch. It is easy to find. Start at either the West Fork Bridge or below Boiling Springs Guard Station. The West Fork put-in cuts out one good drop and several miles of meanders. The take-out is hard to find but worth the search. Just upstream from the Trail Creek Road junction, as the Middle Fork Road starts to climb away from the river, a little unimproved road drops off towards the river. It's marked with a stake numbered 69818. Follow this down to the take-out. The camping and hot springs at the take-out are fantastic.

See graph page 178.

Middle Fork Payette River

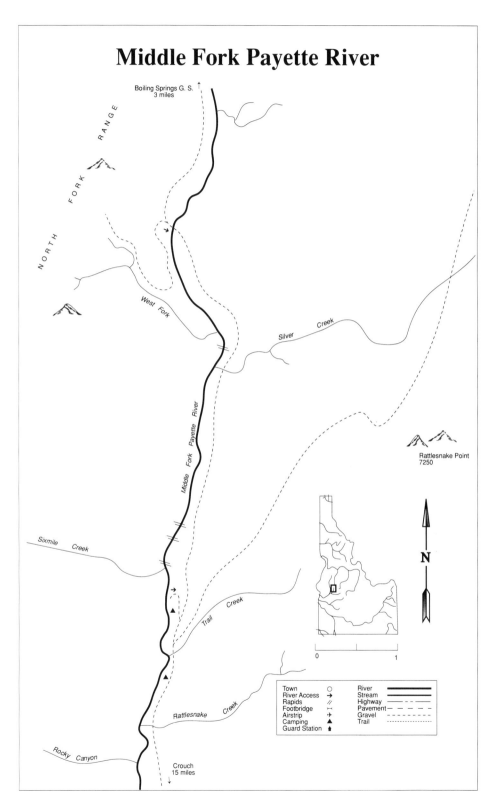

181

DEADWOOD RIVER, LOWER RUN

CLASS	LEVEL	LENGTH	GRADIENT	TIME
III-IV	900-1,200 cfs	10 miles	65 fpm	3 hours
IV	>1,200 cfs			

PUT-IN:	End of road (4,320 ft.)
TAKE-OUT:	Payette Confluence (3,670 ft.)
SHUTTLE:	10 miles
CRAFT:	Kayak
PORTAGES:	1 log
SEASON:	May, June, July
GAUGE:	Deadwood River
PERMIT:	No
MAPS:	Scott Cr., Pine Flat, *Boise NF*
CHARACTER:	Small mountain river, constant gradient, rock gardens, logjams, road, secluded.

DESCRIPTION: In spite of having a road in the canyon, the Lower Deadwood can almost be considered a wilderness run. The dirt road is high enough up the canyon side to keep it out of sight and make access extremely difficult. In addition to the good whitewater, there is wildlife along this run. On one of my first trips down the Deadwood, Eric Straubhar, Dan Givins and I drifted around a sharp corner and almost ran into a bear. He was standing in the water, eating berries off the overhanging bushes. It scared the hell out of all of us, especially the bear. He let out a grunt and showered us with rocks as he scrambled up the bank and into the bushes.

This is a swift, steep river. The rapids are, for the most part, long rock gardens. The water is usually freezing cold, the reservoir releases from the bottom. Don't drift around any of the many blind corners backwards, because like the canyon, the Lower Deadwood is full of logs. Watch out for logjams, they change from year to year. Presently all of them can be safely spotted from the river and quickly portaged. People have been known to duck under two of the logs; reducing the portage number to one and significantly increasing the danger level. Make this decision for yourself.

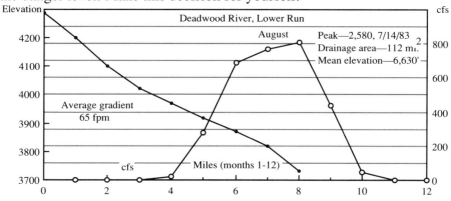

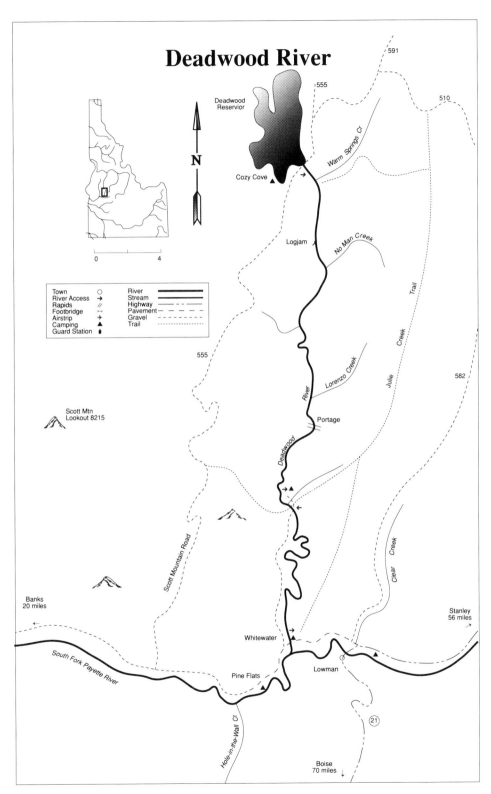

Deadwood River

Deadwood
Reservior

591

555

510

Warm Springs Cr

Cozy Cove ▲

Logjam

No Man Creek

Julie Creek Trail

555

Lorenzo Creek

582

Scott Mtn
Lookout 8215

Portage

Deadwood River

Town ○
River Access →
Rapids //
Footbridge)(
Airstrip ✈
Camping ▲
Guard Station ⌖

River ▬▬▬
Stream ▬ ·
Highway ——
Pavement — —
Gravel – – –
Trail · · · ·

Scott Mountain Road

Clear Creek

Banks
20 miles

Stanley
56 miles

Whitewater ▲

South Fork Payette River

Pine Flats ▲

Lowman ○ ▲

21

Hole-in-the-Wall Cr

Boise
70 miles ↓

DEADWOOD RIVER, THE CANYON

CLASS	LEVEL	LENGTH	GRADIENT	TIME
IV (V)	900-2,000 cfs	14 miles	60 fpm	3 hours

PUT-IN:	Deadwood Reservoir (5,160 ft.)
TAKE-OUT:	End of the road (4,320 ft.)
SHUTTLE:	43 miles
CRAFT:	Kayak
PORTAGES:	2 logs
SEASON:	May, June, July
GAUGE:	Deadwood River
PERMIT:	No
MAPS:	Deadwood Res., Scott Cr., Pine Flat, *Boise NF*
CHARACTER:	Small mountain river, constant gradient, gravel bed changing to rock gardens, logjams, wilderness.

DESCRIPTION: The Deadwood is a secluded wilderness run. It was left alone for years because of rumors of a box canyon and some unrunnable falls. Finally in 1976, Tulio Celano and Roger Hazelwood made the first descent. They didn't find a box canyon or any unrunnable falls. They did find a beautiful wilderness river close to Boise, with a number of dangerous logjams.

The river is fairly steep. It is a mixture of swift water, meanders and several big drops. Unfortunately, because the Deadwood is a small drainage basin saddled with a big dam, the river rarely gets the big spring flush it needs to clear the wood. Most of the big drops on the Deadwood have become filled with logs.

The first couple miles are swift and undefined, then the gradient picks up a bit and there are three good drops as well as a logjam (portage). The whitewater calms down somewhat before coming to the biggest rapid on the run. It's a big class V about three miles above the take-out. It's easy to spot from the river, look for a rocky bar on the left, a horizon line and some logs sticking up in the air. The path is on the right. Most people portage this drop because of the logs. The rapid starts with a big ledge formed by boulders and is quickly followed by a must make move to the left of another boulder and a log suspended just above the water. When the water's low (< 900 cfs) if you blew this move you might be able to fit under the log, (I wouldn't want to be the one to discover you couldn't). Then after coming around to the left of the boulder, there's a second log pinned to the rocks off the left bank. The next log spans the entire river with the exception of a three foot slot on the left bank where the log's submerged. The river pools up briefly and this is where most people get back in. The rapid continues in a steep slot pressed against a cliff which forms the left bank. Two long and complicated rock gardens remain.

The shuttle is a steep dusty hill climb. From the confluence with the South Fork of the Payette, the take-out is 10 miles up the road on the west side of the Deadwood. In the early spring this road is sometimes closed due to washouts. To get to the put-in drive seven miles down the Banks-Lowman Road from the Confluence with the Payette and 26 miles up the Scott Mountain Road. Plan to spend a good part of the morning driving. If you start early, the entire run to the Payette can be done in a day.

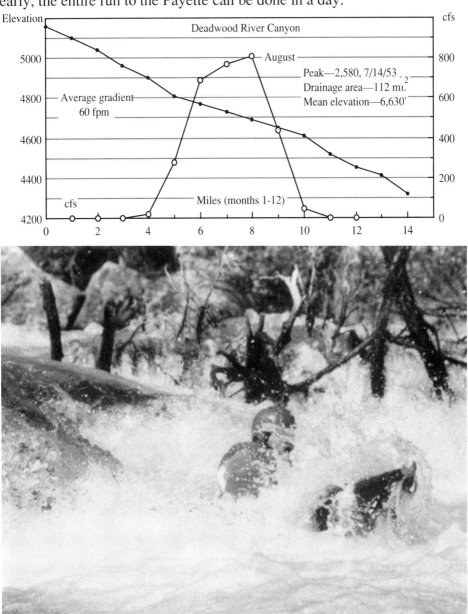

Why do you think it's called the Deadwood?

Photo: Glenn Oakley

Boise River Basin

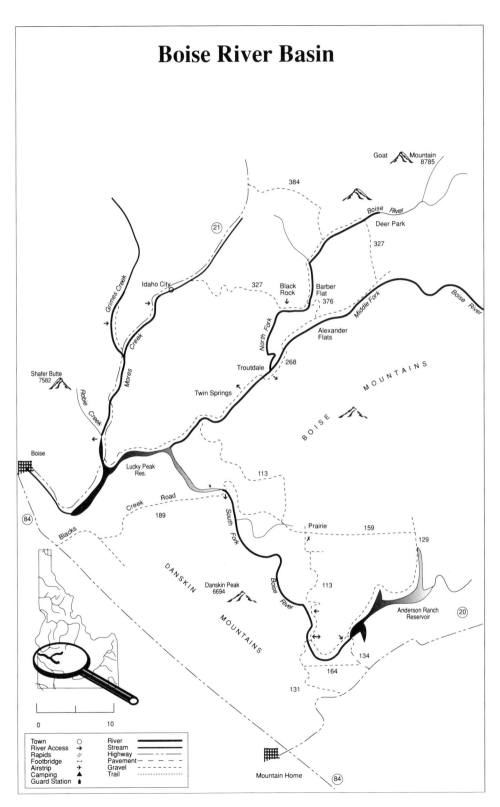

BOISE RIVER, THE WEIR

CLASS	LEVEL	LENGTH	GRADIENT	TIME
III	1,500-3,000 cfs	2 yards	2 fpy	All Day

PUT-IN:	The Weir, mile 3
TAKE-OUT:	The Weir, mile 3
SHUTTLE:	None
CRAFT:	Kayak, canoe
PORTAGES:	No
SEASON:	April, May, June
GAUGE:	Glenwood
PERMIT:	No
MAPS:	Boise City
CHARACTER:	Low-head concrete weir, sticky reversal, laminar waves, shallow, road, dam.

DESCRIPTION: Urban kayaking — side surfing at its best. At flows above 1,500, only in the spring, the Weir becomes heaven for intermediate and advanced hole riders. And like they say in Santa Cruz — "It's breakin' all day." Forwards, backwards, sideways, upside down, the Weir develops some real grip as the water rises. The water is colder than hell, so surfing upside down should be avoided. It's shallow too, shallow enough to wear the nose off a Dancer or scuff your shoulder if your not careful. The best surfing is river right, stay out of the center as flows approach 3,000.

The Weir can be seen from Highway 21 just upstream from the Warm Springs Golf Course. To avoid the poison ivy jungle, park about 50 yards downstream, by the twin power-poles. A trail leads to a dilapidated concrete foot bridge. Put in this side stream and paddle up to the upstream side of the Weir. To take out, get back in the river upstream of the Weir and paddle back the way you came. If it's early in the season, the poison ivy isn't a problem.

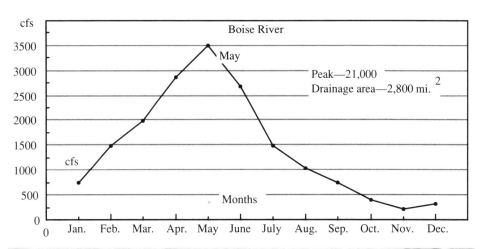

Tony Brennan backsliding.

MORES CREEK

CLASS	LEVEL	LENGTH	GRADIENT	TIME
II-III	600-1,300 cfs	13 miles	45 fpm	3 hours

PUT-IN:	Big Gulch, mile 33 (3,640 ft.)
TAKE-OUT:	Robie Creek (3,060 ft.)
SHUTTLE:	13 miles
CRAFT:	Kayak, canoe
PORTAGES:	0
SEASON:	April, May
GAUGE:	Mores Creek
PERMIT:	No
MAPS:	Idaho City, Warm Springs Pt., Dunnigan Cr., *Boise NF*
CHARACTER:	Swift-water stream, constant gradient, undefined stream-bed, blind corners, road, developed.

DESCRIPTION: Mores Creek is a tight, swift-water run. It never rears back for a good drop, but it never slows down. There aren't any stand-out rapids with moves to remember or lines to be on, only the endless march of water moving downhill. A couple of fences may have to be portaged depending on the water level. If you're going over the fences, you won't be able to make it under the bridges, so be prepared to portage. There is plenty of time to stop and get out, but the eddies are small. The low bridge danger could be worse in the future, because the bridges are being replaced by culverts. The water is in the bushes as well. It goes without saying, this can be dangerous. However, even at high flows, Mores Creek is hardly deep enough to roll. Sound like your idea of fun?

Though Mores Creek runs along the highway, much of it is concealed behind willows and summer homes. Make sure you know what's around the bend before paddling any blind corners.

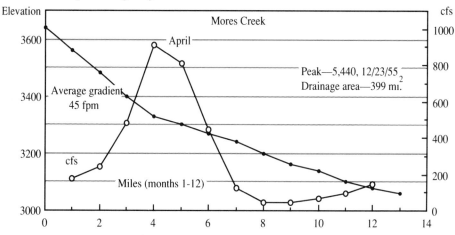

Mores Creek

Peak—5,440, 12/23/55
Drainage area—399 mi.^{2}

Average gradient 45 fpm

Miles (months 1-12)

Mores Creek

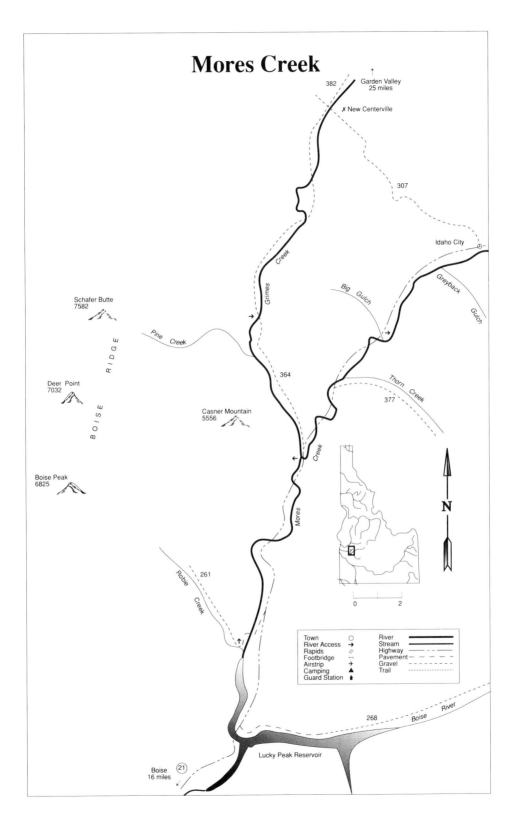

GRIMES CREEK

CLASS	LEVEL	LENGTH	GRADIENT	TIME
II-III	400-1000 cfs	4 miles	48 fpm	2-3 hours

PUT-IN: Four miles up from highway 21 (3,500 ft.)
TAKE-OUT: Mores Creek Confluence (3,310 ft.)
SHUTTLE: 4 miles
CRAFT: Kayak, canoe
PORTAGES: 0
SEASON: April, May
GAUGE: No
PERMIT: No
MAPS: Warm Springs Pt., Dunnigan Creek, *Boise NF*
CHARACTER: Swift-water stream, gravel bed, dredge tailings, road, secluded.

DESCRIPTION: If you've seen it all in the Boise Valley, then put Grimes and Mores Creek on your list, but until you have boated everything else around let these two wait. They are both small creeks with medium gradients that must be boated during the peak of run-off.

Grimes Creek is a straight-forward swiftwater stream. There is one good rapid, formed by the road-cut impinging on the streambed. Close to the run's end an old suspension bridge, that has lost most of its suspension, is hanging in the water; it can be dangerous. Other than this, keep your eyes peeled for deer.

The camping is best above Idaho City. The further the campsite is from the road the better. Black Rock campground on the North Fork of the Boise, 20 miles off the highway, is great . The natural hot water swimming pool at Warm Springs Resort, just south of Idaho City is worth the fee. It's kept clean and the temperature is perfect.

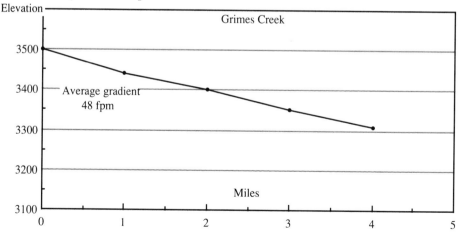

Grimes Creek

Average gradient 48 fpm

Rafting in Idaho.

SOUTH FORK BOISE RIVER, CANYON RUN

CLASS	LEVEL	LENGTH	GRADIENT	TIME
III	600-1,800 cfs	16 miles	26 fpm	4 hours
III-IV	>1,800 cfs			

PUT-IN:	Danskin Bridge (3,640 ft.)
TAKE-OUT:	Neal Bridge (3,220 ft.)
SHUTTLE:	21 miles
CRAFT:	Kayak, canoe, raft
PORTAGES:	No
SEASON:	May, June, July, August, September
GAUGE:	Anderson Ranch Dam
PERMIT:	No
MAPS:	Anderson Ranch, Danskin Pk. 15', Mayfield 15', Long Gulch, *Boise NF*
CHARACTER:	Small river, rock gardens, deep canyon, dam, wilderness.

DESCRIPTION: Driving to the South Fork of the Boise always leaves me with an overwhelming sense of isolation. Prairie Idaho — a bar, a pool table and a prairie — a big prairie.

Tulio Celano and Roger Hazelwood made the first descent of the South Fork Canyon in the early '70s. Both were stationed at Mountain Home AFB. They drove out to Tollgate to check if anyone knew about the river. The people at Tollgate said the rancher who lived in the Boise Canyon came through there once a week and they would ask him about the river. When Tulio and Roger returned a week later, Roger asked, "Well. What did he say?"

"He said to keep the Hell out of there."

Since it didn't look like the locals were going to be any help, Roger convinced a navigator at the airbase to fly down the canyon with a military reconnaissance plane. He returned with a stack of photos, literally covering every inch of the river. The locals, as usual, had overestimated the whitewater.

This is an excellent run through a magnificent canyon cut through the prairie. The water is good and the scenery some of the best. The river starts flat and mellow as it flows through a wide desert canyon. After a mile or two, sheer basalt cliffs close in on the banks. Hiking along or out of the canyon would be extremely difficult.

The rapids are mostly class II-III wave trains. Both the named rapids are about halfway down the run. Raspberry is a long wave train. The other is a class III rapid called Devils Hole. It can be located on the topos because in typical Idaho nomenclature it is named after Devils Hole Creek as Raspberry is named after Raspberry Gulch. Devils Hole can be spotted from upstream, look for a big pool in the river and a tree covered gravel bar on the left. The line is down the left. After this the river picks up and is a splashy class II-III ride almost all the way to the take-out.

Try to get on the river early because the afternoon sunshine doesn't penetrate the canyon. It can get cold in the lower section due to the lack of

South Fork Boise River

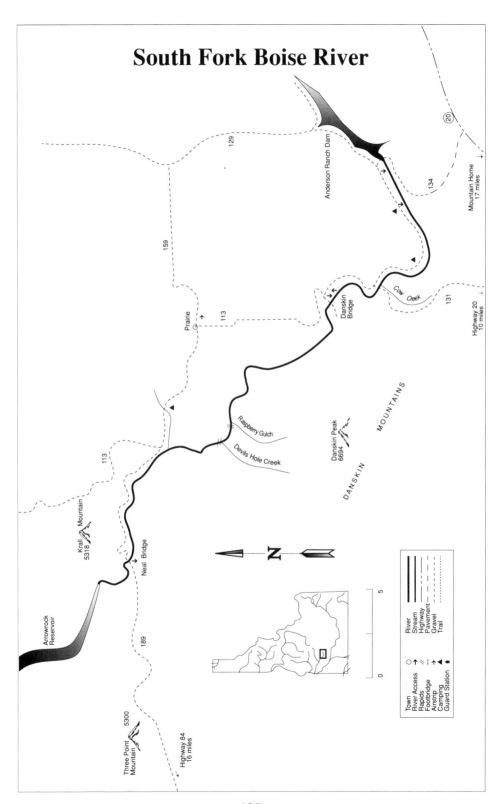

sunshine and all the splashing. There is some great surfing in the lower stretch, so plan your trip to take advantage of it.

The take-out is on the left just up from the Neal Bridge. As soon as it comes into view, pull over and make sure there is room in the small eddy, particularly on weekends.

Finding the river is an adventure in itself. From Boise take 84 east, get off at the Blacks Creek Road Exit, mile 64. Go north/northeast six miles to a junction in a little gulch. There is a home made sign post with directions to ranches and another indicating the area is part of a "Rural Area Watch." So don't be messing 'round. Go left, tò the north. The road climbs over the Danskin Mountains and then drops into the Boise Basin. Continue for 19 miles to the bridge at the take-out.

The put-in is 21 miles from here. Cross the bridge and climb up out of the canyon. Follow the main road to the southeast 11 miles to Prairie. Go right, to the south 10 miles. The road drops back into the canyon. The river and the put-in can be seen at the bottom of the hill. This is a the take-out for the upper run as well.

People coming from the east can get to the put-in off highway 20. Coming up from Mountain Home, take the turnoff to the west at mile post 111, about 16 miles north of the interstate, follow this 10 miles. From here, it drops down a steep grade to the Cow Creek Bridge. There is another turnoff at about milepost 116 used by people coming from the east. It is only five miles to Anderson Ranch Dam and the put-in for that run.

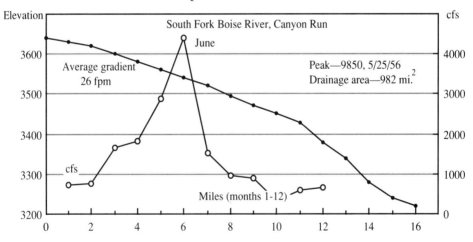

South Fork Boise River, Canyon Run

June

Average gradient
26 fpm

Peak—9850, 5/25/56
Drainage area—982 mi.^{2}

SOUTH FORK BOISE RIVER, UPPER RUN

CLASS	LEVEL	LENGTH	GRADIENT	TIME
I-II	600-2,000 cfs	10 miles	24 fpm	4-6 hours

PUT-IN:	Anderson Ranch Dam (3,880 ft.)
TAKE-OUT:	Danskin Bridge (3,640 ft.)
SHUTTLE:	10 miles
CRAFT:	Kayak, canoe, raft
PORTAGES:	No
SEASON:	May, June, July, August, September
GAUGE:	Anderson Ranch Dam
PERMIT:	No
MAPS:	Anderson Ranch, Danskin Pk. 15', *Boise NF*
CHARACTER:	Small river, swift, continuous, road, dam.

DESCRIPTION: This stretch of the Boise is a nice beginner run. It is relatively flat and straight-forward. The flow is controlled by Anderson Ranch Dam: 1600 cfs is all the turbines can handle and the summer norm.

The river runs through a wide desert canyon with some basalt outcroppings. There are four class I rapids between the put-in and the Cow Creek Bridge. A dirt road parallels the entire run, but it isn't too intrusive because of the willows and the lack of traffic. It also is a very good trail for bicycle shuttles. There is one long class II rapid a mile upstream from the take-out. At low flows, below 1,200 cfs, this rapid is too shallow for a clean run in anything other than a kayak. Expect to see lots of anglers, because this is a blue ribbon trout stream.

The camping along the river is good. There are several big flats in the river bends that are perfect campgrounds and are presently undeveloped. For shuttle directions, or simply to find the place, see the canyon description.

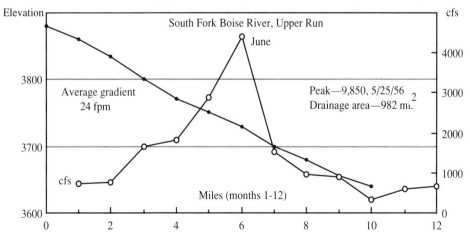

197

MIDDLE FORK BOISE RIVER

CLASS	LEVEL	LENGTH	GRADIENT	TIME
II	500-1,500 cfs	9 miles	12 fpm	3 hours
II-III	>1,500			

PUT-IN:	Troutdale Campground (3,470 ft.)
TAKE-OUT:	Badger Creek Campground (3,360 ft.)
SHUTTLE:	9 miles
CRAFT:	Kayak, canoe, raft
PORTAGES:	No
SEASON:	May, June, July
GAUGE:	Twin Springs
PERMIT:	No
MAPS:	Miner Cr.
CHARACTER:	Beginner canoe, kayak run, road, secluded.

DESCRIPTION: The Middle Fork of the Boise below the North Fork is a wide easy river. This stretch is strictly for beginners. No rapids, no moves and the line is as wide as the riverbed. During the summer the river's shallow and slow. Spring flows will kick up some waves and splash you in the face: no more. The scenery consists of pines, sagebrush and grass. The highlights of this run are the hotsprings at the Sheep Creek Bridge and at Twin Springs. The road along the riverbank, for a road to Nowhere, is busy. The cars kick up a nice dust cloud that floats above the river all day.

To get to the put-in from highway 21 go east past Spring Shores towards Atlanta on road 268, 18 miles to the take-out — Badger Creek Campground. The put-in is up the road nine miles, or 20, or wherever you want.

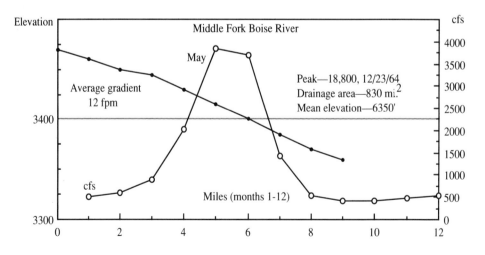

Middle Fork Boise River

Average gradient 12 fpm

May

Peak—18,800, 12/23/64
Drainage area—830 mi.^{2}
Mean elevation—6350'

Miles (months 1-12)

198

Tony Brennan on the North Fork Boise.

NORTH FORK BOISE RIVER, BARBER FLAT

CLASS	LEVEL	LENGTH	GRADIENT	TIME
III-IV	600-1000 cfs	9 miles	57 fpm	3 hours
IV	1000-2000 cfs			

PUT-IN:	Black Rock Campground (3,980 ft.)
TAKE-OUT:	Troutdale (3,470 ft.)
SHUTTLE:	15 miles
CRAFT:	Kayak
PORTAGES:	No
SEASON:	May, June, July
GAUGE:	40% of Twin Springs
PERMIT:	No
MAPS:	Twin Spr., Rabbit Cr., Sheep Cr., Barber Flat, *Boise NF*
CHARACTER:	Small river, rock gardens, scenic, wilderness.

DESCRIPTION: The North Fork of the Boise is a great little whitewater run. It doesn't get much use, which is somewhat of a surprise, because it is only a two hour drive from Boise. The access and shuttle are probably the reasons for the lack of use on this run, but don't be discouraged, the run is well worth the drive. There are plans to build a dam on the Middle Fork, which would inundate most of the North Fork run. This run needs more use and a record of people using it. Check it out and spread the word.

Once on the water the road leaves the canyon just down from the put-in and the river drops into a deep secluded canyon. The rapids are steep, narrow rock gardens. The water is clear and cold. For natural beauty and seclusion this run is a stand-out. One of the first rapids is close to a mile of pure fun, with plenty of surfing and scrambling. There are a couple of turns with some logs in them, so keep your eyes peeled. The river mellows out towards the end. The take-out is at the confluence with the Middle Fork.

To get to put-in from highway 21, go two-and-a-half miles northwest of Idaho City, then go southwest 20 miles on Forest Service Road 327 past Granite Creek Campground to Blackrock Campground, the put-in. Between Blackrock and Barber Flat, another three miles upstream, there are a couple of good drops. To get to the take-out from Barber Flat, go south, across the bridge, up over the mountains, towards Alexander Flats, eight miles on road 376. At the Middle Fork, head back downstream five miles on road 268 to Troutdale, the North Fork Confluence.

The graph is an estimate based on a comparison of the Twin Springs gauge and an old gauge once located upstream from the mouth of the North Fork. By subtracting the flows of this gauge from the Twin Springs gauge, 10 miles downstream, the North Fork flow — roughly 40 percent of Twin Springs — can be estimated.

See graph page 199.

North Fork Boise River

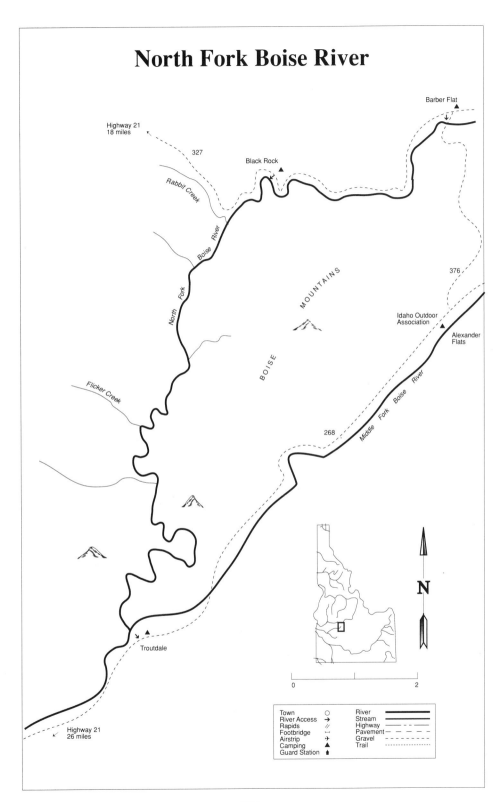

Barber Flat

Highway 21
18 miles

327

Black Rock

Rabbit Creek

Boise River

North Fork

MOUNTAINS

376

Idaho Outdoor
Association

Alexander
Flats

BOISE

Flicker Creek

Middle Fork Boise River

268

Troutdale

N

Highway 21
26 miles

Town	○	River	▬
River Access	→	Stream	▬
Rapids	//	Highway	– –
Footbridge	)-(	Pavement	— —
Airstrip	✈	Gravel	- - -
Camping	▲	Trail	····
Guard Station	♦		

0   2

Owyhee River Basin

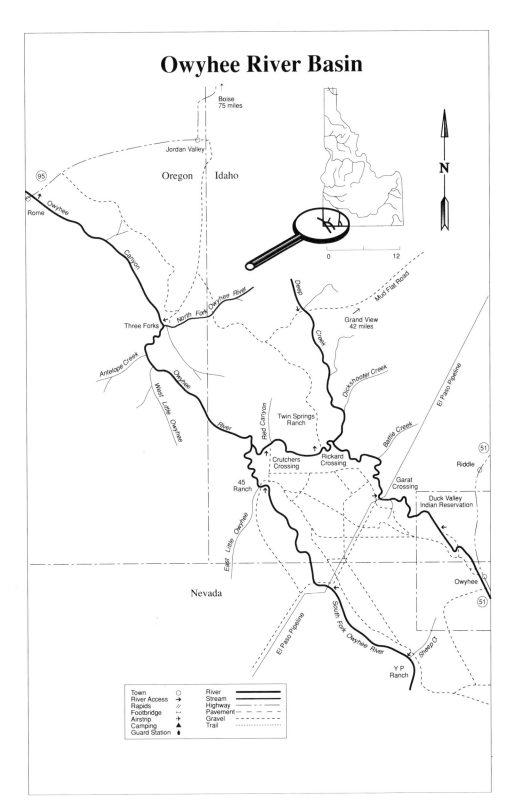

OWYHEE RIVER, THREE FORKS TO ROME

CLASS	LEVEL	LENGTH	GRADIENT	TIME
III (V)	600-1,500 cfs	35 miles	17 fpm	2 days
IV (V)	>1,500 cfs			

PUT-IN:	Three Forks (3,950 ft.)
TAKE-OUT:	Rome (2,360 ft.)
SHUTTLE:	53 miles
CRAFT:	Kayak, canoe, raft
PORTAGES:	0
SEASON:	April, May
GAUGE:	Rome, (503) 586-2612
PERMIT:	No
MAPS:	Three Forks, Whitehorse Btt., Skull Cr., Indian Fort, Dry Cr. Rim, Scott Res. (all Oregon)
CHARACTER:	Desert river, boulder-choked rapids, deep basalt canyon, wilderness.

DESCRIPTION: Unfortunately I've only boated the Owyhee once — I'm no longer welcome in Oregon. We set out to do the Three Forks to Rome stretch in '83 at close to 9,000 cfs. It was pouring rain. The roads were impassable and we had to walk the last mile to Three Forks in the dark. No one wanted to carry the firepan and it was left behind.

The next morning the river ranger woke us and informed us we couldn't build a fire without a firepan. We launched with promises of a cold camp and our fingers crossed.

The first rapid, The Shelf, is around the first bend. At 9,000 cfs it is a gauntlet of huge boulders choking off and stacking up the river. Between the boulders are the most beautiful laminar slides of red-brown water. These drop down about six feet into some big waves and then dump out into a great rock garden. The next stand out is Half Mile. We planned on scouting this long rapid in two sections. We boat-scouted and ran the first half. What happened next is a blurry memory. I remember lots of holes and even more kayaks stuck in them. When I eddied out at the bottom of Half Mile there were lots of swimmers and equipment floating by.

Things went from bad to worse: we camped. There were only two dry sleeping bags in the group. The rest were victims of rain and whitewater. According to BLM regulations, because we'd left our firepan behind, the only logical solution was to freeze to death. Fortunately, we had lots of booze. In the subsequent alcoholic blur, logic was quickly disposed of, and we set up a democracy to decide if our lives were worth drying out a patch of mud. The majority imposed its will, and we built a huge fire. A fire so big it could be seen millions of miles away in space — or at least on the canyon rim, where the river ranger was perched, ready to swoop down on any sign of life.

The river ranger swooped down the thousand feet of cliff and talus, from the canyon rim to our camp, and disposed of our makeshift democracy. He quickly put out our fire and our democratic fervor. Chastised, abjectly

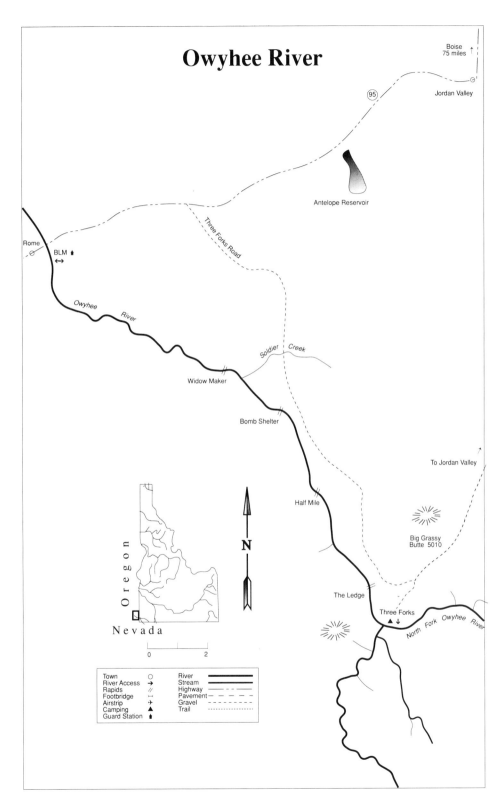

Owyhee River

Boise
75 miles

Jordan Valley

(95)

Antelope Reservoir

Three Forks Road

Rome

BLM ⬆

Owyhee River

Soldier Creek

Widow Maker

Bomb Shelter

To Jordan Valley

Half Mile

Big Grassy
Butte 5010

Oregon

Nevada

N

The Ledge

Three Forks
▲ ↓

North Fork Owyhee River

0   2

Town	○	River	▬▬▬
River Access	→	Stream	▬▬▬
Rapids	//	Highway	———
Footbridge	⊢	Pavement	— — —
Airstrip	✈	Gravel	------
Camping	▲	Trail	········
Guard Station	⬆		

repentant, and still wet, as soon as he left, we built another fire.

Widow Maker, a big class V, was only a mile down from where we camped. The next morning we were more hung-over than warmed-up when it came into view. Out of the group only two ran the drop. After watching Tony and Dick duel it out in the holes, no one else could muster the courage to follow suit. Portaging here is an ordeal, some of us portaged on the right and others on the left. I went on the right. It can't be any harder on the left. It's murder on the right.

There were some rapids left but they're obscured behind my memory of Widow Maker and the impending doom that awaited us at the take-out. Even at 9,000 we had miles of flat water in which to reflect upon our sins before Rome. The ranger wasn't standing alone in the rain. The Oregon State Police flanked him. I thanked God I wasn't the trip leader. He was taken into a BLM building and subjected to God knows what. When he came out he was a changed man. He wouldn't let us drink beer on the bus ride out of Oregon. Even after the police escort left us at the border.

In spite of the fines, flaring tempers and scorched earth, this rates as one of my favorite river trips. There is a moral to this story: observe BLM and forest service regulations.

The shuttle is straight-forward, unless it's been raining. On highway 95, 17 miles south of Jordan Valley or 16 miles north of Rome, look for a little green sign marking the road to Three Forks. It's 36 miles of wild dirt road to the put-in.

*Owyhee River gauge at Rome

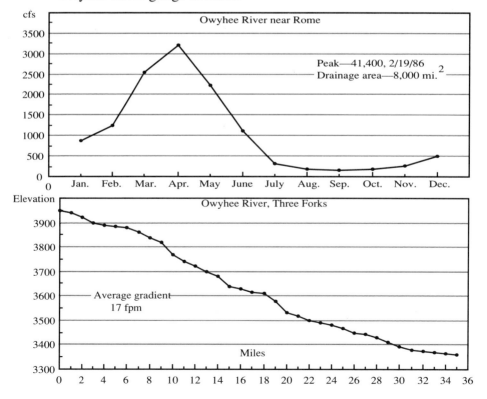

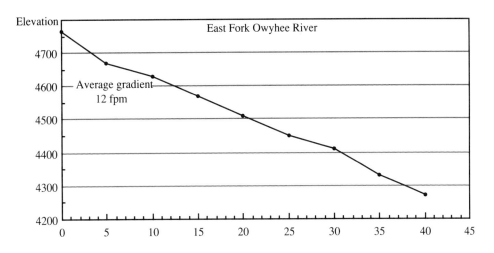

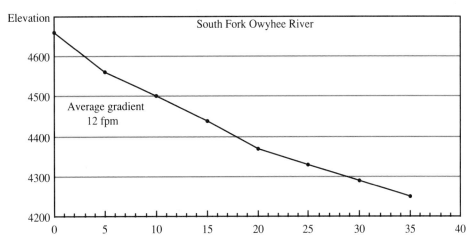

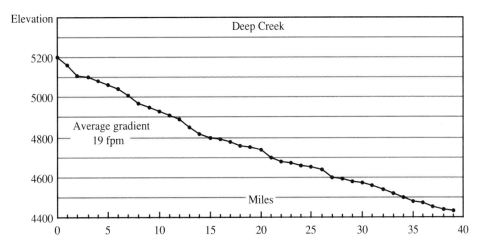

UPPER OWYHEE RIVER

CLASS	LEVEL	LENGTH	GRADIENT	TIME
II (IV)	1,000-6,000 cfs*	36 miles	8 fpm	2 days

PUT-IN:	Crutchers Crossing (4,250 ft.)
TAKE-OUT:	Three Forks (3,950 ft.)
SHUTTLE:	250 miles
CRAFT:	Kayak, canoe, raft
PORTAGES:	0
SEASON:	April, May
GAUGE:	Rome (503) 586-2612
PERMIT:	No
MAPS:	Red Bsn., Bull Bsn. Camp, Beaver Charlie Breaks, Deacon Crossing, Drummon Bsn., Three Forks.
CHARACTER:	Gentle desert river, low gradient, wilderness.

DESCRIPTION: The Owyhee {o-WHY-hee - a phonetic spelling of Hawaii: the river and surrounding area are named after three Hawaiians who disappeared while exploring the area} canyon towers above paddlers with a stark grandeur. Huge spires loom into the sky. A deep canyon in a high altitude desert, almost unvisited except by wildlife and cattle, the Owyhee is unique. Since it's possible to travel for weeks down this river and never see another soul, it is wilder than many designated wilderness streams.

The Owyhee from the East and South Fork confluence down to Three Forks is erroneously called the East Fork on some maps. The easiest access is from the 45 Ranch on the South Fork (by permission).

Be prepared for a bit of strong paddling a mile or so below the confluence at House Rock and Bald Mountain rapids (class IIIs). After approximately 10 miles more of grand scenery, small caves, springs and pleasant floating, keep alert for the Stateline Cabin, set back on the right bank. This marks the beginning of Cabin Rapid, a class IV. Since it is a half-mile long, (longer at lower flows) and has the most juice at the bottom, you will want to scout it on the left.

A couple miles of minor whitewater leads down to Cable Rapid, (IV). Like virtually all Owyhee rapids it was created by a huge rockslide. Look twice at this one from the right and make note of the major siphon and the must-make eddy. The rugged portage (class V) on the right is attractive. If you have a couple of pulleys you might muscle you gear down the aerial cable installed by one of the early outfitters. A solid 2,500 cfs on the Rome gauge is required for lining rafts and drift boats through Cabin and Cable. Since each requires a few hours for even a small party to negotiate, they are best approached early in the day.

Five-Bar Cabins on a flat to the left above Louse Canyon is one of the most interesting historic sites on the river. After inspecting the cabin be sure to wander further back to look at an old forge built into a cave in the draw and at a stack of wooden water pipes.

Warm springs dot the cliffs upstream from Three Forks. Look for a high

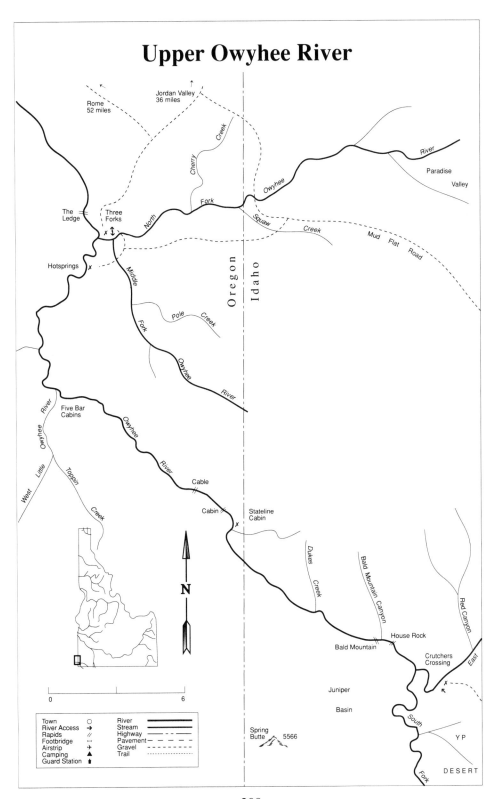

Upper Owyhee River

Rome
52 miles

Jordan Valley
36 miles

Cherry Creek

North Fork

Owyhee

Paradise Valley

River

The Ledge

Three Forks

Squaw Creek

Mud Flat Road

Hotsprings

Oregon | Idaho

Middle

Fork

Pole Creek

Owyhee

River

West Little Owyhee River

Five Bar Cabins

Owyhee

River

Toppin Creek

Cable

Cabin

Stateline Cabin

Dukes Creek

Bald Mountain Canyon

Red Canyon

House Rock

Bald Mountain

Crutchers Crossing

East

Juniper Basin

Spring Butte 5566

Y P

South Fork

DESERT

N

Town	○	River
River Access	→	Stream
Rapids	//	Highway
Footbridge		Pavement
Airstrip	+	Gravel
Camping	▲	Trail
Guard Station		

0   6

spring in a rock outcropping on the left across from a flat with a jeep road just above the forks. This spring is deep enough to swim in.

The canyon is very broad at Three Forks. High clearance two-wheel drive vehicles can get in and out here when its dry. But a solid spring rain can turn the sage steppes into a quagmire and make the thirty six miles out to Jordan Valley into a Class V shuttle adventure.

Trips must be registered with the BLM. Portable latrines and fire pans are strongly recommended. Fire pans are required in Oregon. An Owyhee River Boating Guide complete with maps and hydrographic tables is available from the Bureau of Land Management, Boise District Office, 3948 Development Avenue, Boise, Idaho 83705.

The shuttle distance listed above is almost all on pavement. The 36 miles from Jordan Valley to Three Forks is dirt and gravel. The 30 miles from highway 51 to put in is dirt as well. This route follows highway 78 through Marsing and 95 south to Jordan Valley. The shuttle can be cut to 170 miles by taking the Mud Flat road: 100 miles of dirt. Even when the road is in good condition, this is a questionable shortcut.

*Owyhee River gauge at Rome
P.L.

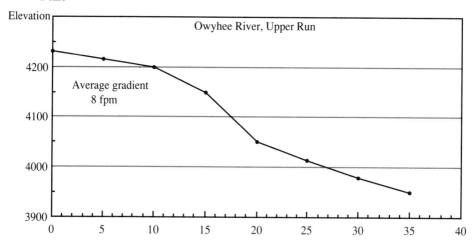

Big water on the Owyhee River. They're not all like this.
Photo: Rob Lesser

EAST FORK OWYHEE RIVER

CLASS	LEVEL	LENGTH	GRADIENT	TIME
II	1,000-3,000 cfs*	42 (40) miles	12 fpm	2 days
II-III	3,000-6,000 cfs			

PUT-IN:	Garat Crossing (4,760 ft.)
TAKE-OUT:	Crutchers Crossing (4,250 ft.)
SHUTTLE:	23 miles
CRAFT:	Kayak, canoe, raft
PORTAGES:	1
SEASON:	April, May
GAUGE:	Rome (503) 586-2612
PERMIT:	No
MAPS:	BLM 30" Owyhee River, Riddle
CHARACTER:	Gentle desert river, low gradient, wilderness.

DESCRIPTION: An East Fork adventure begins on highway 225 (Idaho 51) just north of the Idaho - Nevada line with a search for a gravel road and a little green sign pointing west toward the Owyhee River. The drive across the magnificent high desert can be splendid in fair weather. After a few days of spring rain it can be a nightmare of slick adobe and mired vehicles. In either case keep the maps handy; the trip will put your orienteering skills to the test.

The rugged upper East Fork Canyon is well worth the thrash of getting in. It leads down some of the most remote country left in the lower 48. Paddlers are so few here that desert bighorns wander up to investigate them.

A few remnant rock cabins are all that's left of the Owyhee silver rush of a century ago. Tens of thousands of cattle were grazed on the high desert as food for miners. In a few places the rugged rocks and spires kept the cattle out of the inner canyon preserving the native plants and grasses.

You should plan on arriving at the Lambert gorge in the early morning since it is without good campsites and is a tough passage. Owyhee Falls (approximately seven miles above Crutchers Crossing) is unrunnable and presents a disagreeable choice. River right involves portaging over house rocks and only avoids part of the rapid at higher flows. River left (which the BLM recommends) involves a considerable climb and only a hint of a trail. The falls are not placed with great accuracy on some maps. Watch for a steep creek on the right followed by a rock fall.

Two miles later an initial steep passage just wide enough for a canoe gives Thread the Needle its name. Canoes have been double broached in the narrow run-out from this drop. At low flows these rapids are a maze of house rocks with the river trickling underneath. The East Fork is a demanding trip at any water level.

*Owyhee River gauge at Rome

P.L.

See graph page 207.

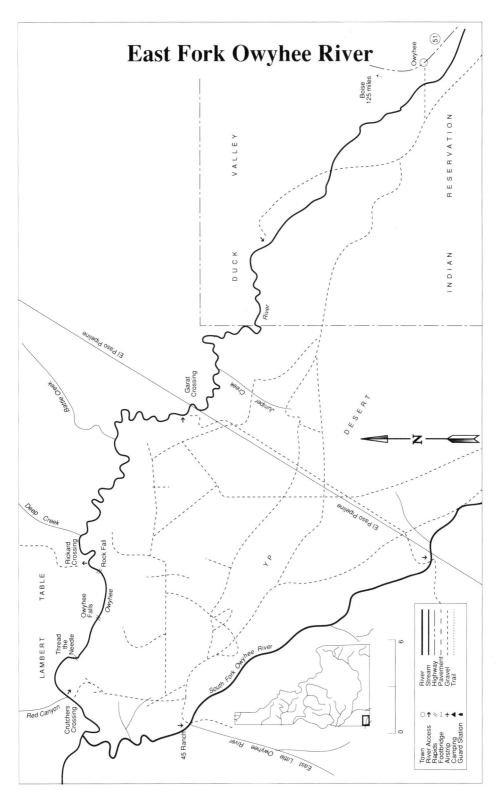

East Fork Owyhee River

SOUTH FORK OWYHEE RIVER

CLASS	LEVEL	LENGTH	GRADIENT	TIME
II	1,000-3,000 cfs*	36 (34) miles	12 fpm	2 days
II-III	3,000-6,000 cfs			

PUT IN:	El Paso Crossing (4,660 ft.)
TAKE OUT:	Crutchers Crossing (4,250 ft.)
SHUTTLE:	27 miles
CRAFT:	Kayak, canoe
PORTAGES:	0
SEASON:	April, May
GAUGE:	Rome (503) 586-2612
PERMIT:	No
MAPS:	BLM 30" Owyhee River, Riddle, Silver Creek
CHARACTER:	Gentle desert river, low gradient, wilderness.

DESCRIPTION: A drive to the El Paso put-in begins like the East Fork journey in the Duck Valley Indian Reservation. Bring a rugged four wheel drive and a good compass. With permission, it is possible to use a less strenuous access point at the YP Ranch approximately 13 miles south of the Idaho - Nevada border.

While not as spectacular as the East Fork, the South Fork offers outstanding vistas and whitewater fun. Starting at the put-in, the whitewater is continuous class II - III all the way to the Idaho Stateline. Good rafters and kayakers should expect no serious problems. Open canoeists should expect to eddy hop and to do a certain amount of judicious scouting. Canoeists may have to line or portage a few spots, depending on the flow.

A little over three miles into Idaho lies Bull Camp where cattle were once wintered along the river. The remains of two rock cabins can be visited on the east bank. On the western side, steel posts and litter mark the camp of the poacher Claude Dallas, who gunned down two game wardens here in 1981. Below lies the beautiful springs and homestead site at Coyote Hole. Sentinel Rapid, two miles downstream, is worth a look.

Taking out at Crutchers Crossing involves paddling two miles upstream on the East Fork. That's right, upstream. At low flows, around 500 cfs, it can be done in two hours. There are some small riffles the boats may have to be pushed up, but otherwise it's flat. Make sure the road to Crutchers is passable before committing to taking out here. It is a jeep trail and subject to wash outs. At high water, take a couple extra days and continue down to Three Forks.

*Owyhee River gauge at Rome

P.L.

See graph page 207.

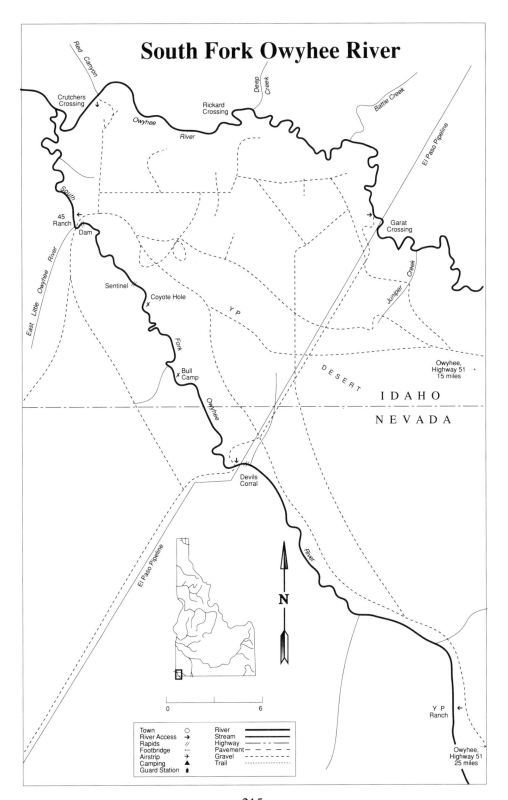

South Fork Owyhee River

Red Canyon

Crutchers
Crossing

Deep Creek

Owyhee River

Rickard
Crossing

Battle Creek

El Paso Pipeline

South

45
Ranch

Dam

Garat
Crossing

East Little Owyhee River

Sentinel

Coyote Hole

Fork

Juniper Creek

Y P

D E S E R T

Bull
Camp

Owyhee

Owyhee,
Highway 51
15 miles

I D A H O

N E V A D A

Devils
Corral

El Paso Pipeline

River

N

Y P
Ranch

Owyhee,
Highway 51
25 miles

Town	○	River	
River Access	→	Stream	
Rapids	//	Highway	
Footbridge	‑‑	Pavement	
Airstrip	✈	Gravel	
Camping	▲	Trail	
Guard Station	⚑		

0   6

DEEP CREEK

CLASS	LEVEL	LENGTH	GRADIENT	TIME
I-II	>2,000 cfs*	39 (35) miles	19 fpm	2 days

PUT-IN:	Mud Flat Road Crossing (5,200 ft.)
TAKE-OUT:	Rickard Crossing (4,430 ft.)
SHUTTLE:	40 miles
CRAFT:	Kayak, canoe, small raft
PORTAGES:	1 fence
SEASON:	April, May
GAUGE:	Rome >2,000 cfs
PERMIT:	No
MAPS:	Slack Mtn., Castro Table, Brace Flat., Dickshooter Rdg.
CHARACTER:	Small desert river, low gradient, scenic, wilderness.

DESCRIPTION: This starts as a little creek, but just downstream from the put-in the flow doubles, and the stream slowly drops into a deep canyon which confines the streambed. After the first mile it is a smooth ride downhill for the rest of the trip. The major obstacles on Deep Creek are sharp turns against cliffs and boulders. The gradient is gradual and slight with a fairly continuous current, but no real rapids. There are some fences spanning the riverbed that may have to be portaged, depending on the water level. Rafts will have to portage Watermelon Seed, a slow squeeze between two boulders.

The scenery is outstanding. In this defacto wilderness area, the desolation is awe inspiring. The Deep Creek Canyon is a miniature Grand Canyon, complete with vertical canyon walls and an oasis-like riverbank. After Deep Creek joins the Owyhee, four miles remain to the take-out at Rickard Crossing.

Deep Creek was first run in 1982. It winds through the second largest roadless area in Idaho and the rangeland of one of the few remaining herds of Desert Bighorn Sheep. Deep Creek is part of the headwaters of the Owyhee River. If someone had the time and desire, Deep Creek could be the first leg of a 200 mile river trip ending in Owyhee Reservoir.

To find the put-in, start in Grand View on highway 78. Go east of town just over a mile to a Y in the road, and the highway turns to the southeast. Take the Mud Flat Road to the south and continue south/southwest about 42 miles to Deep Creek. Start where the road crosses the river. To get to the take-out continue west 11 miles on the Mud Flat Road, take the road to the south 22 miles past Twin Springs to Rickard Crossing. There are several creeks on this road which must be crossed and if full, they will put a four-wheel drive to the test.

*Owyhee River gauge at Rome

R.R.

See graph page 207.

216

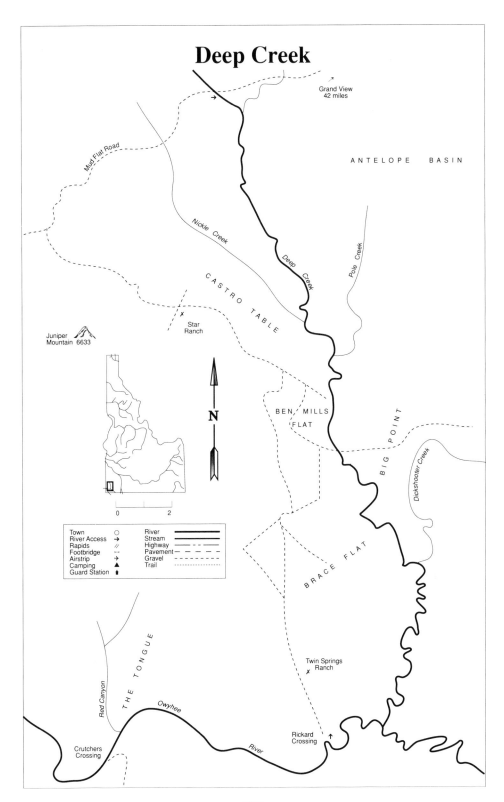

Deep Creek

Grand View
42 miles

ANTELOPE BASIN

Mud Flat Road

Nickle Creek

Deep Creek

Pole Creek

CASTRO TABLE

Star Ranch

Juniper Mountain 6633

N

BEN MILLS FLAT

BIG POINT

Dickshooter Creek

Town	○	River	
River Access	→	Stream	
Rapids	//	Highway	
Footbridge		Pavement	
Airstrip	↗	Gravel	
Camping	▲	Trail	
Guard Station	⚓		

BRACE FLAT

THE TONGUE

Red Canyon

Owyhee

Twin Springs Ranch

Rickard Crossing

Crutchers Crossing

River

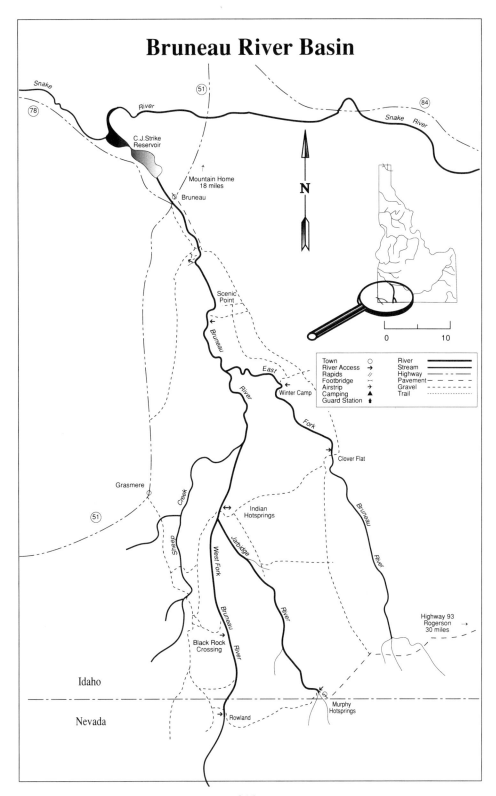

Bruneau River Basin

Snake

River

(51)

(84)

(78)

Snake River

C.J.Strike
Reservoir

Mountain Home
18 miles

N

Bruneau

Scenic
Point

Town	○	River	
River Access	→	Stream	
Rapids	⁄⁄	Highway	
Footbridge	⌐	Pavement	
Airstrip	⇥	Gravel	
Camping	▲	Trail	
Guard Station	♦		

Bruneau

East

River

Winter Camp

Fork

Clover Flat

Grasmere

Creek

Indian
Hotsprings

Bruneau

(51)

Steep

Jarbidge

River

West Fork

Highway 93
Rogerson
30 miles

Bruneau

River

River

Black Rock
Crossing

Idaho

Nevada

Murphy
Hotsprings

Rowland

0   10

THE BRUNEAU

CLASS	LEVEL	LENGTH	GRADIENT	TIME
III	500-1,500 cfs	56 miles	27 fpm	2 days
III-IV	>1,500 cfs			

PUT-IN:	Indian Hot Springs (3,700 ft.)
TAKE-OUT:	Indian Bathtub (2,580 ft.)
SHUTTLE:	45 miles
CRAFT:	Kayak, canoe, small raft
PORTAGES:	0
SEASON:	April, May, June
GAUGE:	Bruneau
PERMIT:	No
MAPS:	Hot Spr., Crowbar Gulch, Austin Btt., Wintercamp, Stiff Tree Draw, Cave Draw, Inside Lakes, Indian H.S.
CHARACTER:	Small river, rock gardens, narrow canyon, wilderness.

DESCRIPTION: The Bruneau River flows through one of the best desert-canyons in the Northern Rockies. The Bruneau is a small river in a narrow and deep canyon, in places only a couple of boat lengths wide with the water filling it from wall to wall. Because it is a small river the season is short, at most April through June. Most years, in April the road to the put-in will usually be a muddy stream. In June the road will be dry, as will the river.

The rapids are generally pool-drop. Most of them are straight forward, and not difficult, however some disappear around corners; you don't want to get in over your head. The first rapid, Kendells Cave, sweeps into a cave cut into the base of a giant cliff and around a large logjam. It's an interesting move, a little scary, but not difficult. Intermediates should be cautious here. In the BLM pamphlet on the Bruneau, the longest rapid, Five-Mile, is rated as a class IV-V. It is more of a III-IV, but requires some scrambling as the water drops.

At the top of Five Mile Rapid, on river right, marked by a dilapidated BLM trail info box, the old Roberson Trail winds up to the canyon rim. The trailhead is approximately two miles south of the Bruneau scenic overlook. It can be used as a put-in to make a day run on the Bruneau. For kayakers or anyone else willing to haul their gear down a very "interesting" trail, the best of the Bruneau's whitewater lies downstream from here. It takes about one-half hour to walk down the trail. As a take-out, it should only be considered by those with an absolute minimum of equipment.

Finding the Bruneau is an adventure in itself. The Bruneau Desert is covered with little dirt trails cutting through the sage. Most of them lead to nowhere. Others look good, but turn into four-wheel drive nightmares. Don't try to just drive to the river by following a road that "looks good." There are only six roads leading to the river: one on each side of Black Rock Crossing, the Roberson Trail and Indian Hot Springs, they do not cross the river. There

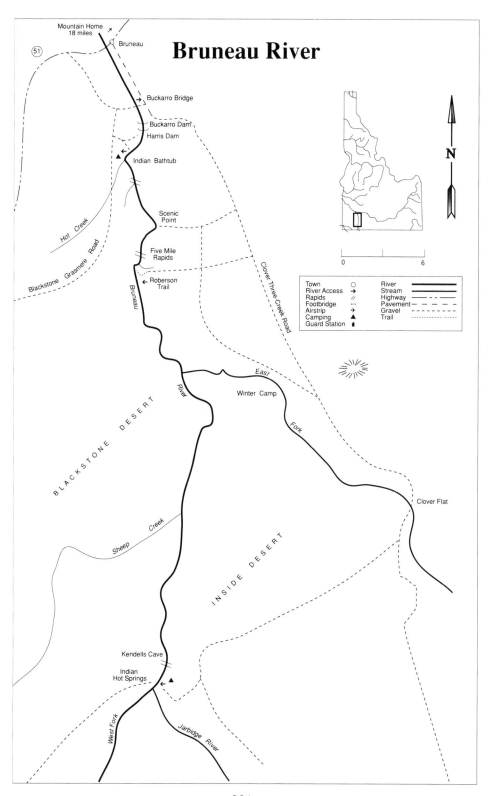

Bruneau River

Mountain Home
18 miles

(51)

Bruneau

Buckarro Bridge

Buckarro Dam

Harris Dam

Indian Bathtub

Scenic
Point

Five Mile
Rapids

Hot Creek

Blackstone Grasmere Road

Bruneau

Roberson
Trail

Clover Three-Creek Road

N

0   6

Town	○	River	
River Access	→	Stream	
Rapids	//	Highway	
Footbridge	⊢⊣	Pavement	
Airstrip	✈	Gravel	
Camping	▲	Trail	
Guard Station	⚑		

East

Winter Camp

Fork

River

B L A C K S T O N E   D E S E R T

Clover Flat

Sheep   Creek

I N S I D E   D E S E R T

Kendells Cave

Indian
Hot Springs

West Fork

Jarbidge River

is a bridge at Indian Hot Springs, but I wouldn't drive my car across it. Don't drive off the road unless you have a four-wheel drive, especially if it has been raining. Carry a jack, a spare and a shovel.

The easiest way to find your way around the Bruneau Desert is to hire a shuttle driver in Bruneau. Ask at Chet's Pastime Bar, prices are negotiable. It takes Parnelli Jones four hours to drive from Bruneau to Indian Hot Springs.

Kayakers can take out at the Buckaroo Bridge, approximately 10 miles south-east of Bruneau on the Clover Three-Creek Road. It's a vertical bank with current, so it would be difficult for rafts. The recommended take-out is upstream near Indian Bathtub. Follow the BLM sign that directs you across the bridge, then after approximately half-a-mile, another sign will direct you to the left. The next turn is the critical one and, naturally, it lacks a sign. As the main road crests the first big hill a little road cuts across the desert to the east, take it and keep to the right. Don't be discouraged if you can't find this place on the first try.

The Indian bathtub is a hundred yards upstream from the take-out, look for a little hollow on river left with a small overhanging cave and a cut bank from an old pipe that once transported hot water downstream. It's worth a stop if you're cold. The low-head dams in the last two miles have been run, but both are easily portaged on the right.

To find the Roberson Trail, start at the Buckaroo Bridge. Go south six miles on the Clover Three-Creek road to the scenic overlook road. Go west 2.5 miles towards the scenic overlook, and take the second road to the south. Go 2.8 miles to the first right, look for a little cairn marking the turn. Continue past the little lake (depending on the time of year the "lake" may be dry) 3.5 miles to the end of the road and the trailhead.

The put-in is 41 miles out the Clover Three-Creek Road and another 15 across the desert to the west. Turnoff about one mile south of the Clover Flat Crossing, where the road takes a diving turn.

For more information and a detailed pamphlet with detailed maps (no stone unturned), write: BLM - Boise District Office, River Coordinator, 3948 Development Ave. Boise, ID 83706, (208) 334-1582.

The gauge is on private property, across and downstream from Indian Bathtub. There is no way to drive to it. Call the Idaho Department of Water Resources, (208) 327-7988 for the current flow data.

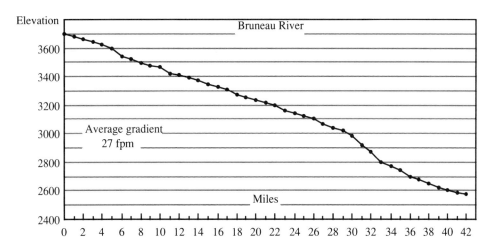

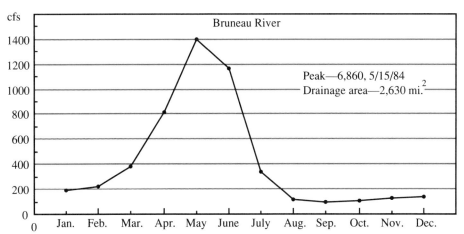

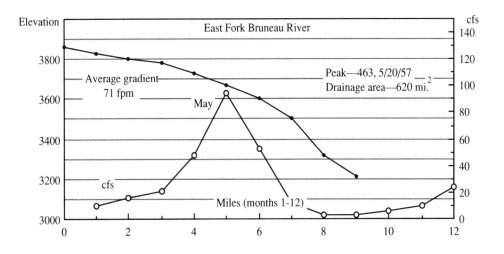

EAST FORK, BRUNEAU RIVER (CLOVER CREEK)

CLASS	LEVEL	LENGTH	GRADIENT	TIME
IV-V	300-500 cfs	17 (9) miles	71 fpm	6 hours

PUT-IN:	Winter Camp (3,860 ft.)
TAKE-OUT:	Roberson Trail {(confl. 3,210 ft.) 2,920 ft.}
SHUTTLE:	13 miles
CRAFT:	Kayak
PORTAGES:	0
SEASON:	April (Peak)
GAUGE:	1951-1960
PERMIT:	No
MAPS:	Hot Springs, Crowbar Gulch, Austin Btt., Wintercamp, Hodge Station, Clover Btt. N., Juniper Ranch
CHARACTER:	Steep creek, rock gardens, deep canyon, vertical cliffs, wilderness, hike-out.

DESCRIPTION: The East Fork of the Bruneau, or Clover Creek, rarely has enough water in it for kayaking. The window is, at most, a week in a high water year, usually it flows at about three cfs. Because of this, it will never be a standard run, and every trip down it will be an exploratory of sorts. Don't put in unless it's bank full and rolling at Winter Camp. If it's bank full and rolling, make sure you are prepared for some dangerous and difficult class IV. Experts only.

To date, the East Fork has been run three times. In 1975, Rick Mellon, Ron Fry, Mike Ferguson and Mark Kuskie made a low water descent. In 1984, John Wasson, Tom Wittaker, Jerry Johnson made a high water run when the Bruneau was flowing at close to 7000 cfs. In 1989 Tony Brennan and I did the desert kayak marathon. We left Winter Camp at noon, pinned and paddled the nine miles of Clover Creek, sprinted the eight miles on the Bruneau to the Roberson Trail, then climbed 600 feet up out of the canyon with our kayaks, biked the 14 mile shuttle across the desert and made it back to Bruneau in time for a couple cold ones and some good natured abuse from the locals.

From Clover Flat to Winter Camp the river meanders through a wide open desert valley. Two miles down from Winter Camp the river enters a gorge. The riverbed becomes constricted and the gradient picks up. Due to the combination of difficult access, sheer-cascading drops, and the constricted canyon, this is an extremely dangerous run. The rapids are boulder-choked mazes. There are tons of undercuts, sweepers and potential pins. The riverbed and boulders are basalt, the kind that dig in and stick to plastic boats.

Winter Camp should be used as the put-in. It cuts the trip to nine miles (plus the eight mile paddle out) and eliminates the meanders. Keep equipment to an absolute minimum if you plan on hiking out the Roberson Trail (See the Bruneau description for details). Winter Camp is about 18 miles south on the Clover Three-Creek Road from the Bruneau take-out at Hot Springs. To get to Clover Flat continue south on Clover Three-Creek Road another 10 miles. See graph page 223.

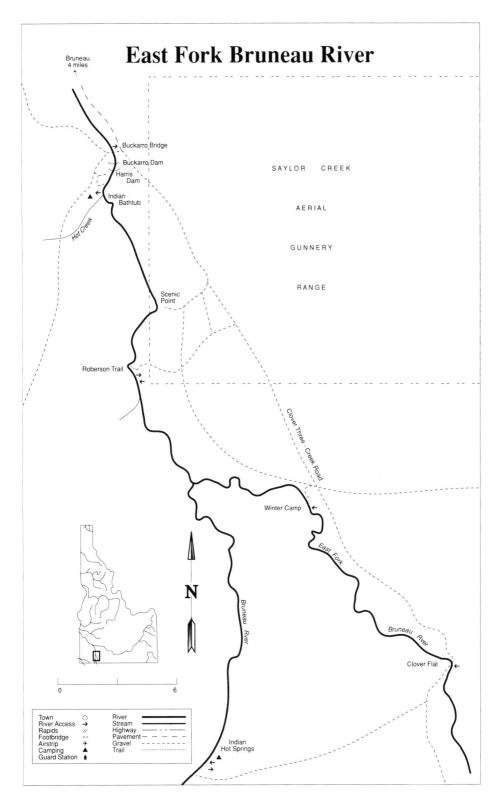

East Fork Bruneau River

Bruneau
4 miles

Buckarro Bridge

Buckarro Dam

Harris
Dam

Indian
Bathtub

Hot Creek

SAYLOR   CREEK

AERIAL

GUNNERY

RANGE

Scenic
Point

Roberson Trail

Clover Three - Creek Road

Winter Camp

East Fork

N

Bruneau River

Bruneau River

Clover Flat

Town	○	River	
River Access	→	Stream	
Rapids	//	Highway	
Footbridge	)(	Pavement	
Airstrip	✦	Gravel	
Camping	▲	Trail	
Guard Station	⬟		

0   6

Indian
Hot Springs

WEST FORK BRUNEAU RIVER

CLASS	LEVEL	LENGTH	GRADIENT	TIME
IV (V)	900-1,500 cfs*	28 miles	43 fpm	2 days
IV-V	>1,500 cfs			

PUT-IN:	Rowland Nevada (4,900 ft.)
TAKE-OUT:	Indian Hot Springs (3,700 ft.)
SHUTTLE:	34 miles
CRAFT:	Kayak
PORTAGES:	0 (3 recommended)
SEASON:	May, June
GAUGE:	Bruneau
PERMIT:	No
MAPS:	Indian H.S., Triguero Lake, Triplet Btt., Rowland
CHARACTER:	Desert river, technical, rock-gardens, ledges, deep canyon, wilderness.

DESCRIPTION: The toughest whitewater in the Bruneau Basin is on the West Fork. Introductions like this keep this run from getting the use it deserves. The West Fork is not run more often because it has a reputation for being nasty: not true. It's a beautiful canyon, filled with wildlife, birds of prey and scenery beyond compare.

It does, however, have some impressive whitewater. The rapids are narrow, long and rocky with eddies large enough for only two or three boats. Some sections are very technical, requiring lots of rock dodging and eddy hopping. The harder sections of this river are also the most difficult to scout.

There are some interesting ledge drop rapids, many have to be run at angles because of the vertical drop and closeness of other boulders. There are lots of blind-corners and blind-drops. Most of the difficult sections are easy to spot, but, take a topographical map and keep a close eye on it.

There are three recommended portages. All of them have been run. However, one is a killer and the others are potential killers. The first, Pintoe, named after yours truly after a toe-crushing vertical pin, is only a few miles below the put-in. The second, Al Beam Falls, is relatively short, about 100 yards, it is more or less a boulder sieve. The basalt boulders and riverbed in this part of Idaho act like glue on plastic boats, so keep this in mind while scouting and planning routes. The feasibility of running the rapid depends on the flow. At any level it's a hard class V. The portage is on the right.

The third portage is Julie Wilson Falls, and it's a long one. It's named after an Atlanta boater who died here in 1974. The entrance is very deceptive. It would be easy to be swept into the rapid before you realized where you were. The take-out for this portage is marked by a bunch of overhanging trees on the left bank after a good length of class II and III water. Right after the trees, the water gets rough fast. Some people run the first half of the rapid. The portage route is up the hill on the left bank. Keep climbing until you find the Julie Wilson gravesite. Then continue across the flat on top until you can see the water below has calmed. Be careful not to come down too soon.

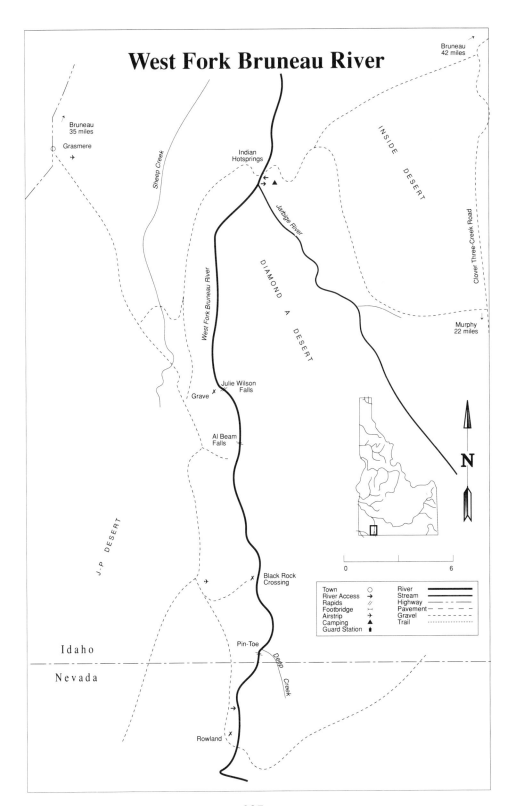

West Fork Bruneau River

The put-in is just south of the state line near Rowland Nevada. From Bruneau go south 35 miles on highway 51 to Grasmere. Less than a mile south of Grasmere, the road to Rowland veers off to the southeast.

*On the Bruneau gauge near Hot Springs.

E.S.

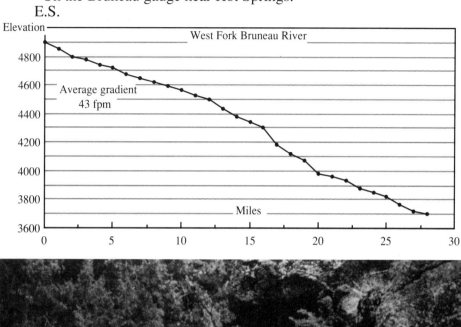

East Fork oasis.

Looking at Julie Wilson Falls. Photo: Rob Lesser

JARBIDGE RIVER

CLASS	LEVEL	LENGTH	GRADIENT	TIME
III-IV	600-1,500 cfs*	25 (24) miles	51 fpm	1 day
IV	>1,500 cfs			

PUT-IN: Below Murphy Hot Springs (4,900 ft.)
TAKE-OUT: Indian Hot Springs (3,700 ft.)
SHUTTLE: 45 miles
CRAFT: Kayak, canoe
PORTAGES: 0 (1 recommended)
SEASON: May
GAUGE: Bruneau
PERMIT: No
MAPS: Indian H.S., Inside Lakes, The Arch, Poison Btt., Dishpan, Murphy H.S.
CHARACTER: Desert creek, technical, boulder-choked rapids, logjams, wilderness.

DESCRIPTION: Jarbidge is a Shoshoni word roughly translated as "devil" or "monster." It has no relation to the whitewater. The scenery needs no translation; the Jarbidge is one of the most beautiful places I've ever been. There is no describing it; you must see it for yourself.

Most of the whitewater isn't difficult, but there are lots of undercuts and sweepers. At all but high flows, expect to bounce off some rocks. Be careful, there is no hiking out. The river can be done in a day, but you'd be missing the point. The start of the run is easy swift water. A few miles down some small rapids start appearing. There are two difficult and tricky rapids as well as a recommended portage, Jarbidge Falls. The major rapids are boulder-choked affairs consisting of steep drops, tight chutes and broach and pin possibilities. The first is about half-way down the run and the second a few miles further. Both are easily portaged. Jarbidge Falls is about five miles up from the confluence with the Bruneau. It can be easily spotted. Look for a giant rock slide on the right bank that comes down and into the river. The trail is on the left. It's rudimentary and surrounded by poison ivy, but not too difficult. Kayakers should be able to be back in their boats in less than 10 minutes. If you like to hike, the side canyons along the Jarbidge are great little places to explore. There is a natural arch three miles up Cougar Creek.

The shuttle is almost all on dirt. If it has been raining, the road into Indian Hot Springs might not be passable. From Bruneau, the take-out is 41 miles out the Clover Three-Creek Road and another 15 across the desert to the west. The turnoff is about a mile south of the Clover Flat Crossing where the road takes a diving turn. See the map. The put-in is another 24 miles south on the Clover Three Creek Road, nine miles west to Murphy and two more downstream.

*On the Bruneau gauge near Hot Springs.

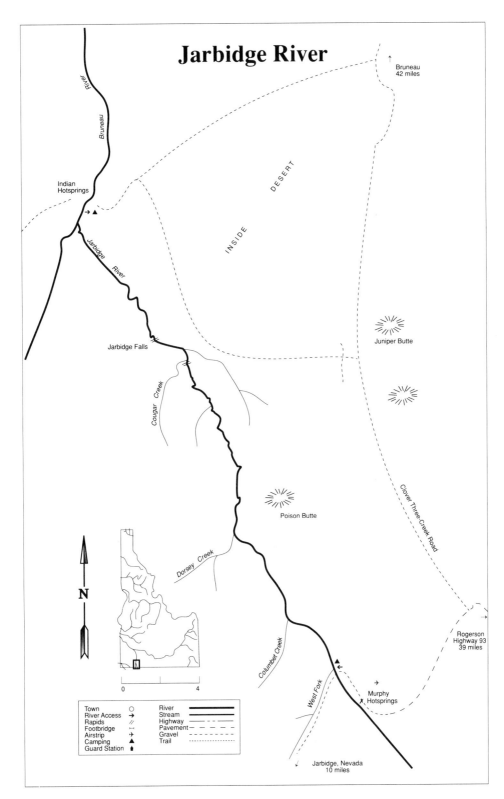

Jarbidge River

Bruneau
42 miles

D E S E R T

I N S I D E

Bruneau River

Indian
Hotsprings

Jarbidge River

Juniper Butte

Jarbidge Falls

Cougar Creek

Clover Three-Creek Road

Poison Butte

Dorsey Creek

N

Columbet Creek

West Fork

Rogerson
Highway 93
39 miles

Murphy
Hotsprings

Jarbidge, Nevada
10 miles

0   4

Town	○	River	▬▬▬
River Access	→	Stream	
Rapids	//	Highway	— —
Footbridge	⊢⊣	Pavement	—
Airstrip	⊣→	Gravel	– – –
Camping	▲	Trail	··········
Guard Station	♦		

Black basalt and whitewater on the West Fork.

232

A typical Jarbidge scene.

The Snake is famous for big surf waves. The Idaho Connection in Murtaugh Canyon. Photo: Rob Lesser

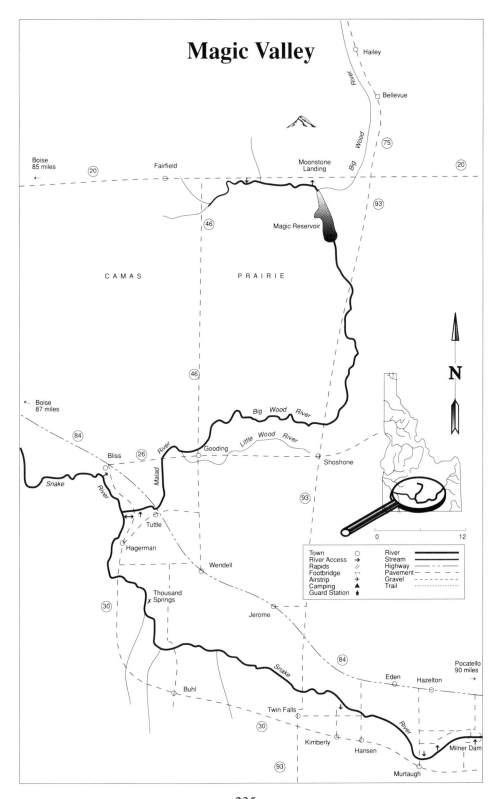

Magic Valley

Hailey

River

Bellevue

Big Wood

75

93

Boise
85 miles

20

Fairfield

Moonstone
Landing

20

46

Magic Reservoir

CAMAS

PRAIRIE

N

46

Boise
87 miles

Big   Wood   River

84

Little   Wood   River

Bliss

26

River

Gooding

Shoshone

Malad

Snake

River

93

Tuttle

Hagerman

Wendell

Thousand
Springs

30

Jerome

Snake

84

Pocatello
90 miles

Eden

Hazelton

Buhl

Twin Falls

River

30

Kimberly

Hansen

Milner Dam

93

Murtaugh

Town	○	River	—
River Access	→	Stream	—
Rapids	//	Highway	—·—
Footbridge	⊢⊣	Pavement	—
Airstrip	✈	Gravel	---
Camping	▲	Trail	⋯
Guard Station	⬥		

0   12

SNAKE RIVER, WILEY REACH

CLASS	LEVEL	LENGTH	GRADIENT	TIME
II-III	5,000-20,000 cfs	5 miles	14 fpm	2-6 hours

PUT-IN: Malad River Confluence (2,730 ft.)
TAKE-OUT: Shoestring Road Bridge (2,660 ft.)
SHUTTLE: 6 miles
CRAFT: Kayak, canoe, raft
PORTAGES: 0
SEASON: All Year
GAUGE: King Hill
PERMIT: No
MAPS: Hagerman, Bliss
CHARACTER: Big gentle river, nice scenery, road, secluded.

DESCRIPTION: Also known as the Bliss Run, this is one of the few runs in Idaho that can be boated year-round. The valley has its own little micro-climate. Both the air and water temperature are mild. Most of the stretch is a pleasant float through the protected farmland of the Hagerman Valley. The world's largest trout ranch is upstream. Thousand Springs, the outlet for the Lost Rivers is upstream as well. There is a house designed by Frank Lloyd Wright along the shuttle route.

What about whitewater? Well, about halfway down the run, marked by a sharp turn in the river, there's a big class III. It's straight forward as long as you go off in the right place. The run's highlight is the big surf waves. They're hard to catch, but once you're up — you'll know why they call it Bliss. They call it the Wiley Reach because the backwaters from the proposed Wiley Dam would inundate this entire run.

To find the put-in, get off Interstate 84 at exit 141 and go five miles on highway 30 towards Hagerman. When you reach the Malad River, cross the bridge, turn right and follow the dirt road down to the Snake River. The take-out is found by going back across the bridge and taking the first road to the left, keeping close to the river until the road crosses the river.

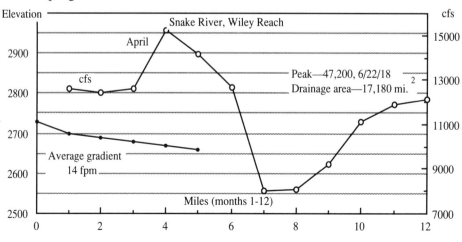

236

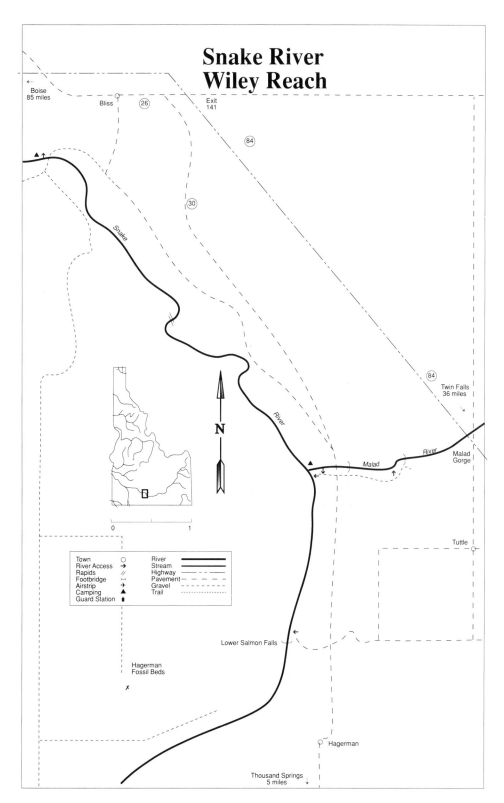

Snake River
Wiley Reach

Boise
85 miles

Bliss

26

Exit
141

84

30

Snake

84

Twin Falls
36 miles

N

River

Malad

River

Malad
Gorge

0   1

Town	○	River	
River Access	→	Stream	
Rapids	//	Highway	
Footbridge	⊢	Pavement	
Airstrip	↦	Gravel	
Camping	▲	Trail	
Guard Station	♠		

Tuttle

Lower Salmon Falls

Hagerman
Fossil Beds

✗

Hagerman

Thousand Springs
5 miles

237

MALAD RIVER

CLASS	LEVEL	LENGTH	GRADIENT	TIME
III-IV	300-800 cfs	2 miles	90 fpm	1 hour
IV	800-1,500 cfs			

PUT-IN:	At the locked gate (3,000 ft.)
TAKE-OUT:	Pool above the Snake Confluence (2,730 ft.)
SHUTTLE:	2 miles
CRAFT:	Kayak
PORTAGES:	1
SEASON:	March, April, May, June
GAUGE:	Malad River
PERMIT:	No
MAPS:	Bliss, Tuttle
CHARACTER:	Steep-creek, extremely rocky, dangerous diversion dams, intrusive power developments, road.

DESCRIPTION: Every whitewater boater should stop at the Malad Gorge when traversing southern Idaho on highway 84. The whitewater run is downstream: the Gorge is for visualization only. The Malad dives through one of the most spectacular river canyons in Idaho. Unfortunately, the guardrails on the bridges prevent highway travellers from seeing the gorge. Thousands of people drive over this little gem every day, cursing the monotony of the desert, oblivious to the beauty directly below them.

Downstream, and out of sight around the corner, is the dam for the Upper Malad Project and the put-in for the Malad run. The Malad consists of two short class IV sluice boxes, they're both a jumble of rocks and ledges. The put-in for the upper is below the first diversion dam, at the locked gate. The hardest rapid is just above the backwater created by the lower dam. The dam's backwater is actually moving swiftly towards the diversion and penstock. This is not a place to swim, or even roll, so be very careful or avoid this altogether.

If the lower section is not dewatered, portage the dam and get back in, otherwise this is the take-out. The lower run starts hard and eases off, opposite of the upper. Get out on the left in the pool at the confluence with the Snake.

If you're looking at the topos and can't find the Malad, don't be discouraged. On some maps it appears as the Big Wood, on others it is the Malad. It was originally named Malad, French for "sick", after a group of trappers became sick while exploring the area. It was changed to the Big Wood by the U.S.G.S. board of names in the '60s. In the '70s it was changed again, back to Malad. For people with erroneous maps here are the directions for finding the Malad: Look for the Big Wood or get off Interstate 84 at exit 141 and follow highway 30 five miles towards Hagerman. The road to the put-in and the take-out is on the east side of the river.

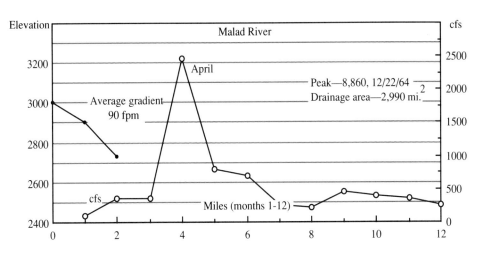

Malad River

Elevation / cfs

Average gradient
90 fpm

April

Peak—8,860, 12/22/64
Drainage area—2,990 mi.^{2}

cfs

Miles (months 1-12)

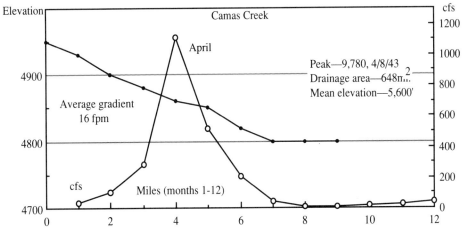

Camas Creek

Elevation / cfs

Average gradient
16 fpm

April

Peak—9,780, 4/8/43
Drainage area—648m.^{2}
Mean elevation—5,600'

cfs

Miles (months 1-12)

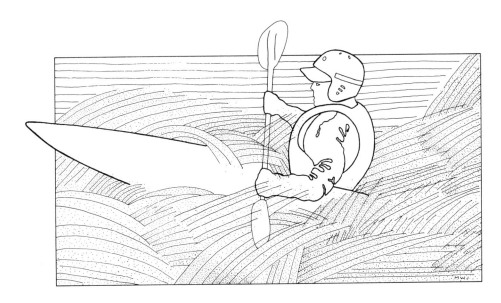

239

CAMAS CREEK

CLASS	LEVEL	LENGTH	GRADIENT	TIME
III	500-2,000 cfs	9 (7) miles	16 fpm	3-5 hours

PUT-IN:	Blain Bridge (4,950 ft.)
TAKE-OUT:	Moonstone Landing (4,800 ft.)
SHUTTLE:	9 miles
CRAFT:	Kayak, canoe, small raft
PORTAGES:	0
SEASON:	April, May
GAUGE:	Near Blain*
PERMIT:	No
MAPS:	Fairfield 15', Blain 15'
CHARACTER:	Small creek, gravel river bed changing to pool-drop, basalt canyon, wildlife, secluded.

DESCRIPTION: Camas Creek is a beautiful little springtime run. It flows through a oasis-like canyon hidden in the expanse of the Camas Prairie. The window on high flows is very brief, unfortunately when the water is high enough to float, the access roads are usually either mud holes or snow covered.

In the canyon, expect to see a variety of wildlife; waterfowl, deer and antelope winter along Camas Creek. This is actually a reason not to make this run; you'll be disturbing pairs of nesting Honkers and exposing their unprotected nests to predators.

From the put-in to the Macon Sheep Bridge (an alternative put-in) there are no major rapids. Beware of the bridge when the water's high, it can be covered, or worse, not quite covered by the water. The banks are willow-lined, so getting out can be tricky. The gauge and a small shrine are on the left bank. Below the bridge the canyon walls close in, and the creek's character changes from swift water to pool-drop. There are six distinct rapids from Macon Bridge to the lake, all obvious, all basically run down the middle.

The shuttle for Camas Creek is on highway 20. From Fairfield, drive 10 miles east on highway 20 to mile 163 and look for the West Magic Road heading off to the south. If you pass the Princess Mine/Blain Road, you've gone too far. Take the road south about a half-mile to the Blain Bridge put-in. If the prairie is covered with snow, start near mile 160 on highway 20, where the creek can be seen from the road.

The take-out at the Moonstone boat ramp is just past mile 170. It's a short drive down to the reservoir. If you want to trade the paddle out on Magic Reservoir for a steep hill-climb, you can drive to the canyon rim above where the creek hits the reservoir's backwaters and hike up the hill. Where the power lines cross the highway, look for a gate, and some corrals, on the south. Take the road through the gate, to a fork in the road, go left to the canyon rim.

*See the appendix for the rating table.

See graph page 239.

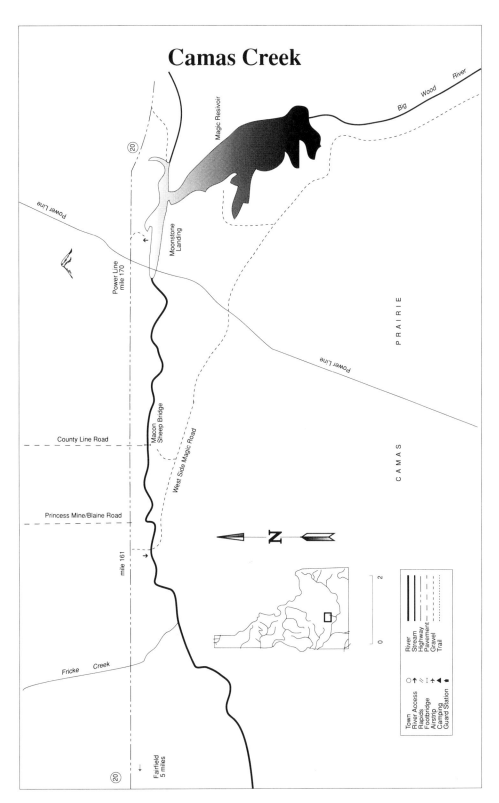

Camas Creek

Big Wood River

Magic Resivoir

Power Line

(20)

Power Line
mile 170

Moonstone
Landing

Power Line

PRAIRIE

County Line Road

Macon
Sheep Bridge

West Side Magic Road

Princess Mine/Blaine Road

mile 161

CAMAS

N

Fricke Creek

Fairfield
5 miles

(20)

Town
River Access
Rapids
Footbridge
Airstrip
Camping
Guard Station

River
Stream
Highway
Pavement
Gravel
Trail

0   2

SNAKE RIVER, MURTAUGH CANYON

CLASS	LEVEL	LENGTH	GRADIENT	TIME
III-IV	900 cfs	13 miles	26 fpm	4 hours
III-IV (V)	1,000-8,000 cfs			
IV (V)	8,000-17,000 cfs			

PUT-IN:	Murtaugh Bridge (3,825 ft.)
TAKE-OUT:	Twin Falls Res. Boat Ramp (3,515 ft.)
SHUTTLE:	14 miles
CRAFT:	Kayak, canoe, raft
PORTAGES:	0 (1 recommended)
SEASON:	All year
GAUGE:	Milner
PERMIT:	No
MAPS:	Murtaugh, Eden, Kimberly
CHARACTER:	Big desert river, ledge drops, big waves and holes, surf insanity, deep canyon, secluded.

DESCRIPTION: Murtaugh Canyon is a great example of what the Snake River has to offer. This is a run with two faces. When the water's high, the rapids are big, and it packs a punch. It also packs some of the best surfing anywhere, including The Idaho Connection. When the water's low, around 1,000 cfs, the river bed shows some character in a series of runnable ledge drops ranging from 5 to 10 feet.

The scenery is framed by the towering cliffs of the Snake River Canyon. Waterfalls spill down the canyon side keeping the surrounding plants green even in the heat of summer.

The river bed is composed of the same jointed basalt that covers the Idaho Desert. The first rapid, right below the bridge at the put-in, is an example of what to expect downstream. Most of the rapids are formed by resistant ridges of basalt running perpendicular to the river bed. The resulting rapids are filled with big waves and sticky holes: approach horizon lines with caution.

The hole on river right at Pair-A-Dice rapid, just up from the Hansen Bridge, is a wicked example of the hydraulics created by these ledges. If no one in your party has done the run before, drive over the Hansen Bridge and have a look at this monster. Bring some binoculars — it's a very tall bridge. Pair-A-Dice is a strong class V, please don't go in the hole. The waves are much larger than they look from the island, and mistake could put you in the reversal.

Scout or portage on the left island. There is a natural cleft in the rock about the size of a small raft. Pull your stuff well up out of the way if you're going to scout or hang out. If another group should pull up and find the take-out jammed, they might be, understandably, somewhat upset.

Just downstream is another big drop, Lets Make A Deal. This is a series of islands, a gauntlet of sorts, that cross the river. The run becomes progressively harder each door to the right, left is easiest, second from the left is best.

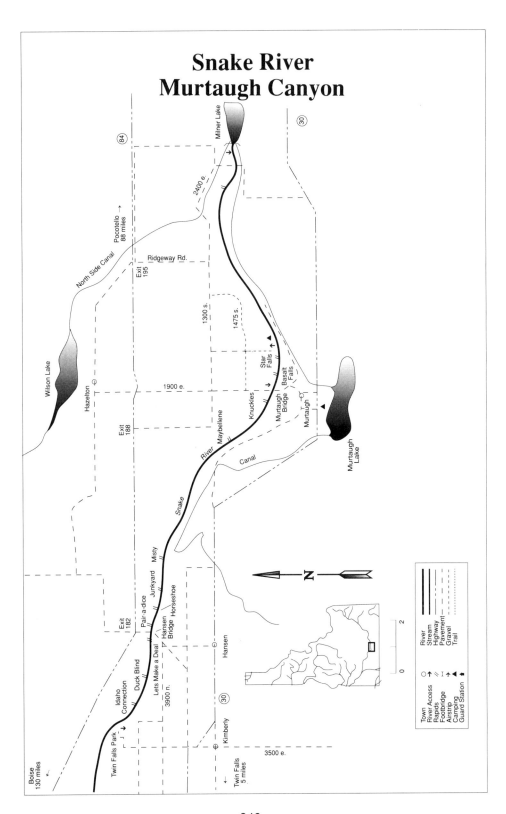

Snake River
Murtaugh Canyon

Milner Lake

(84)

(30)

2400 e.

North Side Canal

Pocotello
88 miles →

Ridgeway Rd.

Exit 195

1300 s.

1475 s.

Wilson Lake

Hazelton

1900 e.

Star Falls

Basalt Falls

Knuckles

Murtaugh Bridge

Exit 188

Murtaugh

Maybellene

River

Murtaugh Lake

Canal

Snake

Misty

Junkyard

Pair-a-dice

Horseshoe

Exit 182

Hansen Bridge

Duck Blind

Idaho Connection

Lets Make a Deal

3900 n.

Hansen

(30)

Kimberly

Twin Falls Park

3500 e.

Boise
130 miles →

Twin Falls
5 miles →

N

Town
River Access
Rapids
Footbridge
Airstrip
Camping
Guard Station

River
Stream
Highway
Pavement
Gravel
Trail

0   1   2

Avoid the ones on the right except when the river is low and the left doors are dry.

The Idaho Connection is about 300 yards up from the end of the run at the backwater of the lake formed by Twin Falls. At flows above 15,000, people have been known to put in at the take-out, paddle the mile up the lake just to surf their brains out.

The shuttles difficult because of the lack of land marks and the millions of farm roads. To find the take-out from highway 84, get off at exit 182. Go south over the Hansen Bridge (look at Pair-a-Dice) take the first right, 3900 n. and go west three miles. Turn to the north on 3500 e. and follow it down into the canyon, through the park, and to the take-out. From Twin Falls there are signs marking the way starting on Blue Lakes Blvd. To find the put-in, drive back out of the canyon and go south to highway 30 and into Kimberly. Follow highway 30 to the west through Hansen to Murtaugh. At mile 237 turn left on 4525 e.. Drive north a few blocks to Boyd St.. Go left again and take the first right (before the post office, zip 83344). Another quick right will take you over the railroad tracks and down to a T in the road. You're almost there, go left and down into the canyon. From the highway it's much easier, get off highway 84 at exit 188, and go south three miles. Then go east one mile, and then south on 1900 e., a little over two miles and the road will drop into the canyon. You can also start a mile upstream, below Star Falls. This will give you an extra mile, and a good sample of the run's character. To get to Star Falls, go back the way you came and follow the signs to Caldron Linn. Once out of the canyon, take 1475 s. to the right, west, one mile. Turn right, across the field and down into the canyon. Look at Star Falls, then put in below it.

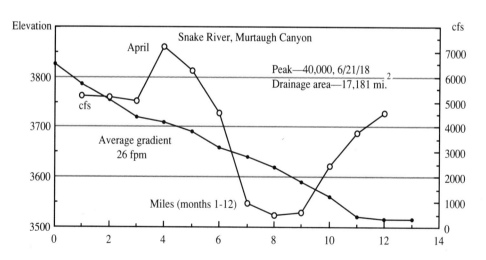

244

Grant Amaral running Pair-a-Dice at 16,000.

SNAKE RIVER, MILNER GORGE

CLASS	LEVEL	LENGTH	GRADIENT	TIME
V	12,000-15,000 cfs	6 miles	28 fpm	2 hours

PUT-IN: Milner Dam (4,075 ft.)
TAKE-OUT: Above Star Falls (3,190 ft.)
SHUTTLE: 9 miles
CRAFT: Kayak
PORTAGES: 0
SEASON: March, April, May, June
GAUGE: Milner
PERMIT: No
MAPS: Milner, Milner Btt., Murtaugh
CHARACTER: Rare steep and big river, huge waves and holes, fractured basalt river bed, remote.

DESCRIPTION: Rob Lesser calls the Milner run on the Snake "the biggest big-water in Idaho." The first mile contains all the ingredients necessary for superlative big water: size, definition and drop. This is a solid class V run for focused experts.

The size is obvious. The optimal flow is big — between 12,000 and 15,000. At higher flows the river becomes even more intimidating. At lower flows, the definition, becomes too well defined, doubling the backwash in the holes.

Don't be deceived by the average gradient, the first mile drops almost 100 feet. The other five miles are a flat water float. Gradients of 100 fpm and flows of 15,000 are a rare combination. Imagine your favorite steep creek flowing at 15,000 cfs.

The river bed is jointed basalt with lots of ledges and sinkholes. These rapids, or rapid because it's non-stop, are big and powerful. The run consists of big waves and huge holes. At the top the line threads down dodging between the holes. The size of the water makes it very difficult to stay on the line, but with some speed, luck and skill, most of the holes can be punched. As the river turns the corner it is important to start the move to line up for the river-wide wall-of-water just downstream. This wave should give you an idea of definition in big water and either make or break your day.

Things start to calm down after this last move and just downstream the whitewater comes to an abrupt end. All that remains is five miles of scenery and flat water. If it's big water you're after, the lower five can be eliminated by taking out where the water flattens out and hiking up the south side of the canyon. A dirt road leads back to the put-in. A pick-up truck and shuttle driver make it possible to run this stretch several times in a day, though you'll probably think better of that.

At the end of the flat water section is Star Falls. Also known as Caldron Linn, this is an unrunnable drop of over 30 feet. Look for the road coming down the right bank signaling the take-out. Get out on the north or river right, above Star Falls. If the whitewater starts to pick up after miles of flat water, smile and wave because you're about to attempt a first descent.

In 1811 this run was, perhaps, the site of the first whitewater accident in Idaho. A group of explorers, known to most high school students as the Astorians, tried to canoe this stretch. The best canoeist in the group, Antoine Clappine, hit a rock, overturned and drowned. The rest of the party walked downstream to scout, looked at Cauldron Linn, abandoned their canoes and portaged the rest of the West.

In 1988, Milner Dam underwent Federal Energy Regulatory Commission review to examine the impact of rebuilding the dam with an additional diversion for a hydro project which will return the water below Star Falls, thus partially dewatering the whitewater stretch and making it too low to paddle except during extremely high run-off years. In the fall of 1988, FERC held a hearing in Twin Falls, on the proposed Star Falls Project. There were about 100 people at the meeting, 95 farmers and 5 kayakers: Rob Lesser, Tom Wittaker, Tony Brennan, Clinton LaTourrette and myself. Surprise — the project was approved.

To find the put-in at Milner Dam, get off highway 84 at exit 194. Go south three miles on Ridgeway Road. Turn left on 1300 south, and go east for 1.5 miles. The road will twist back to the north; don't worry. Cross the canals and turn right on 2400 east. Go a little more than a mile, turn to the right and cross back over the canals and drop down into the canyon and the put-in. To take out at the end of the whitewater, follow the road on the south of the canyon along the canal until you can see the river. To find Cauldron Linn, go back the way you came, except continue west on 1300 s., one mile past Ridgeway Road, then go south one mile. The road will zig-zag to the west and after 3.5 miles, go south one mile and down into the canyon to Cauldron Linn.

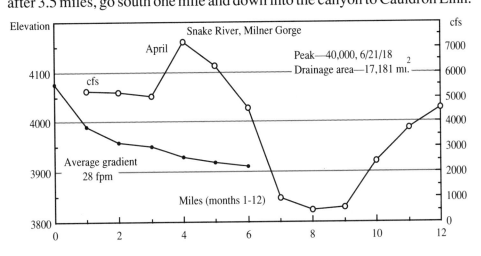

247

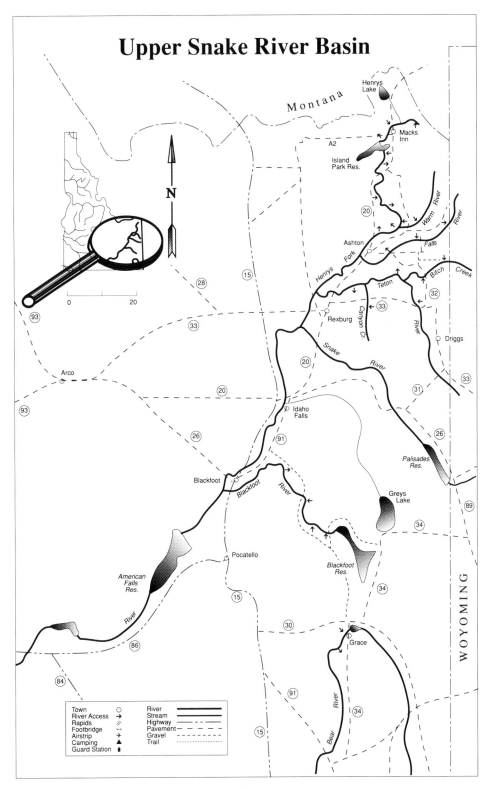

Upper Snake River Basin

BLACKFOOT RIVER, CANYON RUN

CLASS	LEVEL	LENGTH	GRADIENT	TIME
III-IV	350-500 cfs	8 miles	79 fpm	5 hours
IV-V	500-900 cfs			

PUT-IN:	Trail Creek Bridge (5,510 ft.)
TAKE-OUT:	Cedar Creek near Alridge (4,800 ft.)
SHUTTLE:	11 miles
CRAFT:	Kayak
PORTAGES:	0
SEASON:	May, June, July
GAUGE:	Blackfoot Reservoir
PERMIT:	No
MAPS:	Miner Creek, Higham Peak, Goshen
CHARACTER:	Steep creek, canyon, rock-gardens, dam, removed road, secluded.

DESCRIPTION: This is the only major correction for the second printing. The first printing gave the Blackfoot a bad name. It's not true. The rapids have fallen to improved technique and equipment and the poison ivy to my machete. This is a great summer whitewater run.

The rapids consist of steep jumbles of sharp rock. In addition to the countless rock-gardens, there are three standout rapids and another that is usually portaged.

Blackfoot Dam regulates the flow, 500 cfs is the summer average, and prevents the canyon from ever getting a good flush. The result is a huge forest of poison ivy growing right up to and into the river. Don't go in here unless you're immune to poison ivy or can boat class V with a smile on your face.

To get to the take-out from Blackfoot, go north on highway 91. After milepost 110, go east on Wolverine Road (375 n.) 10 miles, at the fork in the road, take the Blackfoot River Road 1400 e., to the right and follow the canyon. After about 3.5 miles the road crosses Cedar Creek, there are some derelict buildings on the right. Go through the gate and follow the primitive road down until you can go no further. You will have to walk your boats 100 yards up Cedar Creek. Or two miles downstream, or on the road back towards town, there's a steep road leading down to a gauge. The put-in is seven miles south of Cedar Creek, below the bridge.

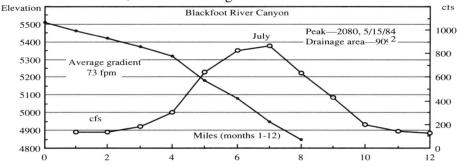

250

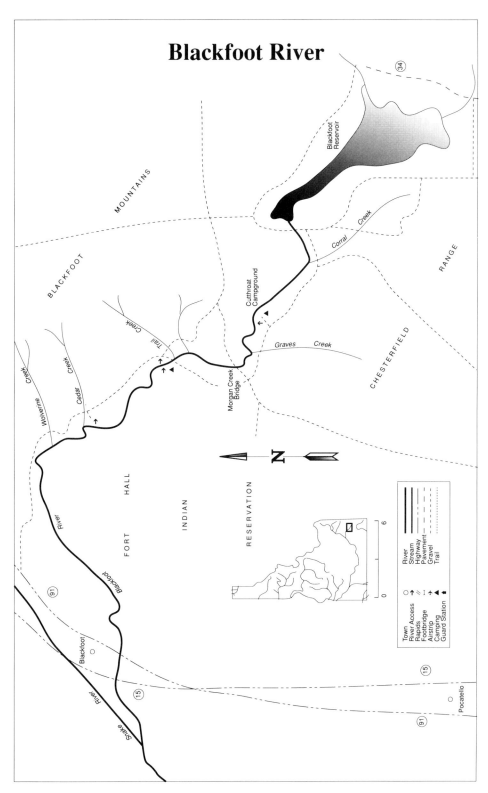

Blackfoot River

BLACKFOOT RIVER, CUTTHROAT RUN

CLASS	LENGTH	GRADIENT	LEVEL	TIME
II	12 miles	28 fpm	550 cfs	8 hours

PUT-IN:	Cutthroat Trout Campground (5,840 ft.)
TAKE-OUT:	Trail Creek Bridge (5,510 ft.)
SHUTTLE:	14 miles
CRAFT:	Kayak, canoe, raft
PORTAGES:	0
SEASON:	May, June, July
GAUGE:	Blackfoot Reservoir
PERMIT:	No
MAPS:	Paradise Valley, Dunn Basin, Miner Creek
CHARACTER:	Low gradient, intermediate river, secluded.

DESCRIPTION: This is a straight forward class II, canoe or beginner kayak run. Summer flows, close to 500 cfs, are controlled by Blackfoot Dam. The river starts off easy and picks up speed. The river bed is wide and littered with rocks. The scenery isn't spectacular, wide open sage covered hills, but it does improve to tolerable by the end of the run. The run can be cut in two at the Morgan Creek Bridge.

Follow the signs for the shuttle. You'll have to figure out the bullet hole punctuation. The scenery will inspire you to drive at a minimum of 70 mph. The sharp rocks in the road will either slow you down or give you a flat tire. If you get stuck out here, maybe one of the locals will take a break from shooting signs and help you out.

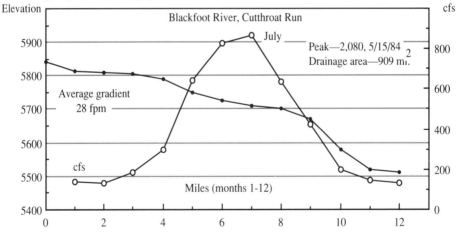

Bob McDougall surveying a highwater dream. Photo: Rob Lesser

CANYON CREEK

CLASS	LEVEL	LENGTH	GRADIENT	TIME
IV-V	100-200 cfs	15 (10) miles	67 fpm	8 hours

PUT-IN: Wright Creek (5,760 ft.)
TAKE-OUT: Old Teton Dam Site {(confl. 5,090 ft.) 5,030 ft.}
SHUTTLE: 10 miles
CRAFT: Kayak
PORTAGES: 10-15
SEASON: July
GAUGE: No
PERMIT: No
MAPS: Linderman Dam, Wright Creek
CHARACTER: Small steep-creek, sustained gradient, sweepers and logjams, technical, secluded.

DESCRIPTION: Jeb Blakely and some other Idaho Falls boaters made the first descent of Canyon Creek in the summer of 1987 at flows between 100 and 200 cfs. The first two miles are easy but covered by brush and trees. Under the highway 33 bridge the whitewater picks up. The drops are sheer boulder chutes into shallow pools. The run is choked with boulders, brush and logs. Running this stretch is a long-strenuous day and will test your equipment, so bring a spare paddle. There are over a dozen portages and twice as many dangerous situations. Be careful of blind corners because of all the sweepers.

The shuttle is straight forward. From highway 91 take highway 33 east to the Teton Dam Road. Go north 1.5 miles to the take-out. To get to the put-in get back on 33 and continue east. Go five miles to Canyon Creek, cross the bridge and drive about three miles up the east side of the canyon. Put in below Wright Creek at the old bridge. Green Canyon Hot Springs (developed with a fee) are up this road a couple more miles if you need to rest your weary bones.

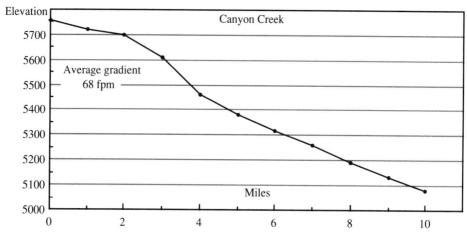

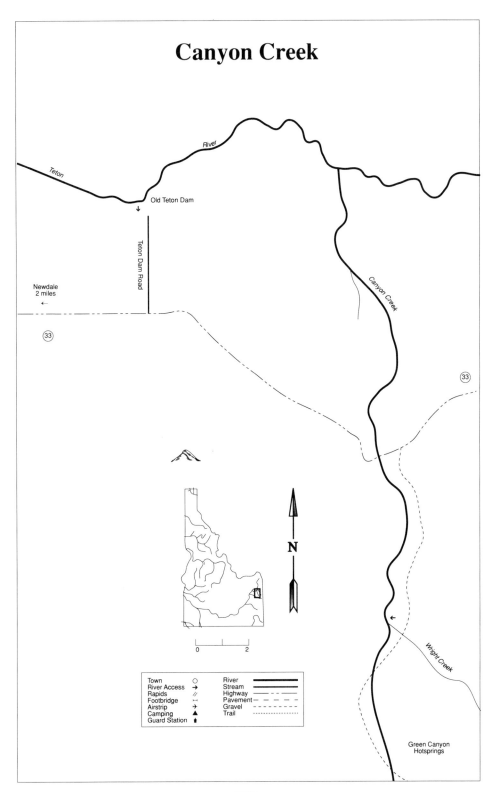

Canyon Creek

Teton

River

Old Teton Dam

Teton Dam Road

Newdale
2 miles

(33)

Canyon Creek

(33)

N

0   2

Town	○	River
River Access	→	Stream
Rapids	//	Highway
Footbridge	⊢⊣	Pavement
Airstrip	✈	Gravel
Camping	▲	Trail
Guard Station	✚	

Wright Creek

Green Canyon
Hotsprings

TETON RIVER

CLASS	LEVEL	LENGTH	GRADIENT	TIME
IV-V	500-2,000 cfs	15 miles	50 fpm	5 hours

PUT-IN:	Highway 33 Bridge (5,925 ft.)
TAKE-OUT:	Spring Hollow, South of France (5,170 ft.)
SHUTTLE:	22 miles
CRAFT:	Kayak
PORTAGES:	1 (2 recommended)
SEASON:	May, June
GAUGE:	Teton near St. Anthony*
PERMIT:	No
MAPS:	Tetonia, Packsaddle L., Drummond, Linderman Dam, *Targhee NF*
CHARACTER:	Small river, boulder-choked rapids, logs, canyon, secluded.

DESCRIPTION: This is not a run for the meek. The whitewater is difficult, class IV and V and even then, only the True Disciples are willing to travel into this country for a good splash in the face. This is the land that made Idaho famous: famous potatoes.

On a clear day the Tetons can be seen from the put-in. Once on the river, they are hidden from view by the canyon walls. The river starts slow with four miles of flat water. This should give you plenty of time to warm up. A farm road parallels the east bank for four miles if you want to avoid warming up. If so, put in near the relay station and warm up in the little play wave. The whitewater starts around the corner with class II-III rock garden that leads into a class V jumble of rocks. At most flows you can bounce down the right. The next rapid is a long and complex rock garden. A mile or two downstream, an eastern Idaho diversion dam creates an ugly class V mess. Don't expect the usual concrete weir, this one is made of boulders positioned across the river. Look for the old pumping platform on the left bank marking the rapid's start. The portage on the left is recommended. Be careful, almost every rock in the river has a log pinned to it.

Several smaller rapids follow and then the Felt Power Plant dewaters the river bed and must be portaged. You can get back in at the top of a long and complicated rock garden where most of the water is returned to the river or at the lower powerhouse. The road from Felt has a locked gate at the canyon rim, so if you want to use this as an access point, you're going to have to do some walking. One big rapid remains before the Bitch Creek Confluence. Below Bitch Creek, there are five more rapids. When the canyon was inundated by the backwaters of Teton Dam, the slumping of the canyon walls created these rapids. They have a pool-drop character: one mile of pool, one short drop. See the Bitch Creek description for directions to the take-out.

See graph page 261.

*See appendix for rating table.

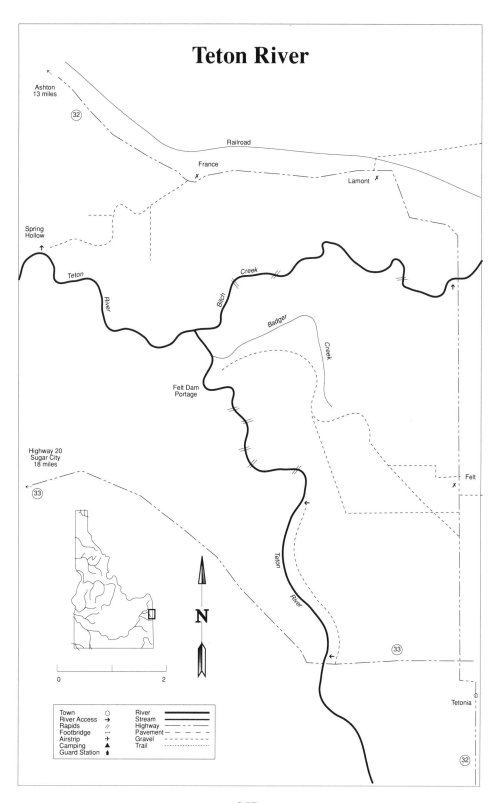

Teton River

Ashton
13 miles

(32)

Railroad

France ✗

Lamont ✗

Spring
Hollow

Teton

River

Creek

Bitch

Badger

Creek

Felt Dam
Portage

Highway 20
Sugar City
18 miles

(33)

Felt ✗

Teton

River

N

(33)

Tetonia

(32)

Town	○	River	
River Access	→	Stream	
Rapids	//	Highway	
Footbridge	⊦	Pavement	
Airstrip	⇥	Gravel	
Camping	▲	Trail	
Guard Station	⬩		

0   2

Roy Piskadlo looking for a soft landing on the Teton.

Mark White making a slow exit from Z-slot on Bitch Creek.

BITCH CREEK CANYON

CLASS	LEVEL	LENGTH	GRADIENT	TIME
IV	600-800 cfs	13 (8) miles	70 fpm	4-6 hours
IV-V	>800 cfs			

PUT-IN:	Highway 32 Bridge (5,850 ft.)
TAKE-OUT:	Spring Hollow {(confl. 5,290 ft.) 5,170 ft.}
SHUTTLE:	12 miles
CRAFT:	Kayak
PORTAGES:	0
SEASON:	May, June, July
GAUGE:	No
PERMIT:	No
MAPS:	Drummond, Lamont, *Targhee NF*
CHARACTER:	Steep-creek, narrow canyon, basalt ledges and long boulder-choked rapids, logjams, secluded, scenic.

DESCRIPTION: From the highway 32 bridge down to the Teton, Bitch Creek is a beautiful class IV-V run. The river starts off in a meadow and drops down into a fantastic gorge of basalt pinnacles and spires.

The whitewater is good as well. The rapids are formed by basalt ledges on the river bed and lots of boulders. There are hundreds of logs in the water, including several sneak-able logjams. If wood in the river makes you nervous, avoid this run. Literally, if there's a rock in the current, you can count on it at least one log being pinned to it. The put-in for Bitch Creek is on private land, so be polite and considerate. The whitewater picks up about a quarter-mile downstream from the put-in. Driscolls Drop is a long steep rapid, just below a right turn with a tall cliff on the right. Scout or portage on the right. Hansens Half-Mile is next: a continuous stretch of class III water, full of logs. The Z-Slot is the boulder choked rapid in the lower part of the river. You should be able to identify it with no hint other than its name. A gauntlet of boulders form the next rapid: Balls to the Wall. Look for the rock wall rising out of the water on the right downstream. It's a river-wide hole, known for trashing kayakers and stuffing them against the wall upside down.

After flowing into the Teton, five rapids remain. This stretch of the river was inundated by the backwaters of Teton Dam during its brief existence and failure in 1976. The rapids were created by the slumping of the canyon walls. Plans to rebuild the dam are currently floating around the Idaho Legislature.

The take-out is on the right after the power lines cross the canyon for the second time. Look for the road coming down a little canyon. It's pretty easy to find the take-out from the river, but to get a shuttle there is another story. From France, the big Pillsbury grain silo and railroad siding (remember the back cover of the Fall, 1988, Patagonia Catalog), go west past milepost 15. The road will start to climb a hill. At the bottom of the hill the road starts to curve to the right, and two roads come in from the left, take the gravel road (going almost due west). Follow it 1.5 miles to a fork in the road, stay left, on the gravel, and continue down into the canyon to Spring Hollow. Drive right over the old boat ramp and down the unimproved dirt road leading to the river. It may take a four-wheel drive to make it down here depending on the time of year and road conditions.

To get to the put-in go back to highway 32 and continue east. The road will swing to the south. Bitch Creek is at mile 8 and a road leads down to the river on the south, downstream of the bridge. Next to the old bridge, there's a stick gauge. The last time Bitch Creek was rated, 1977, 3.5 equalled 650 cfs and 4 equalled 1,100. Someone has been pulling on the upright and the stream-bed has undoubtably changed, but I'll bet this is closer than guessing.

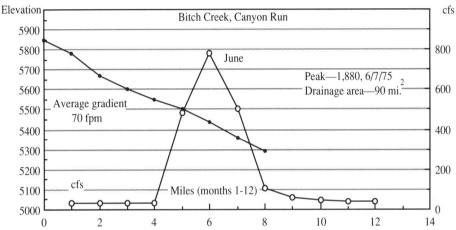

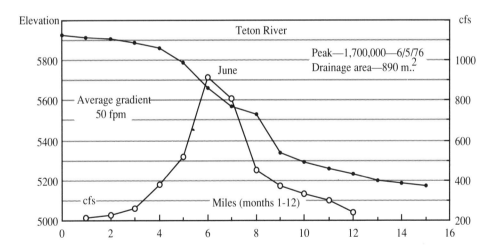

BITCH CREEK, COYOTE MEADOWS RUN

CLASS	LEVEL	LENGTH	GRADIENT	TIME
III-IV	500 cfs	10 miles	57 fpm	6-8 hours

PUT-IN:	Coyote Meadows (6,420 ft.)
TAKE-OUT:	Highway 32 Bridge (5,850 ft.)
SHUTTLE:	16 miles (+2 mile hike)
CRAFT:	Kayak
PORTAGES:	2 logs
SEASON:	May, June
GAUGE:	No
PERMIT:	No
MAPS:	Lamont, McRenolds Res., *Targhee NF*
CHARACTER:	Small scenic stream, meanders mixed with rapids, logjams and sweepers, secluded, wilderness.

DESCRIPTION: The upper run on Bitch Creek, though pretty, is not as spectacular as the other runs in the area. This run is for the boater who has done everything else in the area and wants to see the country.

The run is full of portages in the form of logs and sweepers, so it isn't just a pleasure cruise. There are several good drops mixed in as well, but for most of the run the river meanders through a mix of meadows and mountains.

To get to the put-in drive north at Lamont (mile post 12 on highway 32) one mile, turn to the east on road 700 n. and drive 13 miles to the Coyote Meadows picnic area and a trail head. Follow the trail (on foot) southeast a little over a mile to Crater Creek and the put-in. The take-out is the highway 32 bridge, mile post 8.

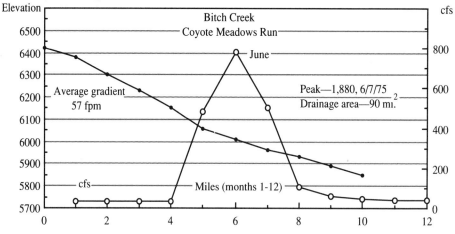

262

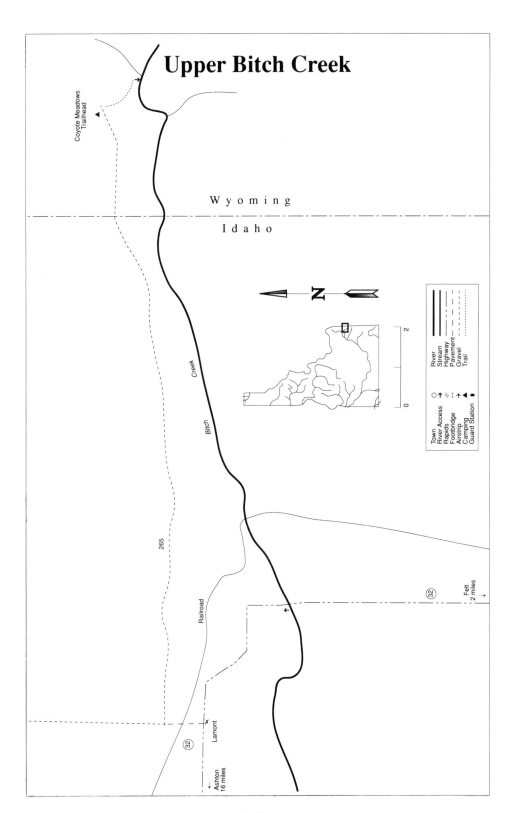

Upper Bitch Creek

Coyote Meadows
Trailhead

W y o m i n g

I d a h o

N

Bitch Creek

265

Railroad

Town
River Access
Rapids
Footbridge
Airstrip
Camping
Guard Station

River
Stream
Highway
Pavement
Gravel
Trail

32
Felt
2 miles

32
Lamont

Ashton
16 miles

FALLS RIVER, LOWER RUN

CLASS	LEVEL	LENGTH	GRADIENT	TIME
III	500-1,200 cfs	6 miles	47 fpm	4-6 hours
III-IV	>1,200 cfs			

PUT-IN:	Concrete C.C.C. Bridge (5,630 ft.)
TAKE-OUT:	Kirkham Bridge (5,330 ft.)
SHUTTLE:	15 miles
CRAFT:	Kayak, canoe, raft
PORTAGES:	0 (1 recommended)
SEASON:	April, May, June, July
GAUGE:	Squirrel
PERMIT:	No
MAPS:	Ashton, Warm River, Warm River Btt. (15'), *Targhee NF*
CHARACTER:	Small river, basalt canyon, secluded.

DESCRIPTION: The Fall River or Falls River — either way there's more at stake here than spelling (a USGS error not mine) — almost became the Dry River and still might. A hydro-power project completed in the spring of 1992 threatened to draw another 500 cfs from the river and essentially de-water this run for all but high water and the Fourth of July (the developer agreed to allow the river this one day of freedom).

Luckily or perhaps unluckily the canal wall failed and, unfortunately, spilled tons of silt into the Falls River and the Henrys Fork. The disaster even upset the folks at FERC. The project license is being reviewed.

The Falls is typical of many of the rivers of eastern Idaho — cutting a narrow basalt canyon through the potato fields. There are three rapids of note: one at the entrance of the canyon, another three miles downstream, and the last, Bobs Nemesis. All are fast, class III rock gardens.

To drive to the take-out, go three miles east of Ashton on 47 to milepost 3. Turn to the south on 3800 e. and go one mile. Turn left on 1200 n. and go two miles to the Kirkham Bridge. Take out downstream and river left. To get to the put-in, continue across the bridge to the east, go five miles to 4525 e.. Go north, one mile, to the concrete bridge. The surrounding land is private property. This is also the Cave Falls Run take-out.

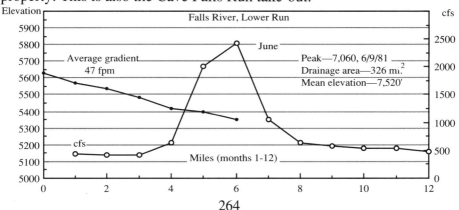

Falls River

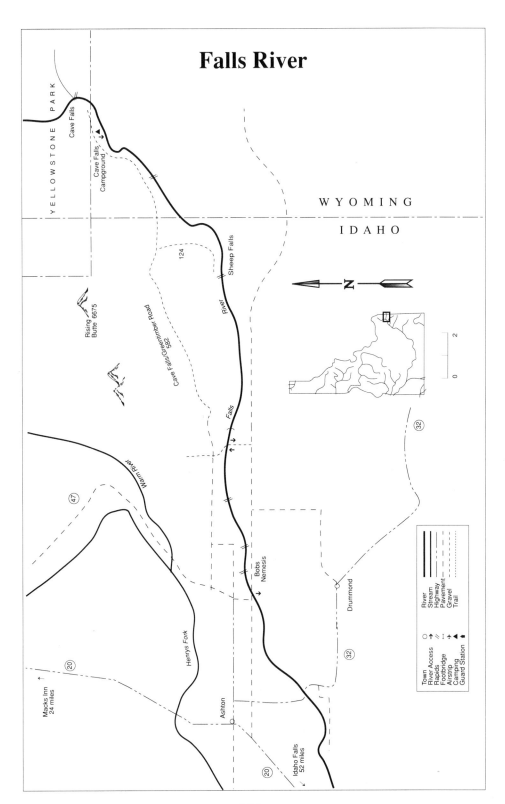

FALLS RIVER, CAVE FALLS RUN

CLASS	LEVEL	LENGTH	GRADIENT	TIME
III	500-1,000 cfs	14 miles	44 fpm	4-6 hours

PUT-IN:	Cave Falls Campground (6,240 ft.)
TAKE-OUT:	Concrete C.C.C. Bridge (5,630 ft.)
SHUTTLE:	20 miles
CRAFT:	Kayak
PORTAGES:	1 (3 recommended)
SEASON:	April, May, June, July
GAUGE:	Near Squirrel
PERMIT:	No
MAPS:	Warm River Btt. 15', Grassy Lake, Montana 15': *Targhee NF*
CHARACTER:	Small scenic river, gravel bed, falls, portage, secluded.

DESCRIPTION: The Cave Falls run on the Falls River starts near the boundary of Yellowstone Park. This is is a scenic run through bear country. It isn't a whitewater run — it's either too steep or too flat.

While the Falls River doesn't have a lot of whitewater, it does have a lot of portages, the first being two or three miles down. The rapid has been run, but it is usually jammed with logs, portage on the left. The second, Sheep Falls, has a big reversal at the bottom. This portage is on the right. Several diversion dams lie downstream. The Marysville Dam, just upstream from the take-out has been run, but the portage on the left is recommended.

The river bed is wide and for most of the run, gravel. The fishing is good and the scenery beautiful. Camping at Cave Falls is nice as well, if you like bears. Be careful, this is prime Grizzly habitat. Bechler Meadows, upstream from Cave Falls, was once the Bad Bear relocation area for misbehaving Yellowstone bears. Cave Falls Campground is subject to "Bear Closures" from time-to-time.

The take-out is the same as the put-in for the lower run, see the lower description for details. To get to the put-in from here, cross the bridge to the north and go one mile to the junction with Cave Falls Road or the Green Timber Road or 1400 n.(they are all the same road spelled differently to confuse tourists) and then go east 19 miles to the put-in.

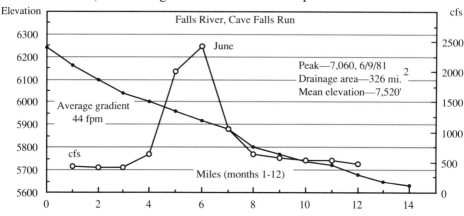

WARM RIVER

CLASS	LEVEL	LENGTH	GRADIENT	TIME
IV-VI	300-800 cfs	5 miles	84 fpm	3-4 hours

PUT-IN: Twisted Draw (5,710 ft.)
TAKE-OUT: Warm River Campground (5,290 ft.)
SHUTTLE: 10 miles
CRAFT: Kayak
PORTAGES: 2-10
SEASON: June, July
GAUGE: No
PERMIT: No
MAPS: Snake River Btt., Warm River, *Targhee NF*
CHARACTER: Extreme steep creek, severe boulder-choked rapids, jagged river bed, logjams, secluded, railroad.

DESCRIPTION: The upper part of this run is not recommended. It is mentioned here only as a record that it has been run and to answer any questions about what the Warm River has for whitewater. Doug Ammons and Monty Morevec made the only descent of the upper stretch in 1987. Below the Bear Gulch Ski Area, the run mellows considerably and contains some low-key whitewater.

The major rapids are formed as the river descends through two thick basalt flows, the same ones that form Upper and Lower Mesa Falls a few miles to the north on Henrys Fork. The rapids are long, complex and steep and all of them have several logs or sweepers. Due to the number of logs, only about 60 percent of this stretch has been run.

The river bed is composed of jointed basalt that is both extremely sharp and forms countless rock sieves. In fact, when judging the flow look at the rapids, not the flow at the put-in or the take-out; the river bed is so fractured that much of the flow percolates through the rock. The flow in every rapid is different and the flow at the take-out is roughly twice the flow of the rapids.

There are two different ways of reaching the put-in: one involves hiking two miles, the other driving right to the put-in. The hiking approach has its advantages, as it provides an opportunity to scout the rapids. To hike to the put-in, park at the Bear Gulch Ski Area and walk down to the railroad bed paralleling the river. Hike upstream two miles (yes, through the tunnel too), and put in where the river flattens and starts to meander. If you just walk down to the river and put in there without hiking upstream, the run is considerably less difficult. To drive to the put-in continue north on 47 to Forest Service road 367, turn right and go approximately two miles to a junction, turn right again and go approximately four miles. The road will start to double back and approach the river. Put in at the point furthest downstream and closest to the river.

D.A.

See graph page 275.

HENRYS FORK, LOWER MESA RUN

CLASS	LEVEL	LENGTH	GRADIENT	TIME
II	1,000-2,000 cfs	4 miles	35 fpm	2-4 hours

PUT-IN: Grandview, **below** Lower Mesa Falls (5,400 ft.)
TAKE-OUT: Warm River (5,260 ft.)
SHUTTLE: 4 miles
CRAFT: Kayak, canoe, raft, driftboat
PORTAGES: 0
SEASON: May, June, July
GAUGE: Near Ashton
PERMIT: No
MAPS: Snake River Butte, Warm River, *Targhee NF*
CHARACTER: Easy class II river, good fishing, secluded.

DESCRIPTION: This is a class V put-in for a class II run. The class V is the steep and long mountainside down to the river, not Lower Mesa Falls. Don't be deceived by the name of this run: Lower Mesa Falls is not part of it. The falls are for visualization only. The put-in is at the bottom of the incredibly steep hill at the lower end of the campground. If getting a kayak or canoe down here seems ridiculous, look at the rope burns on the trees: evidence of die-hard fishermen belaying drift-boats. If you are tough enough to walk down this hill, you don't need a river description. Well maybe a brief one. Look out for Surprise Falls, a small ledge about a mile downstream.

Take out at the bridge across Henrys Fork just out of Warm River. To get to the put-in go north on 47 seven miles to the Grandview Overlook. Make sure you are below Lower Mesa Falls (Yes, people have made this mistake). The camping is good at both the take-out and the put-in.

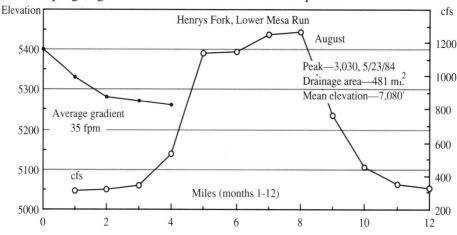

Henrys Fork

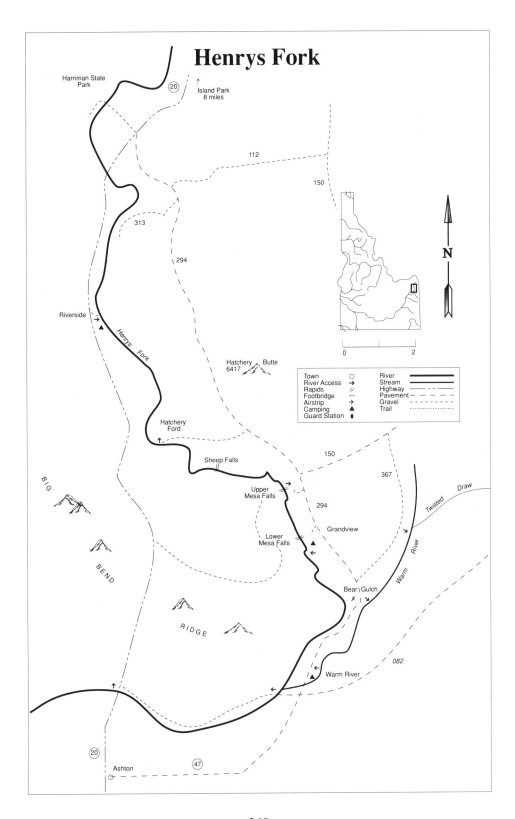

HENRYS FORK, SHEEP FALLS RUN

CLASS	LEVEL	LENGTH	GRADIENT	TIME
III-V	1,000-2,000 cfs	11 miles	38 fpm	4 hours

PUT-IN:	Riverside Campground (6,055 ft.)
TAKE-OUT:	**Above** Upper Mesa Falls (5,640 ft.)
SHUTTLE:	19 miles
CRAFT:	Kayak, canoe, raft
PORTAGES:	0 (2 recommended)
SEASON:	May, June, July
GAUGE:	Henrys Fork near Ashton
PERMIT:	No
MAPS:	Last Chance, Lookout Btt., Snake River Btt., *Targhee NF*
CHARACTER:	Small river, logs, scenic, falls, secluded.

DESCRIPTION: Starting from Riverside Campground this is a fun class III run. The whitewater starts just around the corner. The run starts in on open canyon blanketed with lodgepole pine. This stretch of the Henrys Fork is bear country as well as blue-ribbon trout fishing. Hatchery Ford , about four miles downstream on the left bank is a good take-out to avoid the difficult portages. Sheep Falls and the unnamed falls downstream have both been run, however most people choose to portage. Both are portaged on the left. The Sheep Falls portage is long and difficult .

Upper Mesa Falls is so well marked that only a blind man would fail to notice the horizon line and billows of mist. Have a look at it while setting up the shuttle for insurance. There are warning signs on the river, but they're popular collectors items, so they could be missing the day you decide to make the run. Get out on the left.

To find the take-out from Ashton, go east and then north on 47 for 14 miles. Grandview Overlook and Lower Mesa Falls are on the west. Drive half-a-mile beyond Grandview on 47 to road 295. This leads to Upper Mesa Falls and the take-out. To find the Hatchery Ford take-out, get back on 47 and go four miles further north to the Hatchery Ford Road, number 351, and drive west three miles. In May the road will probably be blocked by snow. The put-in, Riverside Campground, is another eight miles north on 47 and 4.5 miles south on highway 20.

See graph page 275.

Canoeing on Henrys Fork. Photo: Rob Lesser

HENRYS FORK, BOX CANYON

CLASS	LEVEL	LENGTH	GRADIENT	TIME
II	1,000-2,000 cfs	4 miles	18 fpm	2-4 hours

PUT-IN: Box Canyon Campground (6,220 ft.)
TAKE-OUT: Last Chance (6,150 ft.)
SHUTTLE: 4 miles
CRAFT: Kayak, canoe, raft, driftboat
PORTAGES: 0
SEASON: May, June, July
GAUGE: Yes
PERMIT: No
MAPS: Island Park Dam, Last Chance, *Targhee NF*
CHARACTER: Continuous class II river, good fishing, difficult access.

DESCRIPTION: Box canyon is better fishing water than whitewater, it's a swift class II run. There are lots of rocks and the river is wide and shallow. Below the Buffalo River a long class II rock garden will keep you busy.

To find the put-in from highway 20, take the road to the west at Ponds Lodge and drive a mile to Box Canyon Campground. To get to the take-out, go back to 20 and then south four miles to Last Chance, you can take out anywhere close to the road.

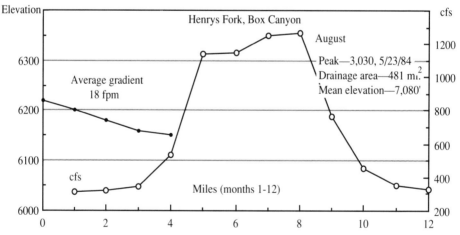

Henrys Fork, Box Canyon

Average gradient 18 fpm

August

Peak—3,030, 5/23/84
Drainage area—481 mi.^{2}
Mean elevation—7,080'

Miles (months 1-12)

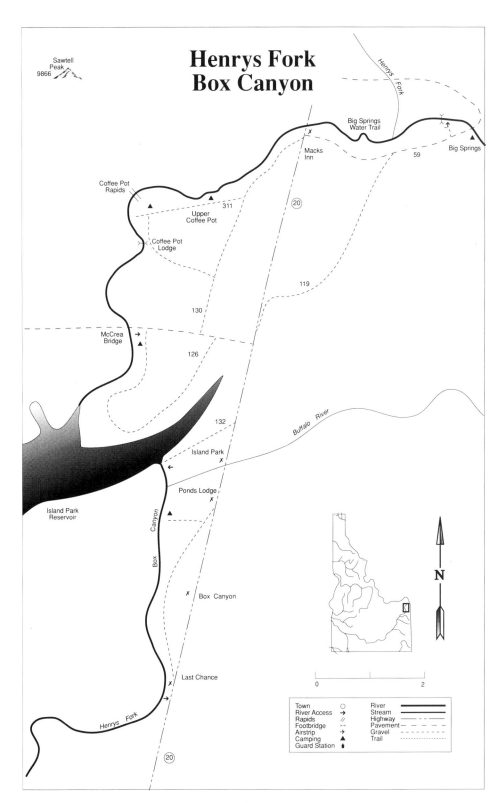

Henrys Fork
Box Canyon

Sawtell Peak
9866

Big Springs
Water Trail

Macks
Inn

Big Springs

Coffee Pot
Rapids

311

20

Upper
Coffee Pot

59

Coffee Pot
Lodge

119

130

McCrea
Bridge

126

Buffalo River

132

Island Park

Ponds Lodge

Island Park
Reservoir

Box Canyon

Box Canyon

Last Chance

Henrys Fork

20

N

Town	○	River	▬
River Access	→	Stream	──
Rapids	//	Highway	─·─
Footbridge	⊢⊣	Pavement	───
Airstrip	✈	Gravel	------
Camping	▲	Trail	··········
Guard Station	⚐		

0   2

HENRYS FORK, COFFEE POT

CLASS	LEVEL	LENGTH	GRADIENT	TIME
III	1,000-2,000 cfs	6 miles	13 fpm	2-4 hours

PUT-IN: Macks Inn (6,380 ft.)
TAKE-OUT: McCrea Bridge Campground (6,305 ft.)
SHUTTLE: 5 miles
CRAFT: Kayak, canoe, raft, drift boat
PORTAGES: 0
SEASON: May, June, July
GAUGE: No
PERMIT: No
MAPS: Island Park, Island Park Dam, *Targhee NF*
CHARACTER: Class II-III river, logs, good fishing, secluded.

DESCRIPTION: If you ask a local what's downstream from Macks Inn he'll probably reply, "Ten-pound trout." Coffee Pot rapids are downstream as well. The river is flat all the way to Coffee Pot and then it's class III water for a mile-and-a-half. Coffee Pot is a long series of pool-drop rapids. It was named by a trapper who overturned his canoe in the rapids and lost everything but his coffee pot. There are always lots of logs in this stretch and at low levels they can span the entire width of the river. After Coffee Pot, there are another two miles of flat water until the take-out at the McCrea Bridge. A footbridge crosses the river a mile upstream from take-out.

If you want to stretch this run-out or just enjoy a very relaxing float, the Big Springs Water Trail starts four miles up from Macks Inn on road 059. Big Springs percolates out of the rock in a beautiful pool filled with big trout. Sorry, no fishing until below the confluence with Henrys Fork. This is flat water meandering through some great scenery. Take out at Macks or continue through Coffee Pot.

To find the Coffee Pot take-out, start at Macks Inn, go 3.5 miles south on 20 to the McCrea Road, then go west two miles to the McCrea Bridge and the take-out.

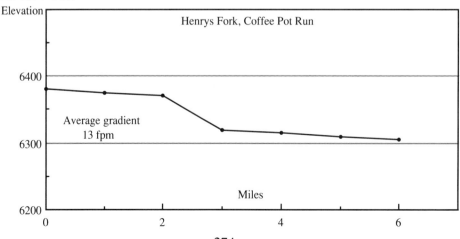

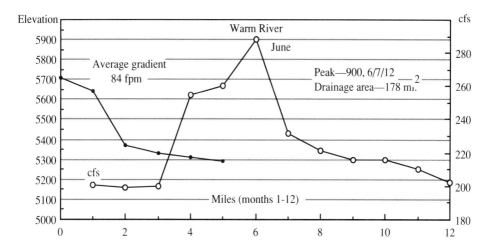

Warm River

June

Elevation / cfs

Average gradient 84 fpm

Peak—900, 6/7/12
Drainage area—178 mi.^{2}

cfs

Miles (months 1-12)

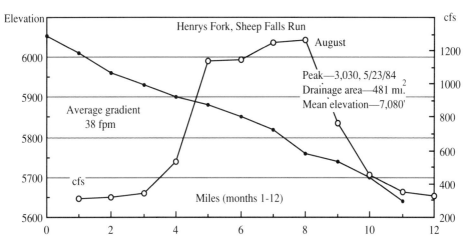

Henrys Fork, Sheep Falls Run

August

Elevation / cfs

Average gradient 38 fpm

Peak—3,030, 5/23/84
Drainage area—481 mi.^{2}
Mean elevation—7,080'

cfs

Miles (months 1-12)

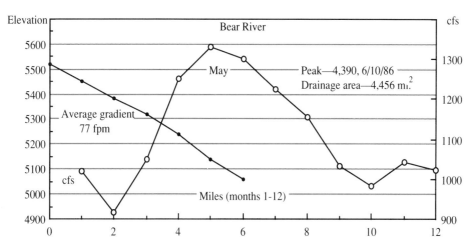

Bear River

May

Elevation / cfs

Average gradient 77 fpm

Peak—4,390, 6/10/86
Drainage area—4,456 mi.^{2}

cfs

Miles (months 1-12)

275

BEAR RIVER

CLASS	LEVEL	LENGTH	GRADIENT	TIME
IV (V)	3'-4'	6 miles	77 fpm	4 hours
IV-V	4'-5.5'			

PUT-IN:	Grace Dam Bridge (5,520 ft.)
TAKE-OUT:	Foot bridge above the Grace Power Plant (5,060 ft.)
SHUTTLE:	7 miles
CRAFT:	Kayak
PORTAGES:	0
SEASON:	April, May, June
GAUGE:	Grace, Utah Power and Light, (208) 425-3511
PERMIT:	No
MAPS:	Grace, Grace Power Plant
CHARACTER:	Narrow, steep-river, basalt ledges and boulder choked rapids, one school bus, secluded.

DESCRIPTION: The Black Canyon of the Bear is a popular class IV - V run with Salt Lake and Eastern Idaho boaters. The river runs through a basalt canyon, cut through fields of famous potatoes. Unfortunately this is a tame bear — flows are controlled by several dams. The water that should flow through the canyon is diverted just upstream from the put-in and finally returned to the river, via a powerhouse, at the take-out. If you hear there's water in the Bear — run it.

The rapids are a mix of basalt boulders and ledges. The first rapid, Grace Falls, is about a mile down from the put-in, just above the Turner Road Bridge. Take a look at it while setting up the shuttle. Grace Falls is a difficult rapid because of the complex entry and the big ledge at the end. Plan your route carefully because it's impossible to see the bottom of the falls from your boat. Close to the run's end is the most difficult rapid on the river, a IV or V depending on the water level, called Boo-Boo — like Yogi's friend. It's above the big bend to the south in the canyon. The rest of the run is full of ledges and holes which can either be a surfing dream or a swimming nightmare.

One of the bridge abutments at the put-in has a gauge painted on it. Flows between three and five feet on this gauge are considered good. At three feet there is still plenty of water left. As the river approaches flows of five feet, the run becomes challenging and above five feet it gets wild.

The shuttle is easy. Go south from the put-in on highway 34, to Grace. Go west on Center Street (Turner Road) two miles. Don't cross the river, unless you want to road scout Grace Falls from the bridge. Follow the Y in the road, before the bridge, to the southwest, two miles. The road will turn to the west because of the penstocks. Go 1.6 miles until the road turns to the south. After two miles it starts to wind around as it drops into the canyon. Keep to the right. Go north, through the company town, one mile. The footbridge is the take-out. The only camping is here.

See graph page 275.

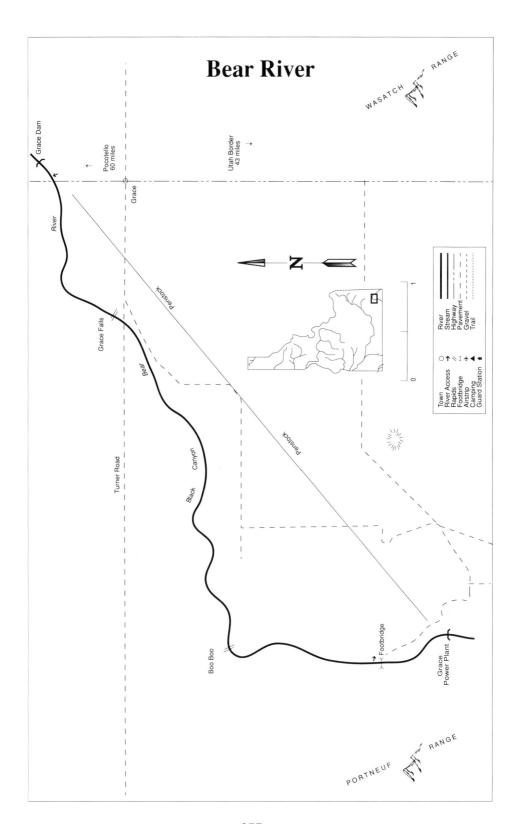

Bear River

WASATCH RANGE

Grace Dam

Pocotello
60 miles ←

Grace

Utah Border
43 miles →

River

Penstock

Grace Falls

Bear

Turner Road

Black Canyon

Penstock

Boo Boo

Footbridge

Grace
Power Plant

N

River
Stream
Highway
Pavement
Gravel
Trail

O Town
↑ River Access
≈ Rapids
I Footbridge
↟ Airstrip
◀ Camping
← Guard Station

0   1

PORTNEUF RANGE

Between a rock and a hard place — Smith Creek, Idaho.

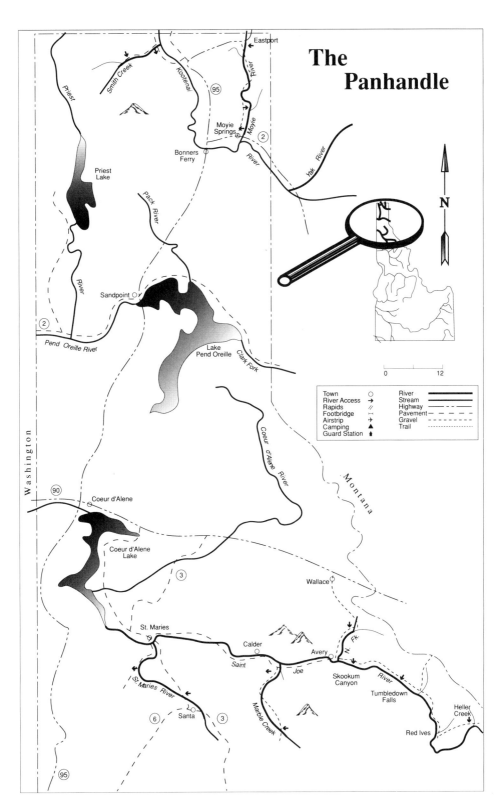

The
Panhandle

Eastport

Smith Creek

Priest

Kootenai

95

Moyie

Moyie
Springs

2

Bonners
Ferry

River

Yak River

Priest
Lake

Pack River

River

N

Sandpoint

Lake
Pend Oreille

Clark Fork

Pend Oreille River

2

Town	○	River	
River Access	→	Stream	
Rapids	//	Highway	
Footbridge	⊣⊢	Pavement	
Airstrip	✈	Gravel	
Camping	▲	Trail	
Guard Station	⬧		

Coeur d'Alene River

Montana

0   12

Washington

90

Coeur d'Alene

Coeur d'Alene
Lake

3

Wallace

St. Maries

Calder

N. Fk.

Avery

Saint

Joe

Skookum
Canyon

River

Tumbledown
Falls

Heller
Creek

St. Maries River

Marble Creek

6

Santa

3

Red Ives

95

SAINT MARIES RIVER

CLASS	LEVEL	LENGTH	GRADIENT	TIME
II-III	600-3,000 cfs	15 miles	29 fpm	4 hours

PUT-IN: Mashburn, (3,210 ft.)
TAKE-OUT: Grassy Flat (2,260 ft.)
SHUTTLE: 22 miles
CRAFT: Kayak, canoe, raft
PORTAGES: 0
SEASON: April, May, June
GAUGE: Near Santa
PERMIT: No
MAPS: Fernwood, Emida, Saint Maries, *Saint Joe NF*
CHARACTER: Swift water, continuous, rock gardens, railroad scenic secluded.

DESCRIPTION: If you're in north Idaho the Saint Maries is a good early spring run. The whitewater is gentle and the surrounding forests are beautiful. Below the put-in the river drops into a deep canyon covered with a thick forest of pine. The rapids are straightforward class II swift water for most of the run. About half-way down the run, the river winds around some big oxbows. The biggest rapid, known as the Loop, is in this stretch. It's a splashy class III on a tight corner just below the first railroad trestle. Below the Loop the river's even flatter than upstream. Its a long paddle to the take-out which is on the left below the third trestle.

The shuttle is easy. You can put in near the bridge at the Mashburn railroad siding on highway 3. This is all private property, so be courteous. From here drive north on highway 3 to Saint Maries. Go over the bridge and turn left just past the IGA supermarket and follow the river upstream just less than eight miles to a small unmarked road crossing the railroad tracks. This is the take-out — known as the grassy flat. If it's been raining it will be the muddy flat — don't get stuck. This is a good place to camp.

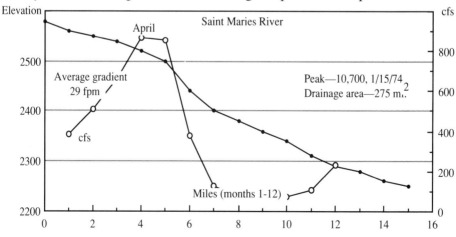

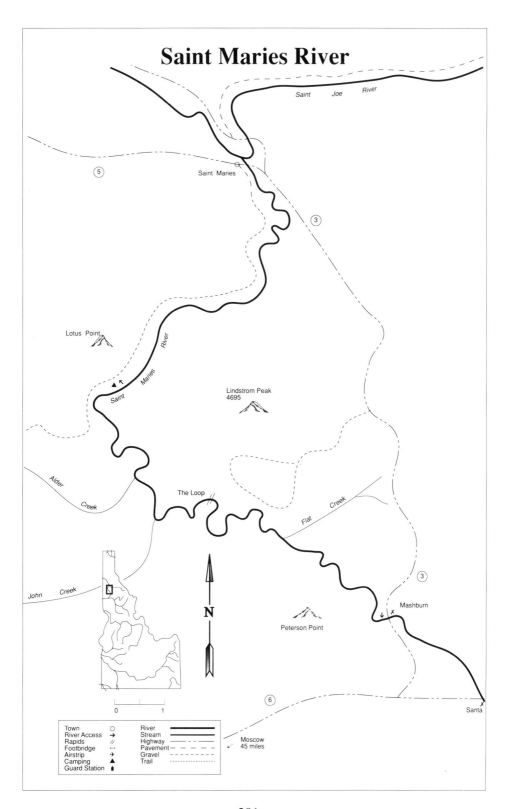

Saint Maries River

SAINT JOE RIVER, MARBLE CREEK

CLASS	LEVEL	LENGTH	GRADIENT	TIME
III-IV	800 cfs	13 miles	73 fpm	2 hours

PUT-IN:	Marble Creek Bridge, mile 14 (3,210 ft.)
TAKE-OUT:	Saint Joe Confluence (2,260 ft.)
SHUTTLE:	14 miles
CRAFT:	Kayak
PORTAGES:	1
SEASON:	April, May, June
GAUGE:	Saint Joe National Forest
PERMIT:	No
MAPS:	Marble Mtn., Grandmother Mtn., *Saint Joe NF*
CHARACTER:	Steep creek, continuous, rock gardens, road, secluded.

DESCRIPTION: Marble Creek is an interesting steep creek, with several good rapids and a ton of history. Marble Creek, like the Saint Joe, was used as a timber transport system just after the turn of the century. The ruins of the Marble Creek splash dams are a reminder of the days of log drives on the St. Joe. If you're interested in history, they are fascinating ruins. If you hate dams and any exploitation of the wilderness, they are an eyesore. The loggers would work the splash dams by filling the dewatered riverbed, downstream from the dam, with logs. Then they would open the gates of the splash dam and flush everything: logs, fish and soil down to the next dam and start the process over again.

Marble Creek starts slowly. Just down from put-in there is an old breakwater built to keep splash-dam driven logs in the current and off the shore. The road climbs away from the river as the canyon becomes steeper. The first rapid is a tight series of ledges and holes with some good play spots for kayakers. The canyon gets wide again and pools up behind an intact splash dam that must be portaged on the right. From here down to just above where the road comes back to the river it's a splashy class II ride. Just above the bridge, the gradient picks up, and the rapids become more difficult. There's a long class III below the bridge, then the river mellows. After floating by the skeleton of another splash dam, there's another mile of flat water before the next rapid. It has an impressive horizon line, but it's straightforward. The next two miles are continuous II-III whitewater with a dangerous class IV, full of piton rocks and jammed with logs. I counted six logs from the top. While scouting I counted a seventh, just under the water in the line I had initially planned. Look carefully at this one. At the Boulder Bridge the river mellows again and the road climbs up the canyon side. It's an easy paddle from here to the Joe.

See graph page 298.

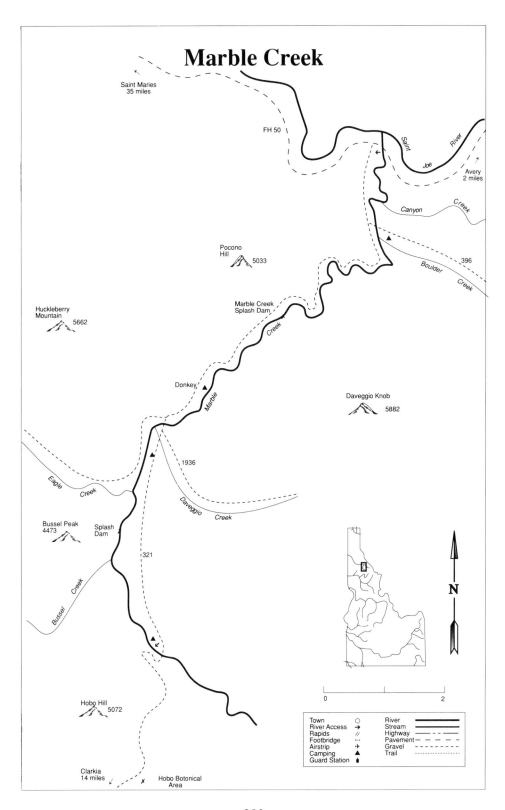

Marble Creek

Saint Maries
35 miles

FH 50

Saint

Joe

River

Avery
2 miles

Canyon

Creek

Pocono
Hill
5033

Boulder

Creek

396

Huckleberry
Mountain
5662

Marble Creek
Splash Dam

Creek

Donkey

Marble

Daveggio Knob
5882

1936

Eagle

Creek

Daveggio

Creek

Bussel Peak
4473

Splash
Dam

321

Bussel

Creek

Hobo Hill
5072

Clarkia
14 miles

Hobo Botonical
Area

N

Town	○	River	
River Access	→	Stream	
Rapids	//	Highway	
Footbridge	‖	Pavement	
Airstrip	✈	Gravel	
Camping	▲	Trail	
Guard Station	⬧		

0   2

SAINT JOE RIVER, NORTH FORK

CLASS	LEVEL	LENGTH	GRADIENT	TIME
III +	500-1,000 cfs	9 miles	89 fpm	3-5 hours
III	1,000-1,500 cfs			

PUT-IN:	Loop Creek Bridge (3,280 ft.)
TAKE-OUT:	Saint Joe Confluence (2,480 ft.)
SHUTTLE:	9 miles
CRAFT:	Kayak, canoe
PORTAGES:	0
SEASON:	April, May, June
GAUGE:	No
PERMIT:	No
MAPS:	Wallace, Saltese (both 15'), *Saint Joe NF*
CHARACTER:	Small river, continuous, rock gardens, road, secluded.

DESCRIPTION: When the water is high, the North Fork of the Saint Joe washes out to a fast and straightforward run. As the river drops, the boulders start appearing, and the river becomes more difficult. The river bed's narrow and congested with rocks. There are at least 10 rapids on the North Fork, most are tight little rock gardens. About a mile down from the top is an underwater snag which must be portaged as the water drops. Another two miles downstream, a second log needs to be portaged. The road is on one side of the river and an old rail bed on the other. There is some good camping at the put-in. Avery: three bars, a gas station and a post office, is just downstream from the take-out and an interesting example of a remote logging town.

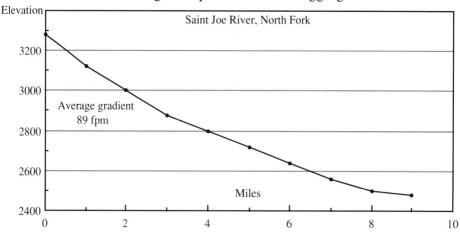

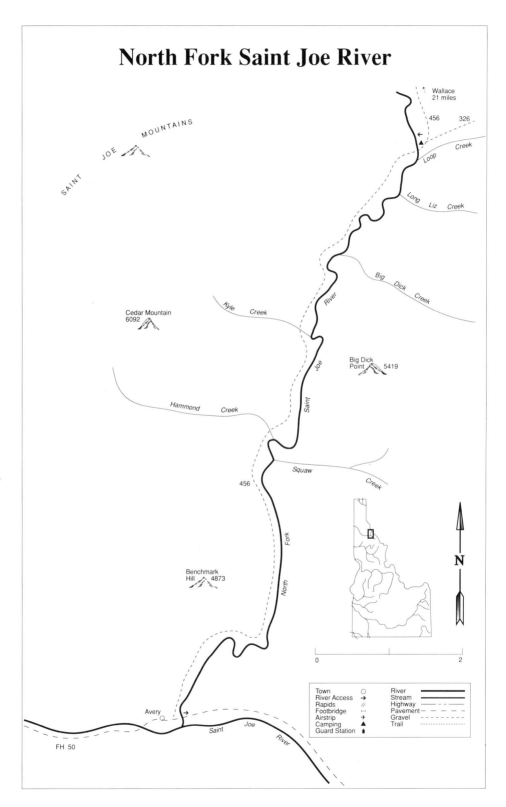

North Fork Saint Joe River

Wallace
21 miles

456   326

Creek

Loop

Long   Liz   Creek

SAINT   JOE   MOUNTAINS

Big   Dick   Creek

Kyle   Creek

River

Cedar Mountain
6092

Big Dick
Point   5419

Joe

Saint

Hammond   Creek

Squaw   Creek

456

North   Fork

Benchmark
Hill   4873

North   Fork

N

Town	○	River	
River Access	→	Stream	
Rapids	//	Highway	
Footbridge	⊥	Pavement	
Airstrip	→	Gravel	
Camping	▲	Trail	
Guard Station	▲		

0   2

Avery

Saint   Joe   River

FH 50

SAINT JOE RIVER, SKOOKUM CANYON

CLASS	LEVEL	LENGTH	GRADIENT	TIME
III	500-1,500 cfs	4 miles	35 fpm	4 hours
III-IV	>1,500 cfs			

PUT-IN:	Turner Flat (2,700 ft.)
TAKE-OUT:	Packsaddle Campground (2,560 ft.)
SHUTTLE:	4 miles
CRAFT:	Kayak, canoe, raft
PORTAGES:	No
SEASON:	April, May, June, July
GAUGE:	Calder
PERMIT:	No
MAPS:	Three Sisters, *Saint Joe NF*
CHARACTER:	Mountain river, moderate gradient, continuous, deep shear canyon, road, secluded.

DESCRIPTION: From Avery to Spruce Tree, the Saint Joe is classified as a Recreational River. At Red Ives the road climbs out of the canyon for 16 miles and the St. Joe becomes an official Wild River as part of the National Wild and Scenic River system. With the exception of the Wild stretch, the road running alongside the St. Joe offers unlimited access to boaters.

The forest service publishes a map dividing the Saint Joe into five runs, unfortunately the map's focus is on access and ignores the actual whitewater runs. Over the years boaters have informally divided the river into three runs: Heller Creek, Tumbledown Falls and Skookum Canyon.

Skookum Canyon runs from Turner Flat to Packsaddle Campground. The whitewater is confined to a shorter stretch in between these two locations. Starting at Turner flat involves paddling two miles of flat water. At most levels the run is class III busy water. The first rapid is short class II rock garden. The biggest rapid, a long class III-IV chute with a splashy run-out, is marked by a gravel island at the top. The last rapid is a little II-III rock garden near Sister Creek. The whitewater take-out is less than a half-mile downstream, look for the trolly crossing the river at Bootleg Creek. When the river is low, the run is rocky but easy. As the water rises, it starts to live up to the translation of "Skookum", a Chinook word meaning strong or powerful.

The freestyle event of the first North Idaho Whitewater Festival was held on a pop-up wave in this stretch. Camping is good at Conrad Crossing, Fly Flat and Spruce Tree.

See graph page 298.

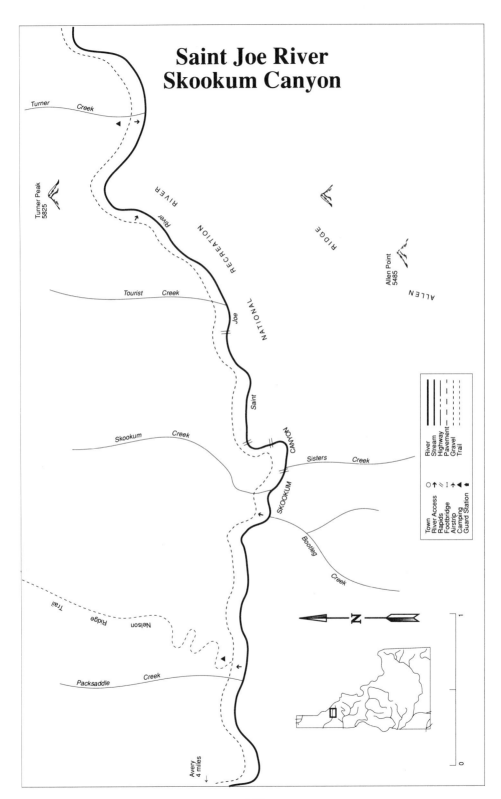

Saint Joe River
Skookum Canyon

Turner Creek

Turner Peak
5825

RIVER

River

NATIONAL

RECREATION

Tourist Creek

Joe

Saint

Skookum Creek

CANYON

Sisters Creek

SKOOKUM

Bootleg

Creek

Allen Point
5485

RIDGE

ALLEN

River
Stream
Highway
Pavement
Gravel
Trail

Town
River Access
Rapids
Footbridge
Airstrip
Camping
Guard Station

Nelson Ridge Trail

Packsaddle Creek

N

Avery
4 miles

1

0

SAINT JOE RIVER, TUMBLEDOWN RUN

CLASS	LEVEL	LENGTH	GRADIENT	TIME
III-IV	500-2,000 cfs	7 miles	46 fpm	3-5 hours
IV	>2,000 cfs			

PUT-IN:	Conrad Crossing Campground (3,360 ft.)
TAKE-OUT:	Bluff Creek Bridge (3,040 ft.)
SHUTTLE:	7 miles
CRAFT:	Kayak, canoe, raft
PORTAGES:	0
SEASON:	April, June, July
GAUGE:	Calder
PERMIT:	No
MAPS:	Simmons Pk., *Saint Joe NF*
CHARACTER:	Mountain river, moderate gradient, continuous, road, secluded.

DESCRIPTION: The Tumbledown run starts easy and gets gradually tougher. Most of the rapids can be characterized as good class II and III depending on the water level. A mile down from put-in is a long II-III rock garden that enters a steep canyon. A couple long rapids lead into Tumbledown Falls, located about 200 yards above Tumbledown Creek. It is a sheer, but runnable ledge. What makes it difficult are the rapids leading into the drop and the sharp left turn just above the ledge that wants to put you into the worst part of the hole. At most levels the hole can be crashed, however the clean line is a tight chute on the left. A small recovery pool forms just below the ledge as the flow drops. Downstream, a half-mile, a log spans the river above the water. Rafts might have a problem going under it when the water is high. A long class III S-turn is downstream, and when the water's high a river-wide breaking wave forms at the bottom of this rapid. After this, a couple smaller rapids remain. You should get out below the Bluff Creek Bridge on the right. It's steep and rocky, but the next good access point is 14 miles of flat water downstream.

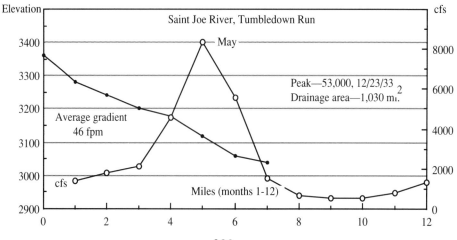

288

Saint Joe River
Tumbledown Run

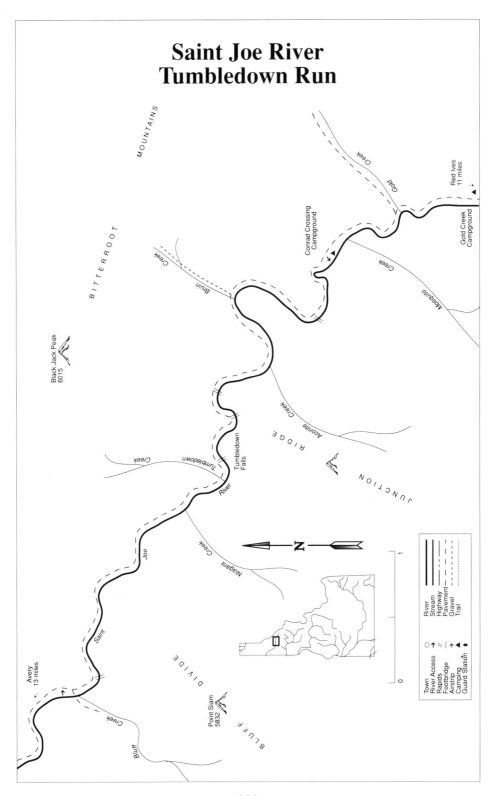

SAINT JOE RIVER, HELLER CREEK RUN

CLASS	LEVEL	LENGTH	GRADIENT	TIME
III-IV	800 cfs	16 miles	62 fpm	2 days

PUT-IN:	Heller Creek (4,690 ft.)
TAKE-OUT:	Spruce Tree Campground (3,700 ft.)
SHUTTLE:	12 miles
CRAFT:	Kayak
PORTAGES:	Logjams
SEASON:	July
GAUGE:	Calder
PERMIT:	No
MAPS:	Illinois Pk. 15', Simmons Pk. 15', Bacon Peak, *Saint Joe NF*
CHARACTER:	Small river, rock gardens, blind corners, trail, logs,wilderness

DESCRIPTION: The 16 miles from Heller Creek downstream to Spruce Tree Campground qualify the Saint Joe for "Wild" status in the nations Wild and Scenic River System. Below the take-out, the road winds out of the canyon and gives the Heller Creek run a remote wilderness character. The run is typical of a young Idaho stream, swift, undefined and plagued by deadfall and logjams. A trail runs the length of the run on river right to make portaging easier.

Besides the logjams, the biggest problem with this run is snow. The road to the put-in is a primitive dirt affair winding around the north slope of Red Ives Peak. It's usually blocked by snow until the middle of June, and unfortunately by then, the run-off has come and gone.

Below the bridge at Red Ives there's a modern stick gauge. In addition, there's an old gauge on one of the bridge abutments dating from the pre spray-paint era. It is both useful, and in a rustic way, artistic. Whoever painted it took the time to mark the flood waters of 1948 and 1973. River runners should note this compromise between stencils and the "José loves whitewater" schools of bridge gauges. Keep it in mind if you ever paint a bridge gauge.

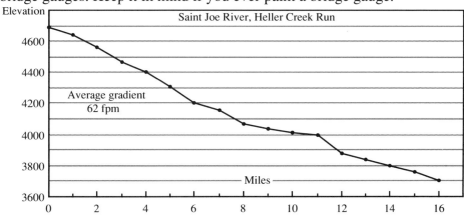

290

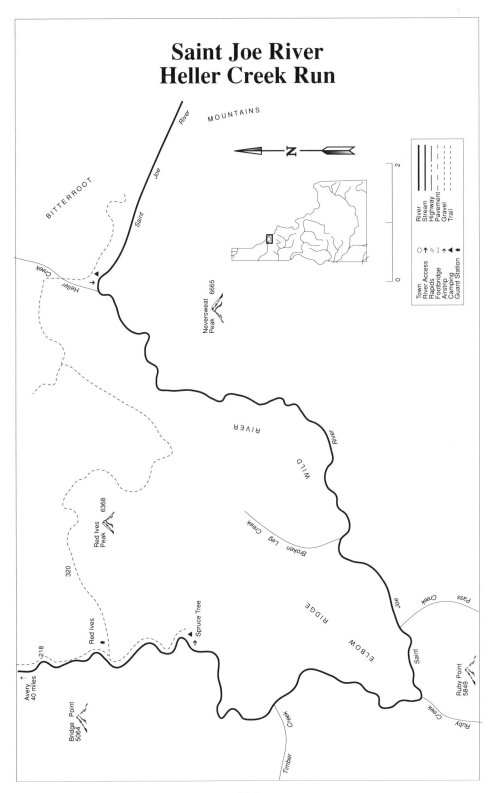

Saint Joe River
Heller Creek Run

MOUNTAINS

River Joe Saint

BITTERROOT

Heller Creek

Neversweat Peak 6665

RIVER

WILD River

Broken Leg Creek

Red Ives Peak 6368

320

Spruce Tree

Red Ives

218

ELBOW RIDGE

Joe Saint

Pass Creek

Ruby Point 5849

Avery 40 miles

Bridge Point 5064

Timber Creek

Ruby Creek

Town
River Access
Rapids
Footbridge
Airstrip
Camping
Guard Station

River
Stream
Highway
Pavement
Gravel
Trail

2

0

N

MOYIE RIVER

CLASS	LEVEL	LENGTH	GRADIENT	TIME
II	500-1,500 cfs	18 miles	31 fpm	1 day
III	1,500-2,500 cfs			

PUT-IN:	Copper Creek (2,580 ft.)
TAKE-OUT:	Back waters of Moyie Dam (2,030 ft.)
SHUTTLE:	19 miles
CRAFT:	Kayak, canoe, raft
PORTAGES:	0
SEASON:	May, June
GAUGE:	Eastport
PERMIT:	No
MAPS:	Eastport, Moyie Springs, *Kaniksu NF*
CHARACTER:	Spring river, shallow rock gardens, road, logs, developed.

DESCRIPTION: The Moyie has a quick and early spring run-off, this is the only time for whitewater. The rest of the summer, the river is too low to float. During the peak the Moyie is a fun class II-III. The run is usually divided into two stretches. From Copper Creek to Meadow Creek, the Moyie is a class II canoe run, with shallow, rock-filled rapids and riffles. Below Meadow Creek, the river enters a canyon containing two class III rapids. The old Eileen Dam, breached on the left, forms the first rapid. If the river is above 2000 cfs approach Eileen Dam with caution because it becomes difficult and dangerous. The other rapid is called Hole-in-the-Wall.

A gravel road runs along the length of the river, but most of the lower run is hidden from view. The camping at Meadow Creek and Copper Creek is good.

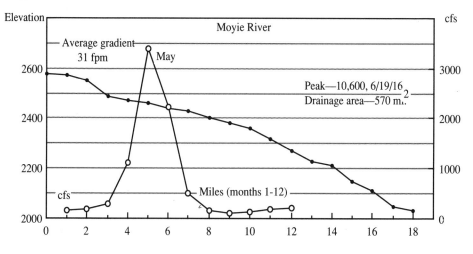

Moyie River

Peak—10,600, 6/19/16
Drainage area—570 mi.^{2}

Moyie River

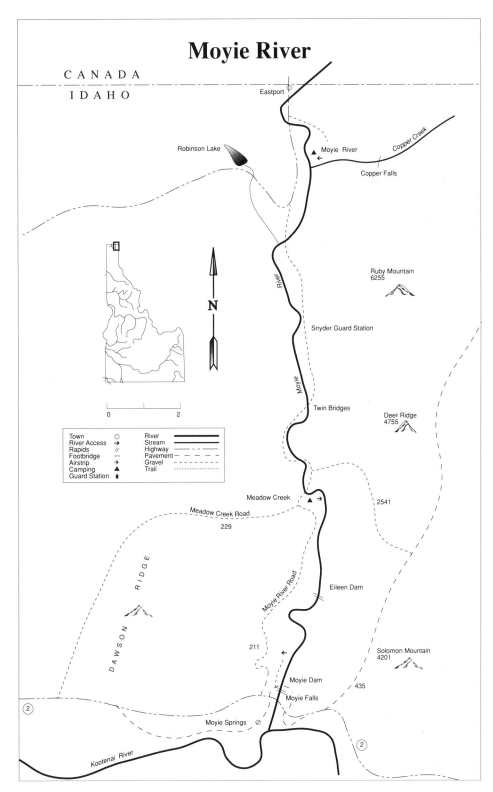

SMITH CREEK

CLASS	LEVEL	LENGTH	GRADIENT	TIME
IV+-V+	150-250 cfs	6 miles	282 fpm	1 day
IV+-VI	250-500 cfs			

PUT-IN:	Smith Creek Bridge (3,450 ft.)
TAKE-OUT:	Above Smith Falls (1,760 ft.)
SHUTTLE:	6 miles
CRAFT:	Kayak
PORTAGES:	8-12
SEASON:	April, May, June
GAUGE:	Smith Falls
PERMIT:	No
MAPS:	Smith Falls, *Saint Joe NF*
CHARACTER:	Extreme class V steep creek, granite riverbed, continuous, ledges, falls, logs, remote.

DESCRIPTION: This is one of the best steep creeks in the Northwest and perhaps one of the best in the States, but don't start loading your kayaks without reading the entire description and cooling your heels for a moment. This is not a run for paddle twirling and thrill seeking. Teams of experts with an intense focus on safety are the only ones who should seriously consider this run. Teamwork and safety should be the key words for any Smith Creek run.

The gradient is continuous, ranging between 250 through 500 fpm, with the last five miles averaging 320 fpm. The rapids are created by the smooth granite river bed and huge polished boulders. Smith Creek starts with an easy mile of class II and III whitewater, with several large rapids thrown in to give a hint of what lies downstream. After this stretch the gradient jumps to 350 fpm for the next three miles. The result is an endless series of long granite waterslides, complex rapids and bizarre hydraulics formed by exfoliated granite ledges. Perhaps the most amazing aspect of this run is practically all the rapids are runnable if the flows are right and you are paddling well.

The gems of the run are two long sections of class V whitewater comprising approximately the third mile. The first is named "One Thousand Moves per Mile." The name alone should tell you what to expect. It's a crazy mix of scrambling ferries, must-make eddies and tight-steep drops. Done right it will leave you grinning. The second gem is called "Too Much (is what I love)." Like MPM upstream, this one is a long series of rapids without any real break between them. A half-mile of technical class V ends in a dramatic, but runnable, sliding-waterfall approximately 50 feet long and dropping perhaps 30 feet. The falls flow over a large polished slab of exposed granite bedrock at about a 30 degree angle. At flows of 250 cfs or greater, the lead-in is difficult and a mistake might be fatal, but at low flows (150-200 cfs) the entrance mellows, with the holes in the entrance and the bottom losing some punch.

The next two-thirds of a mile are solid class IV and V whitewater, with

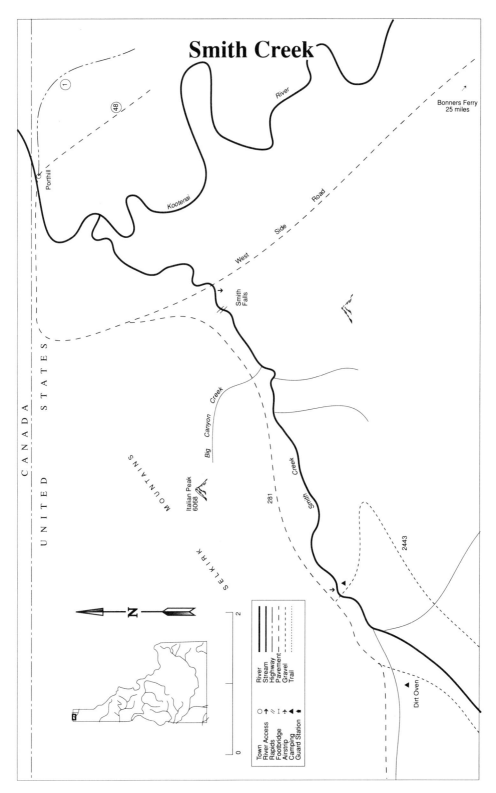

Smith Creek

River

Kootenai

Porthill

① ⊕48

CANADA
UNITED STATES

Bonners Ferry
25 miles

West   Side   Road

Smith
Falls

Big   Canyon   Creek

Italian Peak
6068

281

Smith   Creek

2443

Dirt Oven

SELKIRK   MOUNTAINS

N

Town
River Access
Rapids
Footbridge
Airstrip
Camping
Guard Station

○ River
╌ Stream
↑ Highway
⫽ Pavement—
I Gravel
↑ Trail
◀

0   2

several probable portages, depending on the water level. Notable among them is "Cover Shot." It is a S-turn rapid with three closely spaced four to six foot ledge holes leading into a 12 to 14 foot drop around a constricted corner. The crux of the rapid is the corner. At flows >250 cfs, a deep whirlpool-like eddy forms against a rock wall on one side, while the main flow smashes into a fence of boulders. At lower flows it is less menacing and has been run.

The run's character changes downstream at a place marked by a large avalanche path on the south (river right) slope of the canyon. Be extremely careful coming into this stretch, the gradient increases and a series of class V+ and VI cascades lead right to the lip of an unrunnable 20 foot falls. Portage all of this high on the left bank. Get back in by climbing down the mossy gully below the second falls. Immediately downstream is a short, rocky class IV-V. For the remaining two miles the stream's bedrock is packed with boulder debris and rubble from the avalanche. Lots of good rapids remain as well as several portages, depending upon the water level. The congested, boulder-choked rapids suddenly stop in the last quarter mile and the stream literally drops through the bedrock in five major waterfalls. The first is unrunnable — at low flows the water falls 20 feet into a pothole, and at high flows it smashes into a rock outcrop. The next three falls are in the 10-15 foot range and can be managed. Smith Falls is the finale. It is a straight forward (and straight down) 35 foot plunge into a deep pool — unrun as of yet.

Some final words of warning: even at what appear to be ridiculously low flows (150-500 cfs) Smith Creek is a demanding run and any party tackling it should be composed of experienced and cautious paddlers. The gradient and constriction combine to form some large and unusual hydraulics. Although the season is from April to June (In April you'll be scouting in waist-deep snow), it is difficult to predict a safe flow because the stream fluctuates from 150 up to 200 cfs — often in less than two days. The difficulty in prediction may increase with the completion of a lowhead dam this year.

There are several turn outs along the canyon road and some developed campgrounds above the put-in where you can camp. While you're in the area, you can also run the Yaak, Moyie and a short big water class IV stretch on the Kootenai River below Kootenai Falls in Northwestern Montana.

POSTSCRIPT: Unfortunately, last summer, 1989, Smith Creek was dammed and developed as the largest privately owned hydroelectric site in the US. Dominian Hydroelectric built a low-head dam about two thirds of a mile below the put-in, and buried a penstock under the road down to a power plant just above Smith Falls. Most of the physical run has not been changed, although several rapids between the put-in and the dam have been ruined. The real damage is to the wilderness quality of the canyon and the river's natural flow. The dam and pipe are capable of diverting up to 350 cfs. Since all the runs to date have been made with flows between 150-500 cfs, it may drastically affect the paddling season by dewatering the run at the times when the natural flow is predictably in this range. However, it is still unclear what effect the diversion will have, and will depend upon the run-off and power demand.

The Duff in a quiet moment on Smith Creek.

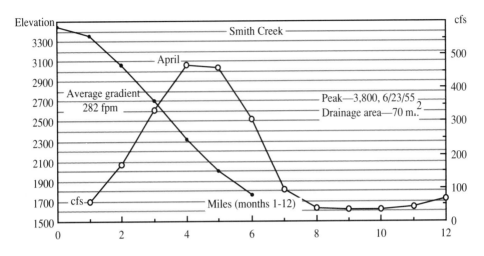

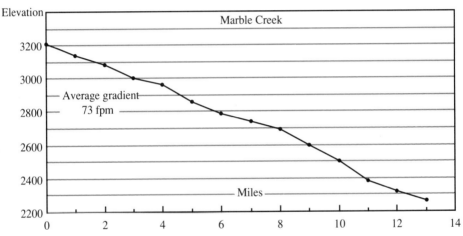

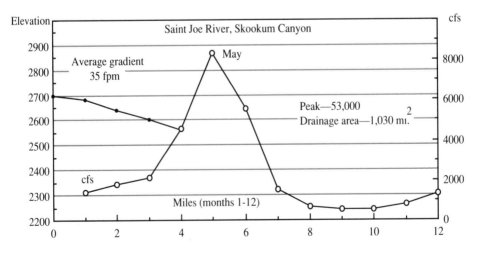

298

Asking the classic kayak question: "Are you sure you want to start here?

Flying in Idaho

Idaho puddle jumpers can fly you and your whitewater gear to a number of remote rivers and streams at a fraction of the cost of a day of heli-skiing. Because of the mountains, rivers and huge tracts of wilderness, Idaho is a tough place to drive around in. A large and competitive air force of puddle jumpers has developed to deal with the long distances and rough roads in the central Idaho mountains.

The best planes are a Turbo Cessna 207, a Twin Islander, and a DeHavilland Otter. The 207 can handle three kayaks and passengers. The Islander is big enough for five kayaks and passengers with room to spare. The Otter can haul a small invasion force and their jeep.

Middle Fork Mail Service

For self contained kayakers this is a mail call you won't want to miss. You can mail yourself a cache of goodies, important, but heavy stuff, like beer, to pick up at Indian Creek or Loon Creek. The fee is the standard US Postal rate, delivered once a week on Thursday. All you have to do is allow time to make it to Arnold Aviation in Cascade before the Thursday you plan on being on the river. Wrap it in weather proof packaging and address it to yourself at the proper airstrip, care of

Arnold Aviation
Cascade, Idaho 83611
(208) 382-4844

Call for all the details or to insure your package is waiting to fly before Thursday. They deliver at other airstrips as well, but most of these are private and you'll have to make arrangements with the folks on the receiving end. Don't send any thing you can't afford to lose because the pilot just sets the package down at the end of the airstrip. There's no one there to guard your stash from any river scum who may wander by before you arrive for the connection.

The following airstrips are the ones of importance to river runners. Prices are approximate for a 207 starting in Salmon:

Big Creek:	snowbound access to Big Creek. $160
Indian Creek:	low water access to the Middle Fork of the Salmon. $160, Middle Fork mail drop
Upper Loon Cr.:	snowbound access to Loon Creek. $160
Lower Loon Cr.:	Middle Fork mail drop
Running Creek:	snowbound Selway access

Selected Air Taxies

Arnold Aviation
Cascade, Idaho, 83611
(208) 382-4844
Middle Fork mail service

Wilderness Aviation
Box 1535
Salmon, Idaho, 83467
(208) 756-4713
Turbo Cessna 207

Salmon Air Taxi
Box 698, Dept. O
Salmon, Idaho, 83467
(208) 756-6211
Twin Islander

McCall Air Taxi
Box 771
McCall, Idaho 83638
(208) 634-7137

Whitewater Equipment

Idaho River Sports
1521 N. 13th St.
Boise, Id. 83702
(208) 336-4844

Boise Water Sports
3204 Overland
Boise, Id.
(208) 342-1378

Northwest River Supplies
Box 9186
Moscow, Id. 83843-9186
800-635-5202

Blackadar Boating
Highway 93 North
Salmon, Id. 83467
(208) 756-3958

Gravity Sports
503 Pine St.
McCall, Id. 83638
(208) 634-8530

Holiday Sports
126 W. Main St.
Grangeville, Id. 83530
(208) 938-1518

Backwood Sports
Ketchum, Id. 83340
(208) 726-8818

Shuttles

All rivers:................River Rat Express, Stanley ....(208) 774-2265

Bruneau: ....Jumbo's Service, Bruneau ....(208) 845-2150

Owyhee: ....Ken Haylett, Jordan Valley, Ore.......(503) 586-2406

Secesh:....................Contact: Gravity Sports, McCall .....(208) 634-8530

South Fk.Boise: ......Conny Carrico, Prairie ....(208) 868-3255

South Fk. Salmon: ..Contact: Gravity Sports, McCall .....(208) 634-8530

National Forests

Boise National Forest
1750 Front St.
Boise, Idaho 83702
(208) 364-4100

Caribou National Forest
Suite 294, Federal Bldg.
250 South Fourth Ave.
Pocatello, Idaho 83201
(208) 236-7500

Challis National Forest
Forest Service Bldg.
Highway 93
Challis, Idaho 83226
(208) 879-2285

Clearwater National Forest
12730 Highway 12
Orofino, Idaho 83544
(208) 476-4541

Idaho Panhandle National Forests
1201 Ironwood Drive
Coeur d' Alene, Idaho 83814
(208) 765-7223

Nez Perce National Forest
Highway 13
Route 2, Box 475
Grangeville, Idaho 83530
(208) 983-1950

Payette National Forest
106 W. Park St.
P.O. Box 1026
McCall, Idaho 83638
(208) 634-1333

Salmon National Forest
Highway 93
P.O. Box 729
Salmon, Idaho 83467
(208) 756-2215

Sawtooth National Forest
2647 Kimberly Rd. East
Twin Falls, Idaho 83301
(208) 737-3200

Targhee National Forest
420 North Bridge St.
Box 208
St. Anthony, Idaho 83445
(208) 634-3151

River Permits

Bruneau and Owyhee Rivers
BLM
3948 Development Ave.
Boise, Id. 83705
(208) 384-3300

Salmon River, Lower
BLM
Rt. 3, Box 181
Cottonwood, Id. 83522
(208) 962-3245

Salmon River, The Main
North Fork Ranger District
Box 180
North Fork, Id. 83466
(208) 865-2383

Salmon River, Middle Fork
Middle Fork Ranger District
Box 750, Challis, Id. 83226
(208) 879-5204

Selway River
West Fork Ranger District
Darby Mt. 59829
(406) 821-3269

Snake River, Hells Canyon
Hells Canyon Nat. Rec. Area
Box 699
Clarkston, Wa. 99403
(509) 758-0616
River reservation line:
(509) 758-1957

Bibliography

Boone, Lalia. *Idaho Place Names*. The University of Idaho Press, Moscow, Idaho, 1988.

Carry, Johnny and Cort Conley. *The Middle Fork and the Sheepeater War*. Backeddy Books, Cambridge Idaho, 1977.

Carry, Johnny and Cort Conley. *River of No Return*. Backeddy Books, Cambridge Idaho, 1978.

Carry, Johnny and Cort Conley. *Snake River of Hells Canyon*. Backeddy Books, Cambridge Idaho, 1979.

Conley, Cort . *Idaho for the Curious*. Backeddy Books, Cambridge Idaho, 1982.

Garren, John. *Idaho River Tours*. The Touchstone Press, Beaverton, Oregon, 1980.

Idaho Department of Parks and Recreation. *A River Runner's Guide to Idaho*. Idaho Department of Parks and Recreation, 1980.

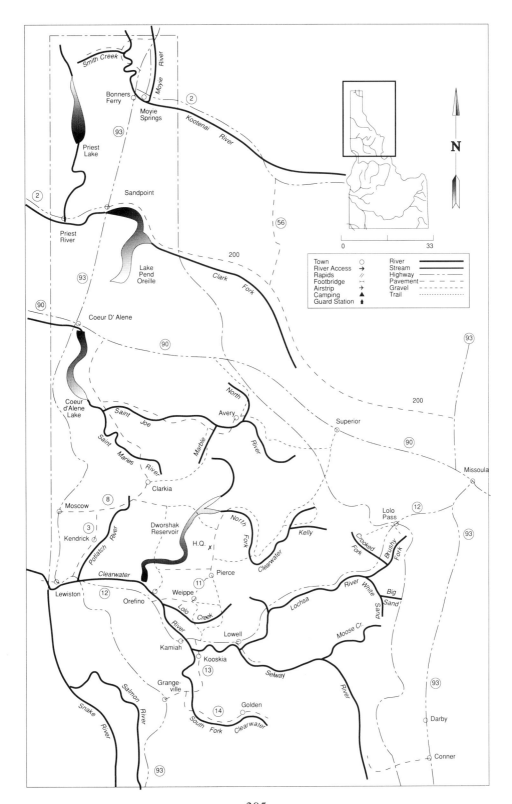

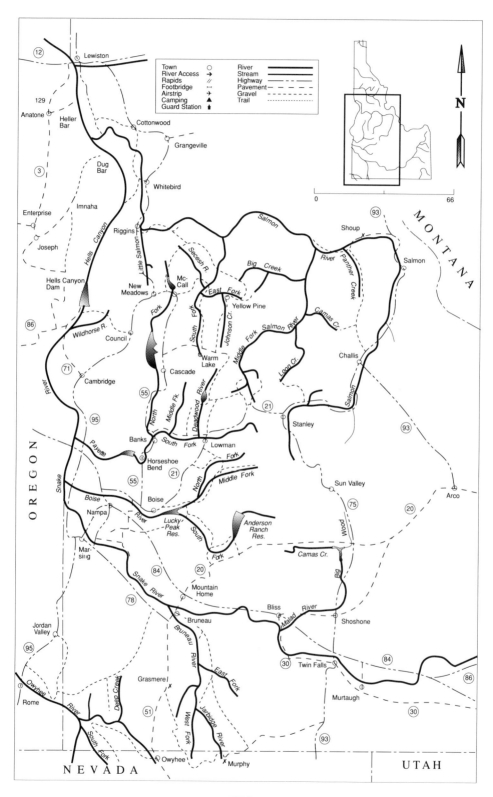

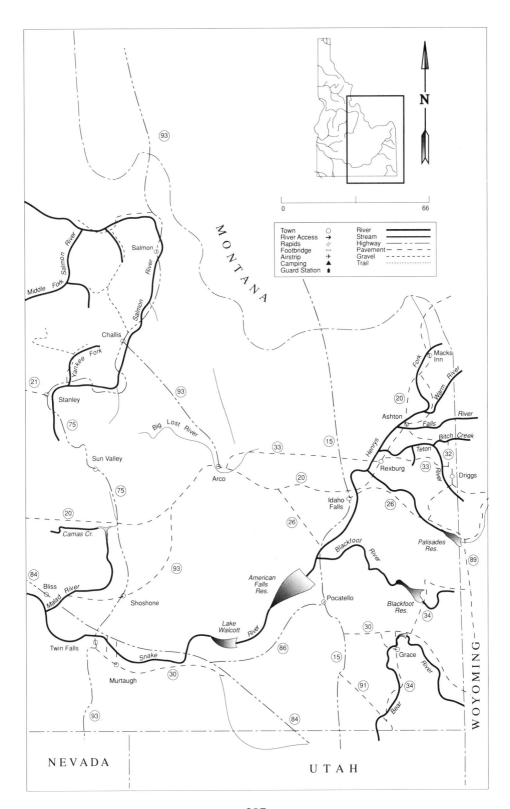

Rivers on the Whitewater Recording:
(208) 327-7865

Saint Joe at Calder
Snake at Milner
Bruneau at Hot Springs
Snake near Murphy
Owyhee River at Rome, Oregon
South Fork Boise at Anderson Ranch
North Fork Boise at Twin Springs
Boise at Glenwood
South Fork Payette at Lowman
North Fork Payette at Cascade
Payette at Horseshoe Bend
Salmon at Salmon
Middle Fork Salmon at M. Fk. Lodge
Little Salmon at Riggins
Salmon at Whitebird
Grande Ronde at Troy, Oregon
Selway at Lowell
Lochsa at Lowell
South Fork Clearwater at Stites

Selected Rating Tables

	Camas Creek near Blain — Left bank, 2.6 mi. upstream from maximum level of Magic Reservoir, four miles east of Blain	Blackfoot River near Shelly — right bank, 1.2 miles downstream from Wolverine Creek.	Boise River at Glenwood — left bank, 175 ft. upstream from Glenwood Bridge	Boise River near Twin Springs — right bank, 3.2 mi. downstream from Twin Springs	Bruneau River near Hot Spring — right bank, 1.5 mi. upstream of Hot Springs	North Fork Clearwater River near Canyon Ranger Station — left bank, immediately upstream from forest road bridge 1.7 mi. downstream from Canyon Ranger Station	South Fork Clearwater River at Stites — left bank, 0.4 mi. upstream from county road bridge	Johnson Creek at Yellow Pine — right bank, 700 ft. upstream from mouth
1.00								
1.50								
2.00								
2.50								
3.00								
3.50							670	690
4.00				543			1096	1054
4.50				767			1875	1464
5.00				1065	467		2721	1914
5.50	524		440	1561	672	598	3700	2401
6.00	730		710	2156	896	958	4785	2923
6.50	944	436	1067	2852	1140	1430	5963	3476
7.00	1165	736	1514	3650		2030	7209	4059
7.50	1392	1130	2057	4552		2731	8494	
8.00	1624	1650	2702	5558		3530	9841	
8.50	1860	2260	3454			4444		
9.00	2101	3010	4318			5461		
9.50	2345		6406			6580		
10.00	2593		7637			7800		
10.50	2844					9097		
11.00	3098					10490		
11.50	3355					11980		
12.00	3615					13560		
12.50	3877					15230		
13.00	4141					17000		
13.50	4407					18900		
14.00	4676					20900		
14.50	4947					22910		
15.00						25000		
15.50								

	Lochsa River near Lowell right bank, 0.7 mi. upstream from Lowell	Lochsa River on Three Rivers Bridge downstream left side of right piling	Malad River near Bliss right bank, 700 ft. upstream from mouth	Mores Creek above Robie Creek left bank, 1.7 mi. upstream from Robie Creek	Moyie River at Eastport left bank, at Eastport, 1000 ft. downstream from border	Payette River, North Fork near Banks right bank, 300 ft. downstream from highway bridge 2.5 mi. north of Banks	Payette River, South Fork near Lowman right bank, 0.5 mi. downstream 200 ft. upstream from summer home area	Salmon River below Yankee Fork left bank, 700 ft. downstream from Yankee Fork
1.00								
1.50		3000						
2.00	443	3500						309
2.50	818	4000						613
3.00	1340	4500	445					853
3.50	2000	6500	643				608	1128
4.00	2780	8000	929	538			1057	1437
4.50	3660	9750	1307	773	542		1621	1779
5.00	4660	12250	1780	1044	920	528	2301	2154
5.50	5760	13250	2323	1349	1377	725	3093	2560
6.00	6980	14000	2947	1689	1910	960	3997	2998
6.50	8300	15000	3656	2061	2500	1235	5010	3466
7.00	9680	15750	4450	2464	3161	1557	6138	3965
7.50	11100	17000		2899	3880	1920	7400	4493
8.00	12600	18250		3364	4656	2311		5057
8.50	14160	19500		3859	5508	2739		5638
9.00	15800				6420	3211		6254
9.50	17560				7320			6899
10.00	19400				8300			7571
10.50	21360							8272
11.00								
11.50								
12.00								
12.50								
13.00								
13.50								
14.00								
14.50								
15.00								
15.50								

	Salmon River, Middle Fork on bridge at Middle Fork Lodge	Salmon River, South Fork near Krassel right bank, 1.2 mi. downstream from Krassel	Selway River near Lowell right bank, 7 mi. upstream from Lowell 0.2 mi. upstream from O'Hara Creek Bridge	Selway River near Paradise Guard Station right bank, at Selway launch site	Snake River at Milner left bank, 200 ft. downstream from highway bridge	Teton River near St. Anthony left bank, 0.5 mi. north of Teton 60 ft. upstream from county road bridge		
1.00				857				
1.50	376			987				
2.00	688			1140		466		
2.50	1080		280	1468		708		
3.00	1570	468	582	1608		992		
3.50	2150	676	1030	2001		1370		
4.00	2820	927	1650	2429		1950		
4.50	3570	1223	2437	2904	512	2700		
5.00	4410	1564	3380	3411	1015	3740		
5.50	5340	1953	4480	3964	1816	5080		
6.00	6380	2391	5710	4562	2664	6780		
6.50	7530	2878	7088	5144	3548	8830		
7.00	8760	3415	8600	5844	4551			
7.50	10100	4003	10240	6669	6928			
8.00	11500	4644	12000	7683	8208			
8.50	13000	5338	13870	9044	9543			
9.00	14500	6086	15870	10780	10930			
9.50	16200		17980		12490			
10.00	18000		20220		14540			
10.50	19700		22570		16730			
11.00			25030		19060			
11.50			27610		21520			
12.00			30300					
12.50			33140					
13.00			36090					
13.50			39160					
14.00			42340					
14.50			45640					
15.00			49050					
15.50								

Flow Information

www.idaho.usgs.gov/public/h2odata.html

Department of Water Resources whitewater recording: ...(208) 327-7865

All rivers: National Weather Service.........................(208) 334-9860
During regular business hours the flow information for any river with a
gauge is available. After four, a recording of all the popular whitewater
runs.

Hydrology Dept . Current flow information for any river with a gauge
Monday - Friday, 8:00 - 5:00 ....(208) 327-7900

Bear River: Utah Power and Light.........................(801) 535-2174
....(208) 425-3511

Blackfoot River: Fort Hall Indian Reservation ....(208) 238-6264

Lochsa River: Lochsa Ranger District ....(208) 926-4275

Owyhee River: BLM Rome...............................(503) 586-2612

Middle Fork of the Salmon: M. Fk. Ranger District.......(208) 879-5204

Salmon River, The Main: N. Fk. Ranger District ....(208) 865-2383

Salmon River, South Fork, McCall Ranger District ......(208) 634-4525

Selway River: W. Fk. Ranger District ....(406) 821-3269

Snake River, Hells Canyon ....(800) 422-3143

The Idaho Statesman, Thursday Rec Section

Water Supply Outlook Report: Published monthly,, January through June.
Contains snowpack an runoff estimates for individual rivers and basins
throughout Idaho. Write:

> Soil Conservation Service, Attn. Snow Survey
> 3244 Elder St.
> Boise, ID 83705

For additional rivers, updates and ordering information:

www.aguaazul.com/watershed

Watershed Books
PO Box 111
Garden Valley, Idaho 83622